Jan 2014   Caroline Andrée-Marie

LUXURY MINIMAL

LUXURY MINIMAL

MINIMALIST INTERIORS
IN THE GRAND STYLE

Fritz von der Schulenburg

Text by Karen Howes

with 300 colour illustrations

For Angela

COVER A contemporary staircase and an 18th-century sleigh in the hall of Heinrich Graf von Spreti's country house in Bavaria.

PAGE 1 An English Regency Brighton lantern (c. 1820) hangs above the original Georgian stone staircase with wrought-iron balustrade in the London home of designer John Minshaw.

PAGES 2–3 The Arcade Hall of the Neoclassical Roman baths at Charlottenhof, the estate outside Potsdam built by Karl Friedrich Schinkel around 1830 for Crown Prince Frederick William of Prussia. Schinkel also designed the marble-topped table with a cast-zinc frame, as well as the cast-iron bench. The plaster relief (c. 1840) is from the workshop of Christian Daniel Rauch.

PAGE 6 The Palladian Bridge was built by Emilio Terry, from watercolour impressions created by Alexandre Serebriakoff, in the grounds of the Château de Groussay in France, the erstwhile home and lifelong passion of Charles de Beistegui.

PAGE 7 Inspired by Palladio's Villa Capra on the outskirts of Vicenza, entrepreneur Sebastian de Ferranti commissioned artist Felix Kelly in 1982 to draw up the architectural plans for this new rotunda 'as if Vanbrugh were interpreting Palladio'. Julian Bicknell was the architect who pulled the design together, and the building was developed on the foundations of a Victorian house in the grounds of the Henbury estate near Macclesfield in Cheshire.

First published in the United Kingdom in 2012 by Thames & Hudson Ltd, 181A High Holborn, London WC1V 7QX

Luxury Minimal copyright © 2012 Thames & Hudson, London

Photographs copyright © 2012 Fritz von der Schulenburg

Text copyright © 2012 Karen Howes

All Rights Reserved. No part of this publication may be reproduced or transmitted in any form or by any means, electronic or mechanical, including photocopy, recording or any other information storage and retrieval system, without prior permission in writing from the publisher.

British Library Cataloguing-in-Publication Data
A catalogue record for this book is available from the British Library

ISBN 978-0-500-51583-9

Printed and bound in China by Toppan Leefung Printing Limited

To find out about all our publications, please visit www.thamesandhudson.com. There you can subscribe to our e-newsletter, browse or download our current catalogue, and buy any titles that are in print.

CONTENTS

Introduction
THE ART OF ELEGANCE
by *Fritz von der Schulenburg*   8

RHYTHM   14
with *Nicholas Haslam* and *John Minshaw*

COLOUR   62
with *John Stefanidis*

LIGHT   110
with *David Collins*

SPACE   152
with *Anthony Collett* and *Annabelle Selldorf*

TEXTURE   208
with *William Sofield*

COMPOSITION   258
with *Axel and Boris Vervoordt* and *Robert Kime*

DIRECTORY   313
ACKNOWLEDGMENTS   315
INDEX   316

Introduction THE ART OF ELEGANCE

'Minimalism in the Grand Style' would appear to be a contradiction in terms. Grand Style, with its richness, opulence and expensive materials, is the polar opposite of Minimalism; and yet good proportion and exquisite design, when pared down, comprise precisely these concepts.

This book has come about as a result of the way I see, and ultimately photograph, an interior. I see everything in wide angle. By enlarging a picture, or pulling back from the focal point, I give context to the objects and furniture within a room, revealing the space in between and thereby adding a Minimalist perspective to their composition.

Minimalism is about space and light. Vast space, intimate space, grand space, simple space, whether created by man or by nature: light gives life to that space. Photography is also about space and light, and, whether one is photographing interiors, exteriors or landscapes, these are the two most important influences. Both are essential in creating the mood and atmosphere of an image.

From space and light comes rhythm: rhythm is the space in between. An avenue of tall beech trees has a natural perspective – the pale grey trunks planted at regular intervals; the damp darkness at the heart of the avenue, illuminated intermittently by shafts of light that pierce the canopy of leaves: combined, these create rhythm. In just the same way, the architectural structure of an interior must have rhythm. Arches, columns, statuary and windows create rhythm through shape and repetition. The reflection of light on walls and floors enhances this effect, together with the use of contrasting materials and colours in creating repeating patterns.

I am not a black and white photographer; I see and dream in colour. Without colour film, it would be impossible for me to capture the subtleties in design and decoration, or to do justice to the way in which architects and interior designers use tone and shade. Whether it is the Pompeiian red of a Neoclassical interior created by Schinkel, the vibrant wall panels in primary colours used by the architect Hans Scharoun in the interior of his Schminke house, or the daring and often surprising combinations created by interior designer John Stefanidis, colour brings things to life! I have always identified with the subtlety of Neoclassical colours – the blue-greens and pale greys and those natural, slightly distressed shades. (At the other end of the spectrum, I love red: fire red and the ox-blood red that I have applied to furniture, objects and walls.)

A sense of proportion and composition has always come to me naturally, but over the years the experience of photographing so many wonderful interiors has helped me to understand a space in a matter of minutes. Irrespective of the size of the property, before unpacking my cameras, I do a rapid tour. I see how the light falls, identify the important areas, and find the individual pieces of furniture, paintings and objects that help to define the spirit of the place. Decisions are immediate and unhesitating, and the secrets of the building are revealed in that first sense of discovery.

My main rule of thumb is to follow the light, which is always changing. The rhythm of my photography I liken to the various movements in a symphony, as I try to capture the play of light and shadow, as well as the variations in colour, pattern and texture that can be seen around a room. At the end of a shoot there is only ever one photograph that captures the essence of a house.

According to Antoine de Saint-Exupéry, 'perfection is achieved, not when there is nothing more to add, but when there is nothing left to take away'. Elimination is a key requirement of a Minimalist style, and, although confidence comes with experience, I believe that either we are born with a sense of visual balance and the ability to compose, or we are not. This is not something we learn.

I inherited very little, so the belongings I choose to surround myself with are pieces that I have collected over the years and that are full of personal memories. Each one has a story, not only when it comes to its provenance, but also because of its shape, form, colour or texture. Decoration must always have a meaning.

This book looks at ways in which architects and designers allow a sense of self to be part of the Minimalist interpretation. For me, there should always be a sense of life – a reflection, however subtle, of the person who has created and who occupies the space.

On one occasion, I was working with the interior designer Stephen Sills on an apartment in Manhattan. It was newly decorated and lacked life. It was autumn and Stephen disappeared into Central Park and returned with bags of multicoloured fallen leaves and filled the empty fireplace with them. As a consequence the photograph and the apartment came to life.

For a photographer, composition is fundamental, but displaying and combining objects and furniture is an art form. It is the proportion of objects as a collection, as much as the objects themselves, that influences how they should be displayed. Fashion designer Bill Blass had a great eye for composition and his collaboration with antiques dealer Christopher Gibbs at both his apartment in New York and his house in Connecticut was legendary. Bill Sofield is a designer with a similar talent for creating a harmony between old and new, while Robert Kime, although not an obvious Minimalist, has an unerring eye for composition.

My choice of designers, who I believe to be the best interpreters of 21st-century Minimalism in the Grand Style, is more visual than intellectual, though each makes a convincing and assured argument for this style of decoration. Each has a unique confidence and a feeling for rhythm, colour, light, space, texture and composition, combined with an approach to design that allows them to be generous rather than rigid.

Influenced by years of travel, they have experienced many different styles of architecture and design and have discovered a plethora of extraordinary spaces around the world. Most important of all, they each have the ability to incorporate these impressions into their designs. There is very little that is new in design; everything has been done at least once already, so it is really a question of delightful reinterpretation that gives it all a new look for the 21st century.

ABOVE Photographer Fritz von der Schulenburg, standing in the kitchen of designer John Minshaw's London home. He is reflected in a massive 1920s mirror placed on the polished stone floor of the entrance hall.

OVERLEAF In one of Axel Vervoordt's signature compositions, a large 18th-century table made out of a single plank of elm and displaying a Chinese scholar stone is juxtaposed with a 2nd-century AD Roman draped female figure and a contemporary artwork by Kazuo Shiraga in a restrained yet elegant interpretation of Minimalism in the Grand Style.

RHYTHM

Rhythm, scale and proportion determine our visual perception of a building. Our ability to move through an architectural space amplifies our appreciation of its structure and order. It also reinforces the importance of light, colour and composition in the achievement of structural harmony in an interior.

Architects and interior designers create rhythm by using many different elements: by repeating features such as arches, columns, doors, staircases and windows; by using shapes, including circles, semi-circles, lozenges, squares and triangles; by gauging the quality of light, whether natural or artificial; and by deploying colour and pattern to emphasize perspective.

The way in which the eye sees and makes sense of a space is influenced by the discipline of the space's construction. While the Parthenon is believed to have established the concept of harmony in Western-style architecture, Neoclassical architect Karl Friedrich Schinkel, an important influence in Minimalism in the Grand Style, is responsible for introducing a period of Greek Revival, with its Classical rhythm, before moving on towards the end of his life to a Modernist style that was way ahead of its time.

The Grand Gallery in Stockholm's Royal Palace (opposite) illustrates perfectly how each element of a room's design contributes to the overall rhythm of the space. The row of ornate arches and paired Classical columns punctuates the gallery at regular intervals, drawing the eye up to an impressive barrel-vaulted ceiling that resonates with rhythm. Natural light, falling in through floor-to-ceiling windows, floods the space from one side of the gallery, illuminating a series of statues that has been arranged along the length of the opposite wall. A black and white marble floor, laid in a chequerboard pattern, reinforces the perspective established by the symmetry of the arches, and the eye is transported effortlessly to the far end of the room.

Architect Annabelle Selldorf introduces dramatic rhythm to her renovation projects by using skylights to create a rhythmic lighting

OPPOSITE The Grand Gallery in Stockholm's Royal Palace epitomizes a visual sense of rhythm, with its paired columns and vaulted ceiling, punctuated by seven windows. The walls are painted grey to provide a contrast to the white marble of the sculptures. The black and white marble floor creates a repetitive and rhythmic pattern.

effect; supports, pillars and floating walls to create conscious intervals; as well as textured or coloured materials that distinguish further the old from the new building.

Vistas and enfilades are additional architectural conceits that enforce a sense of rhythm. The visual perception of an enfilade is enhanced by its disappearing perspective, yet interrupted by the outline of doorframes and archways or a piece of furniture that has been placed deliberately out of alignment.

The staircase is possibly the one architectural element in which rhythm is absolutely intrinsic to its construction. Space and light bring out the full architectural impact of the shape of a stairwell, whether it is spiral, helical, cantilever, floating or open, transforming the individual treads into complex rhythmic patterns, often lit by skylights and cupolas from above or by artificial up-lighters from below.

Natural light energizes an interior. Its ever-changing quality transforms space, highlighting certain areas while casting others into shadow. This ceaseless play of light affects the colours in which an interior has been decorated. It creates patterns and reflections on floors and walls and, as the sun moves around a property during the day, it influences the theatre of a space. In between space and light, there is always rhythm.

OPPOSITE Rhythm is created through the repetition of doors and windows opening onto this simple corridor in the Courtiers' Wing of Gripsholm Castle in Sweden, a Neoclassical extension that was built between 1780 and 1782 by Count Fredric Cronstedt.

ABOVE A contemporary spiral staircase (LEFT) benefits from a skylight at the top of the narrow stairwell, which adds light to the rhythm created by the swirl of regularly spaced concrete treads. The open staircase in a converted farmhouse in Majorca (RIGHT) has a rhythmic simplicity.

LEFT The unique marble interior at Elveden Hall in Suffolk is the legacy of the Maharajah Duleep Singh, exiled ruler of the Punjab, who purchased the estate in 1863 and rebuilt the house to resemble one of the Mughal palaces of his youth. During the Second World War, the house became one of the headquarters of the US Air Force, the resulting incongruous signage of this occupation still in evidence on the walls and doorframes seventy years later.

OPPOSITE AND ABOVE The dining room is situated on the ground floor of a five-storey wood and glass tower designed by architect Annabelle Selldorf. The floor-to-ceiling windows afford spectacular views of the Dolores Mountains in Colorado. A set of dining chairs by Josef Frank is matched with an antique wooden table and with 1960s-style pendant lights bought at auction.

LEFT Kremsmünster is a Benedictine monastery in Austria. One of its architectural idiosyncrasies is a large fish tank, which was built in the 17th century to house the monastery's requirement of fresh fish to feed the monks. Designed by Carlo Antonio Carlone, the series of three basins, punctuated with Classical statuary and fountains, is enclosed by a columned walkway lined with hunting trophies.

Stripes of colour – a traditional combination of dark red, black and cream – are seen on the painted walls of this hammam, or bathhouse, in the grounds of the Palais Sursock in central Beirut (ABOVE). The living room in Kenyan artist Joni Waite's former home in Lamu Town (OPPOSITE) is decorated with colourful striped local fabrics.

OVERLEAF At Schloss Marienburg (LEFT), designed for King George V of Hanover in the 19th-century Neo-Gothic style, each tread of the spiral staircase is lit by a tea-light, which accentuates the shape. The spiral staircase at the Hotel Amigo (RIGHT), on the Grand Place in Brussels, dates from 1957.

IN CONVERSATION WITH NICHOLAS HASLAM

'I compose an interior like a musical score. It starts on paper and I gradually build up the layers, adding and eliminating as that initial sketch takes shape.

Dorothy Draper was among the first women in America to see interior decorating as a commercial profession. I'm mad about her strong style! A room she did at Rockefeller Center in New York was immediately hailed as 'frozen music'.

My first interpretation almost automatically starts with a 'classic' plan, and progresses using light and reflection for balance, as only then can one start minimalizing. People now are fixated on 'light', and want far too much. Rooms should not be glaringly floodlit; they should sparkle with light.

Colour is more my thing, and it is influenced both by natural and artificial light, so, by applying paint and pattern in textures and layers, I can create endless different effects and permutations. It is important in any decorative scheme to remember that the eye needs to absorb the atmosphere of a room and to create its own interpretation of the whole.

Depending on the project or my mood, I can be influenced by both designers and architects. Yet I consider myself to be neither. Both professions tend to be somewhat bloodless, lacking passion. I am essentially a decorator, a beautifier. I add drama and the unexpected.

A decorator's approach to colour must be self-assured. Whereas confidence is commonplace and often misplaced, assurance is both bold and subtle.

Nancy Lancaster was one of the assured combiners of colour. In one house she painted one room pink, the one next to it blue. When complimented on the unlikely combination, she pointed out that it was the colour of the air, where the colours met, that was beautiful. Mrs Lancaster also had the one really successful yellow room in England, which, much to her annoyance, I described once as 'butter yellow'! Yellow isn't a colour I use much in this country, despite the old nonsense about 'sunny'; the reflection of so much natural green and grey outside works against it.

My favourite colour, one which I use over and over again, I call 'ashes of lilac'. It's a kind of grey violet tinged with a sable brown. It's the colour of shadows in old French floral chintzes. I love greys and browns and dull mauves, 'grauve' in my mind. They work for both Neoclassical and Minimal projects.

While some may raise an eyebrow at the mere suggestion of my being considered a Minimalist, designers haven't ever learned Maximalism.

My work hasn't become stuck in a rut; never a recipe. It's important for designers often to critique their output, change their style, their aims, even in my case their appearance. Besides, Minimalism is essentially a case of elimination, of paring away. It is static as opposed to fluid, and creates a void in which the decorator has to create an atmosphere. If one gets it right, the barrenness will be eliminated.

I do not set out to achieve a restrained grandeur in my decoration, but an interior must evolve if it is to be successful, until a certain point is reached at which it is obvious that a degree of restraint needs to be reintroduced. It can be as simple as walking into a room and recognizing that a certain piece of furniture or an object needs to be removed, or, conversely, that a shape or a piece is missing from a composition.

———

Paradoxically, some of the most elaborate rooms in the past have a Minimal quality about them, and I suspect that is what this book sets out to prove. For example, Empress Maria Theresa enlarged the royal castle in Prague in the 18th century in the most sumptuous Baroque style, yet every inch of the room was decorated entirely in white. Marie Antoinette's dairy at Rambouillet had a simple five-footed white marble table in a white room before a rock-wild grotto, and much of the Louis XVI furniture and decoration is as pared down as contemporary stuff. Just look at it without a jaundiced eye.

———

One of my recent interiors in London was commissioned by the client under the soubriquet of 'Minimalist Baroque': plain and pared down, but with a twist of Haslam exuberance! The project had a Minimalist beginning: it was a complete gut job. A classic four-bedroom townhouse was reconfigured, luxuriantly, as the echt one-bedroom city pied-à-terre.

———

I interpreted the unusual pairing of styles by exaggerating the scale of the decoration: from elaborate, ornamental plasterwork around the doorways, which is pure homage to Draper, to wide stripes of marble in black and white on the floor of the entrance hall.

———

Schinkel was a fabulous architect in Neoclassical Berlin and is a constant point of reference. Frances Adler Elkins was an American designer celebrated in the 1930s for her unorthodox approach to interior design. She integrated different styles and periods in a manner that had not been attempted before, juxtaposing Classical with sleekly modern decorating techniques; she used a shimmering colour palette, particularly blues, taupes and pinkish whites.

———

It must have been much easier to create breathtaking interiors, say, a hundred years ago. People understood that quality took time. Now, they want everything yesterday. Marie Antoinette was happy to wait a decade for her furniture. Well, I presume she was happy! Perhaps she was endlessly sending chivvying letters.

———

I was once offered the chance to create an ephemeral interior. Where things do not have to be decorated to last, it can feel extraordinarily liberating and I can experiment with different materials. We covered the floors in lengths of painted canvas, for example: temporary, yes, but imaginative … and also Minimal!

———

I love it when a design comes together quickly. A project can lose its impetus.

———

Artists have influenced, and continue to influence, the references we use to design and decorate our homes, as well as the ways in which we combine colour, texture and pattern. The walls of my office are covered in mood boards pinned with an ever-changing collection of sources of inspiration and ideas to interpret.

———

Decoration today is still about bravery; the courage not to copy either yourself or others, but to take elements, to mix them up and to create something new.'

ABOVE This bedroom, designed by American William Sofield, has as its focal point a white marble fireplace based on a design by Sir John Soane. Folding doors of Venetian plaster conceal a plasma screen, and the chimneybreast is flanked by a pair of mica-panelled, bronze-framed armoires.

ABOVE The scale of this double doorway in a house in London is exaggerated by its monumental plasterwork surround. It was created by Nicholas Haslam in homage to the 1930s American decorator Dorothy Draper.

A trio of white-painted and gilded Neoclassical chairs with dainty white seat covers lines a wall of the dining room of Pavlovsk Palace outside St Petersburg (OPPOSITE). Chairs can be hung easily from wooden pegs along the walls of this living room in the Hancock Shaker Village in Massachusetts (ABOVE).

'Artistic expression is a manifestation of the unity of design and material. This once again underlines the necessity for incorporating works of sculpture (or painting) creatively into the interior setting from the outset. In the great epochs of cultural history this was done by architects as a matter of course and, no doubt, without conscious reflection.'

LUDWIG MIES VAN DER ROHE, ARCHITECT (1886–1969)

OPPOSITE Hill House, outside Glasgow, is considered to be Charles Rennie Mackintosh's greatest domestic project. In the entrance hall, rhythm is achieved through the repetition of pattern: shapes and motifs are picked out in the murals, the pendant light and the rug, as well as in the glazing of the doors.

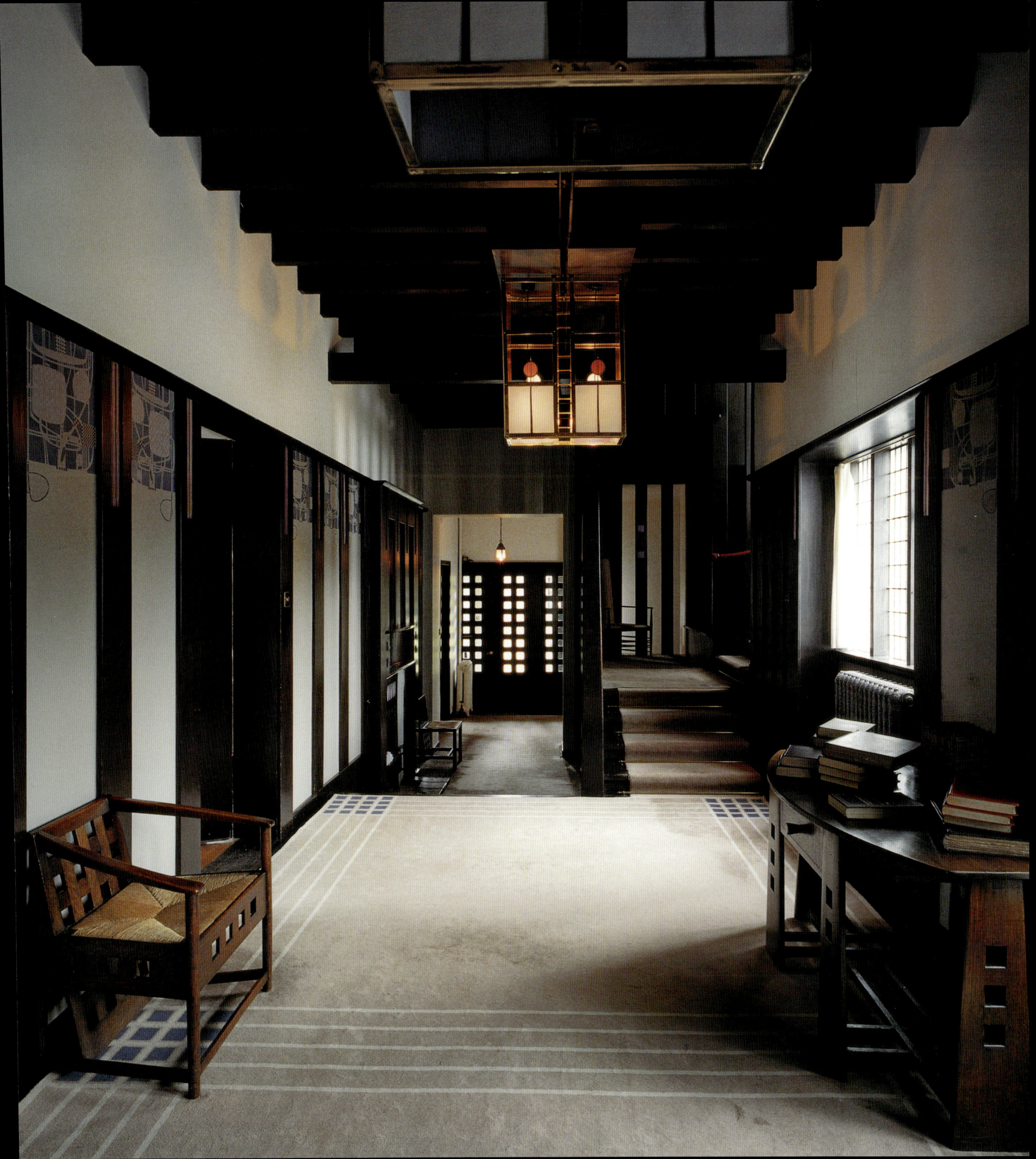

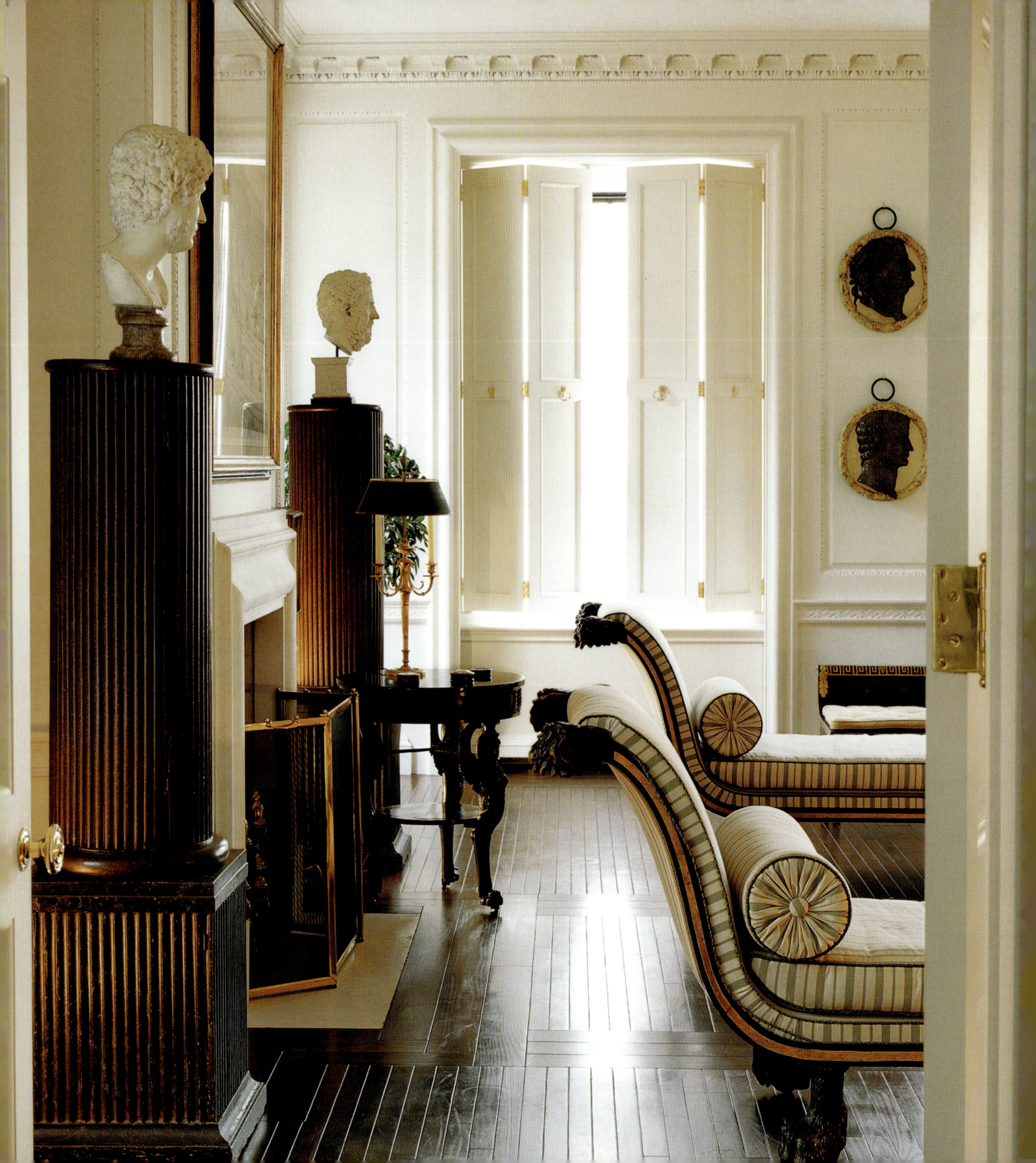

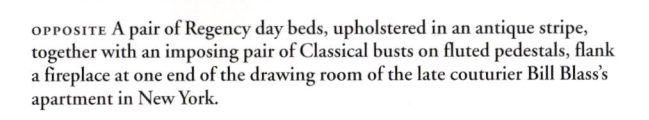

OPPOSITE A pair of Regency day beds, upholstered in an antique stripe, together with an imposing pair of Classical busts on fluted pedestals, flank a fireplace at one end of the drawing room of the late couturier Bill Blass's apartment in New York.

CLOCKWISE FROM TOP LEFT Designer Nicholas Haslam creates exaggerations of scale in a London apartment: a small curved connecting hallway; an entrance hall laid with fat stripes of marble; illuminated vases cut in half and displayed in an oversized plaster frame; a tall narrow double door, opening into a bedroom at the top of the stairs.

RHYTHM

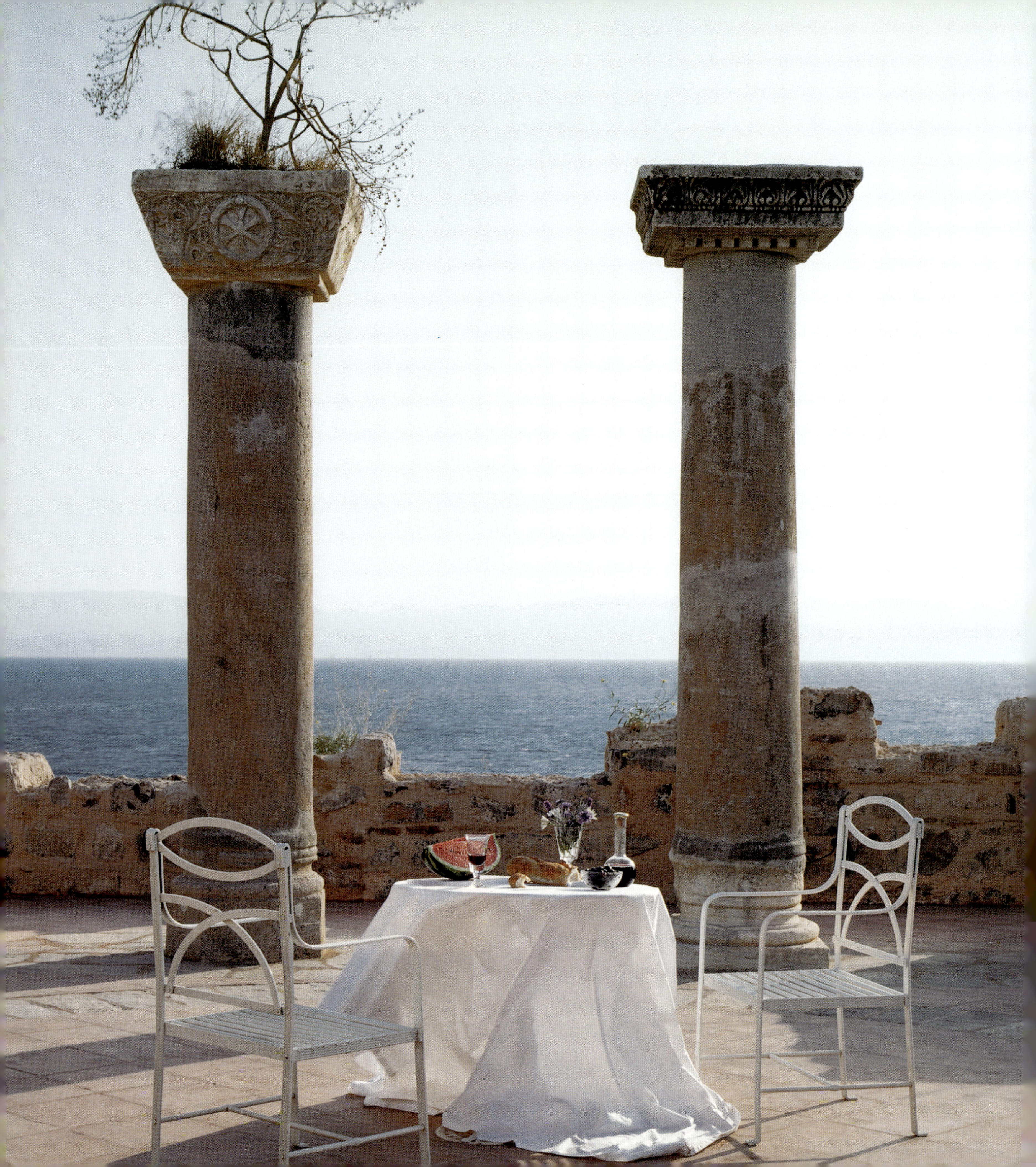

OPPOSITE A pair of stone columns from the Museum of Turkish Antiquities frame the impromptu meal that has been served on this sunlit terrace with views over the Sea of Marmara.

ABOVE At the foot of the Spanish Steps in Rome is the Fontana della Barcaccia ('Fountain of the Old Boat'), designed by Pietro Bernini between 1627 and 1629.

RHYTHM

'To create, one must first question everything.'

EILEEN GRAY, ARCHITECT AND FURNITURE DESIGNER (1878–1976)

OPPOSITE Sunloungers are lined up to dry against a wall of the horizon pool at Finca Buenvino in Huelva, a hotel and cookery school owned and run by Sam and Jeannie Chesterton, which has views over the Sierra de Aracena National Park.

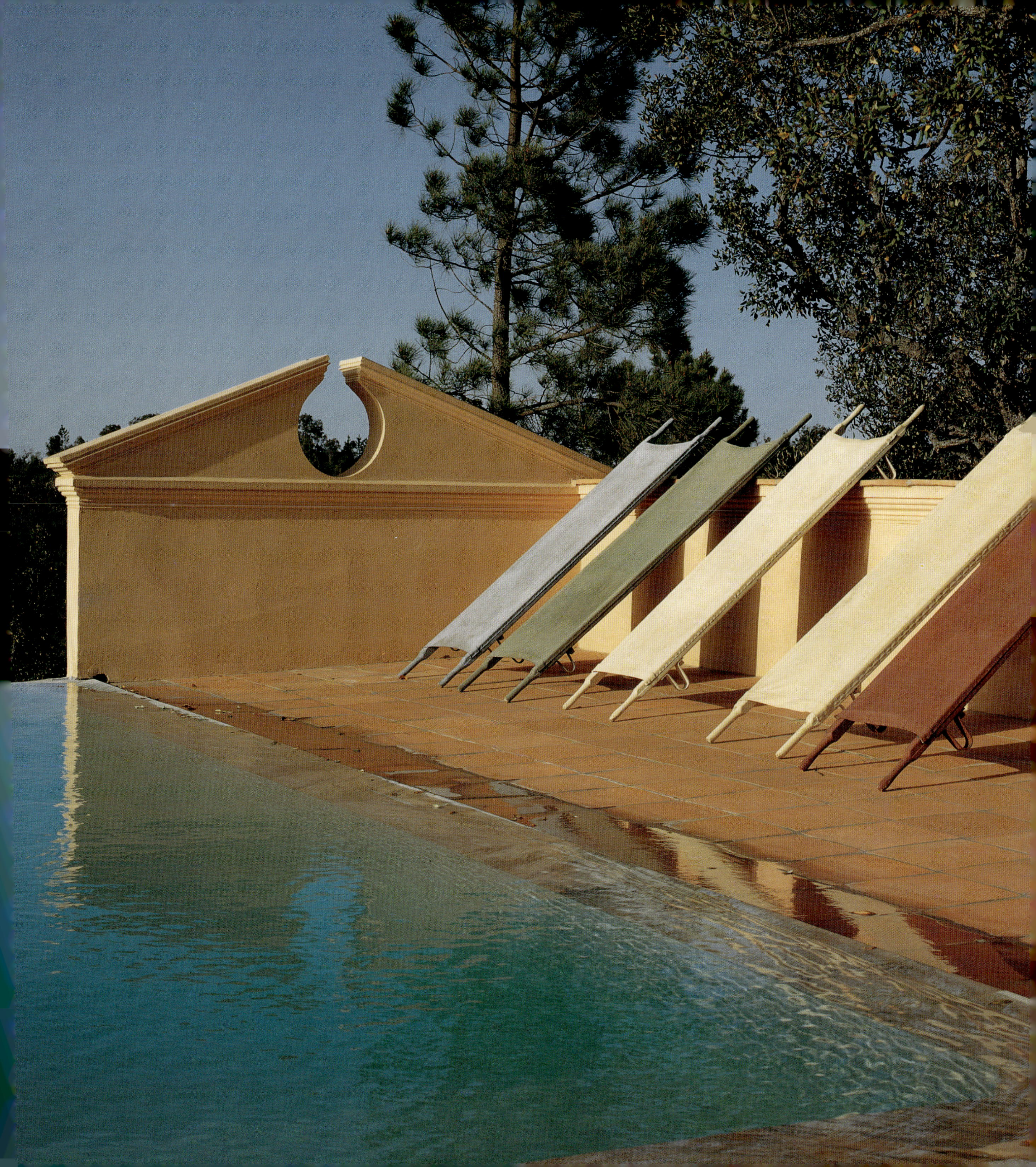

Rhythm is created with repeated pattern and exacting placement. The pale green wall of this simple Swedish living room (ABOVE) has been hand-painted to resemble panelling. A row of Biedermeier chairs beneath a painting (OPPOSITE) has been placed in precise fashion.

43

ABOVE This dramatic 1920s-style bathroom was designed by William Sofield for a house in New York and is graced with an original Lalique 'Rinceaux' chandelier in clear and frosted glass. The custom-made bath, washbasin and shower cabinet, in a black nickel finish with rock crystal handles, were made by P. E. Guerin.

OPPOSITE The walls of the magnificent library at Althorp, in Northamptonshire, are lined with bookcases. The books inside represent the remains of a collection of 40,000 volumes amassed in the 18th century by the Second Earl Spencer and now kept in the John Rylands Library in Manchester.

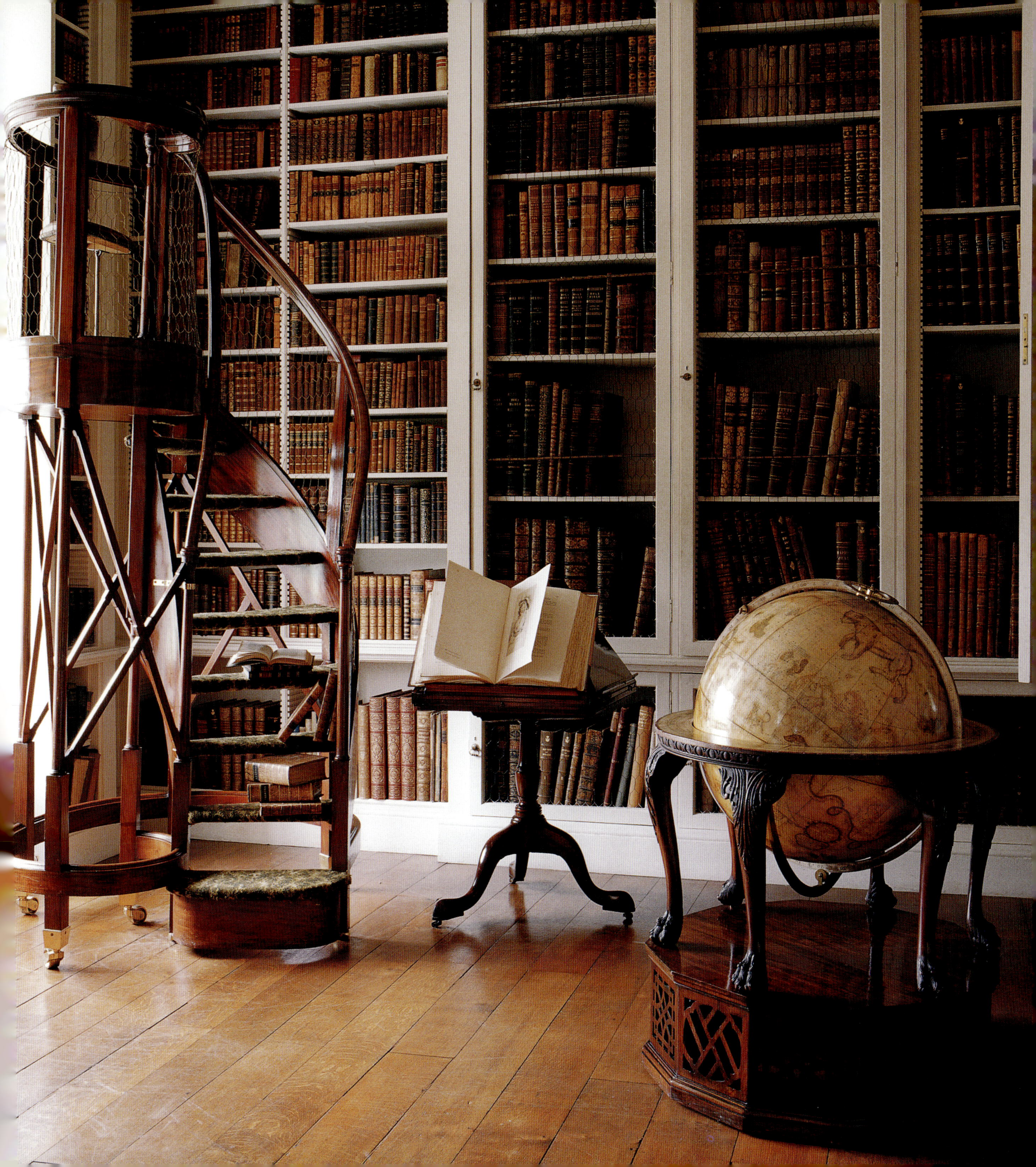

IN CONVERSATION WITH JOHN MINSHAW

'Colours can be used to great effect to create perspective and rhythm.

———

There is no real right or wrong when it comes to using colour. You can't say yellow is better than black; it is simply a question of interpretation. I use a lot of blue, deep mauve and Bible black, which when you put light onto it turns pink. More recently I have also taken to using a collection of bronze paints in a series of five muddy shades of olive. I use these as a processional palette, so I start off light and then get darker. I also decorate many of my interiors in one base colour, such as a strong white, which I use in a variety of finishes. Even though it is essentially the same colour, the layering of emulsion, eggshell and flat oil reflects the light differently.

———

I have only built a handful of buildings from scratch so far, and it is a great freedom. I am currently working on a house that I am transforming in an interpretation of an 18th-century interior, one in which all the rooms would have led off a central corridor. In contemporizing the historical layout, there is in fact no corridor, just interrelating rooms which create a splendid modern enfilade, and in which there is the added joy of being able to play with and progress the colour in its decoration.

———

Fabric and textiles also play an important role in any design scheme. For instance, there can be softness and elegance in the way that fabric drapes which cannot be achieved with sacking. I work with a lot of 'plains' – using texture in the same colour way, much as I do with paint – and the contrasting textures of chenille, velvet, linen and cotton reflect light differently.

One trick I have developed is to make a rough linen curtain with a fabulous silk curtain beneath it, so you can draw one or the other, or both, for a different textured effect. A contrasting lining to a curtain is another good trick; like a man's suit, traditional and sober on the outside, vibrant and unexpected on the inside. I give cushions the same treatment, where one side might be velvet and the reverse plain linen.

———

Subtlety is underrated in our business. Pattern is often used as camouflage, and an ornate design employed to confuse the eye. If you have a white room with one dot in it, you tend to fixate on the dot; but if you covered the wall with a million dots, you would dissipate the whole effect.

———

'Minimalism' is a word invented to make sparse into a concept. I don't consider what I do to be Minimal; I am just very sparse. I am a 'bones' person.

———

A building is about volume and I like to get the structure right, the design done and everything fitted into its correct place, and to leave the resulting interior as clean and as spare as possible. This level of exposure makes it much more difficult to create an empty space in which every part of the design is essentially on show. In a pared-down interior, the finish is everything.

———

I have an art-school background and learned at an early age how to revolve an object three-dimensionally in space and to be able to draw it from any angle. I have always been crazy about proportion, yet I think that a true understanding of proportion is not something you learn; you are simply born with it.

I have made furniture for over twenty years, and as a result have a strong sense of balance and scale. If you look at Georgian and Victorian architecture, the façade of a building will reveal that the window size diminishes proportionately up the elevation. Nowadays, if a house is designed using a computer, the windows of a three-storey building will all be the same size. In my opinion these nuances of scale are fundamental to an overall design, like the difference between a plastic and a horn button on a man's suit. A plastic button may look just as good, but it will not deceive an expert eye.

———

The greatest compliment I can be paid when someone walks into a house for the first time is the thought that I have done nothing to its structure. My own home in London was a dental laboratory with three floors of tiny cubby-holes and we were obliged to move or rebuild everything in the house except the staircase.

———

A sense of history is incredibly important to a designer and I remember a lecture I attended at the Soane Museum when the house was lit entirely with candles. In that wonderful yellow drawing room, a mirror placed behind each candle sconce and a mirror on the opposite wall ensured that a single candle was reflected a thousand times. In the flickering light, sculpture and artwork became theatrical in their composition: I have never forgotten the impact.

———

I am sure that I reference my work subliminally to Soane, particularly when it comes to lighting and his sense of theatre. Light, when it is misunderstood, can ruin an interior. When I visited Greece for the first time and saw the quality of the light, I understood why the Greeks were so big on mouldings. Shape reflects light in so many different ways and in Greece there is an extraordinary clarity of light. While I understand today's technology, I don't tend to get ritzy with lighting and, rather than playing with artificial light, prefer to let natural light do the work and to keep it simple.

———

I love the element of surprise you still get sometimes when you first enter a building. Hawksmoor and Vanbrugh were brilliant when it came to playing with space and proportion, and in their hands massive proportions became theatrical.

———

I love to buy furniture and art, and still buy for houses that in essence are finished. While I hate the term 'organic', I do like the slow way in which an interior can be developed. For me, objects and furniture are touchstones that reveal what other people were thinking and creating years ago. I love the connection, and the pleasure associated with discovering a new way of displaying someone else's genius is enormous.

———

I try not to overfill a house, but I am a sucker for paintings, ceramics and pots. We have a lot to thank Axel Vervoordt for. In the old days, antiques dealers would cram their showrooms with stuff. The trick as a designer is to take an object out of context and to view it in a new light. Axel has led the way in how to display objects in a sparse interior.

———

No matter my love of historical and particularly Neoclassical reference, as a designer I am delighted to be living in the 21st century. We have so many possibilities and options to play with that if Sir John Soane were alive today, he would be unable to contain himself!'

ABOVE According to designer John Minshaw, the dining room is one of the most complete rooms in his London home and was configured to form a perfect cube. The table and benches were made to his own design in macassar ebony; the ceiling light is Italian, 1960s; and the painting on the mantelpiece is from the school of William Nicholson.

OPPOSITE John Minshaw's study is a conservatory space that was originally occupied by a 1960s building separated from the main house. The 1930s Danish black leather wingchair is matched with a 19th-century French library desk, a Charles Eames lobby chair and a Klismos chair. The bookcases are by John Minshaw Designs.

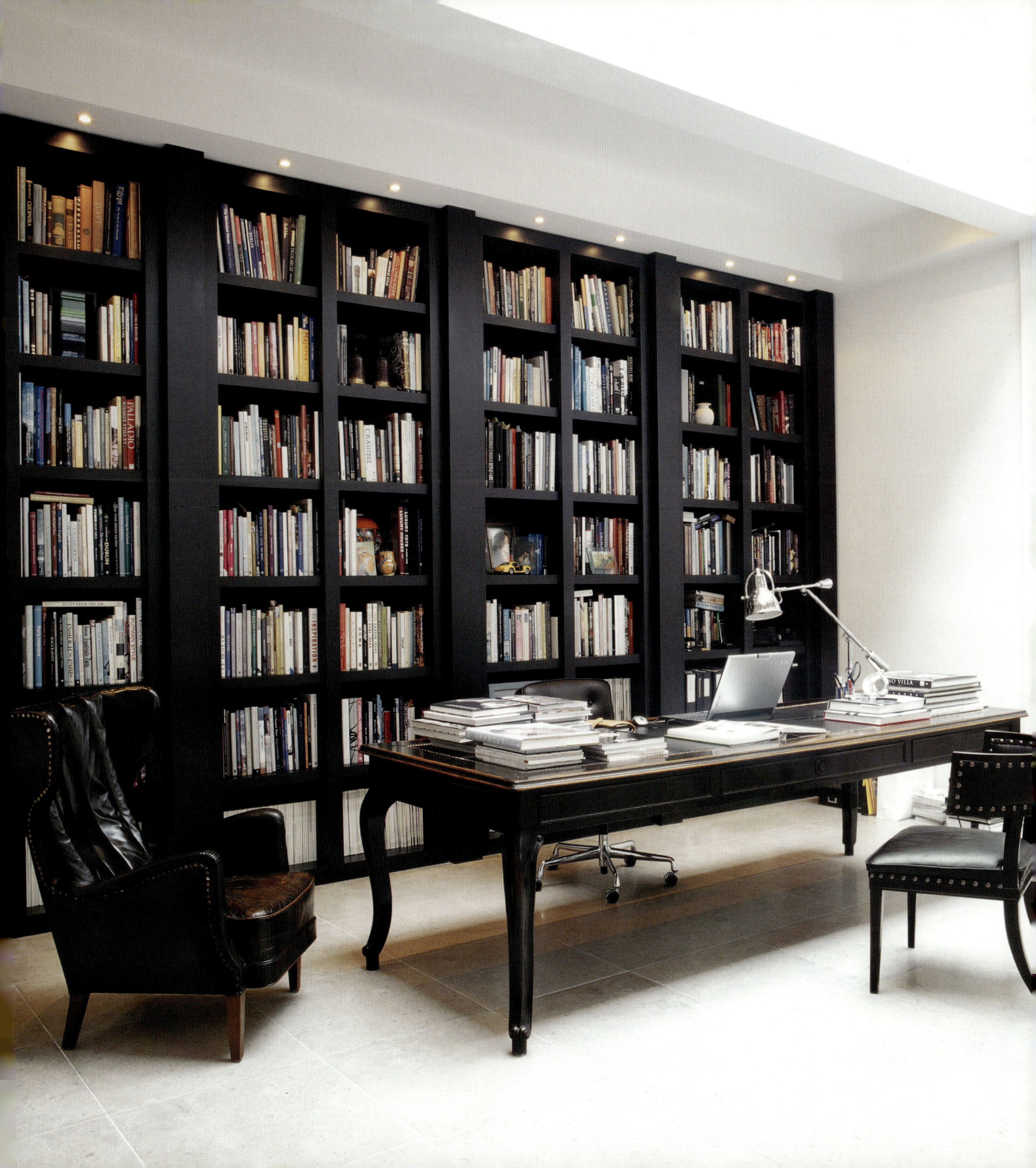
PALLADIO
INSPIRATION

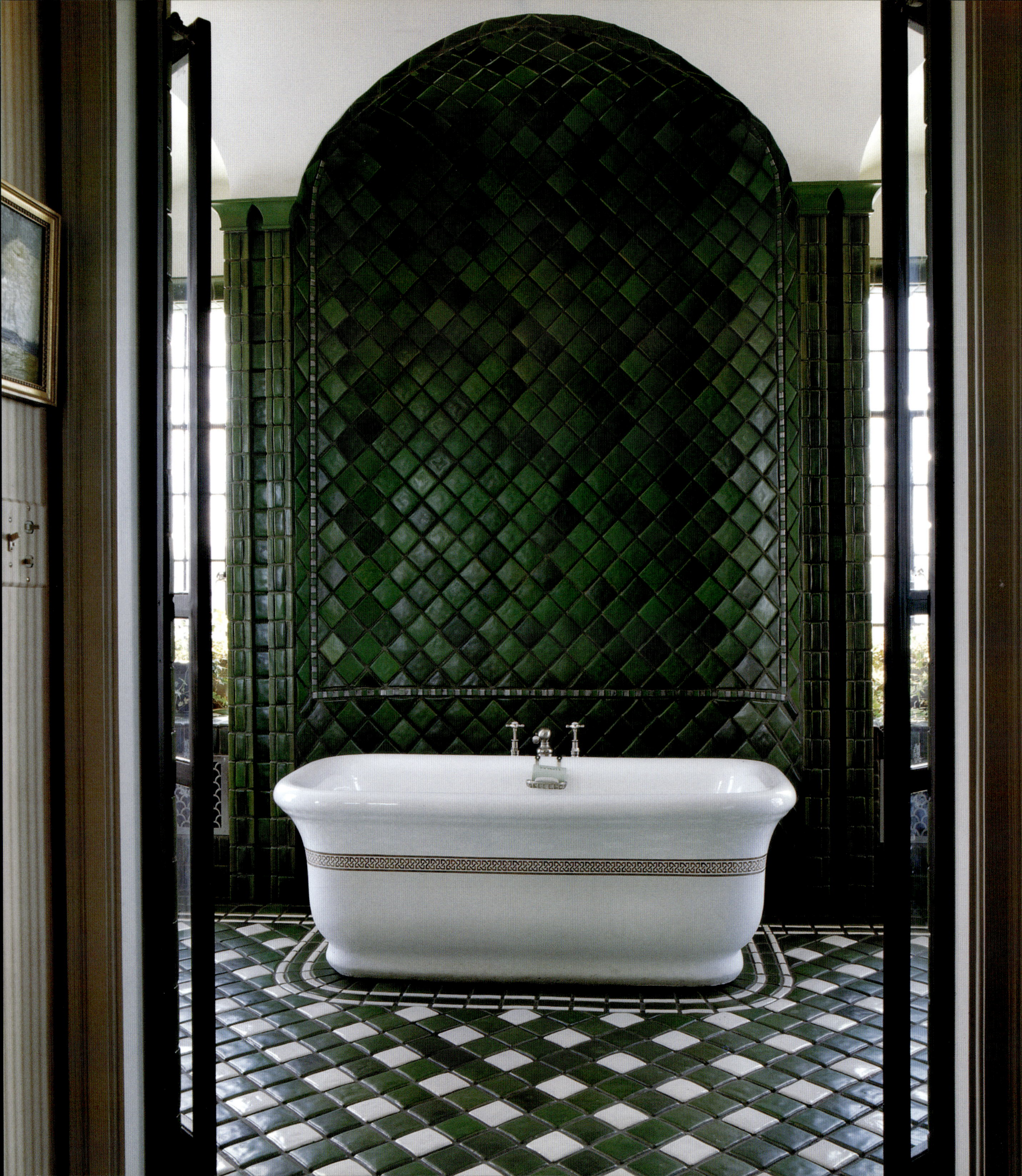

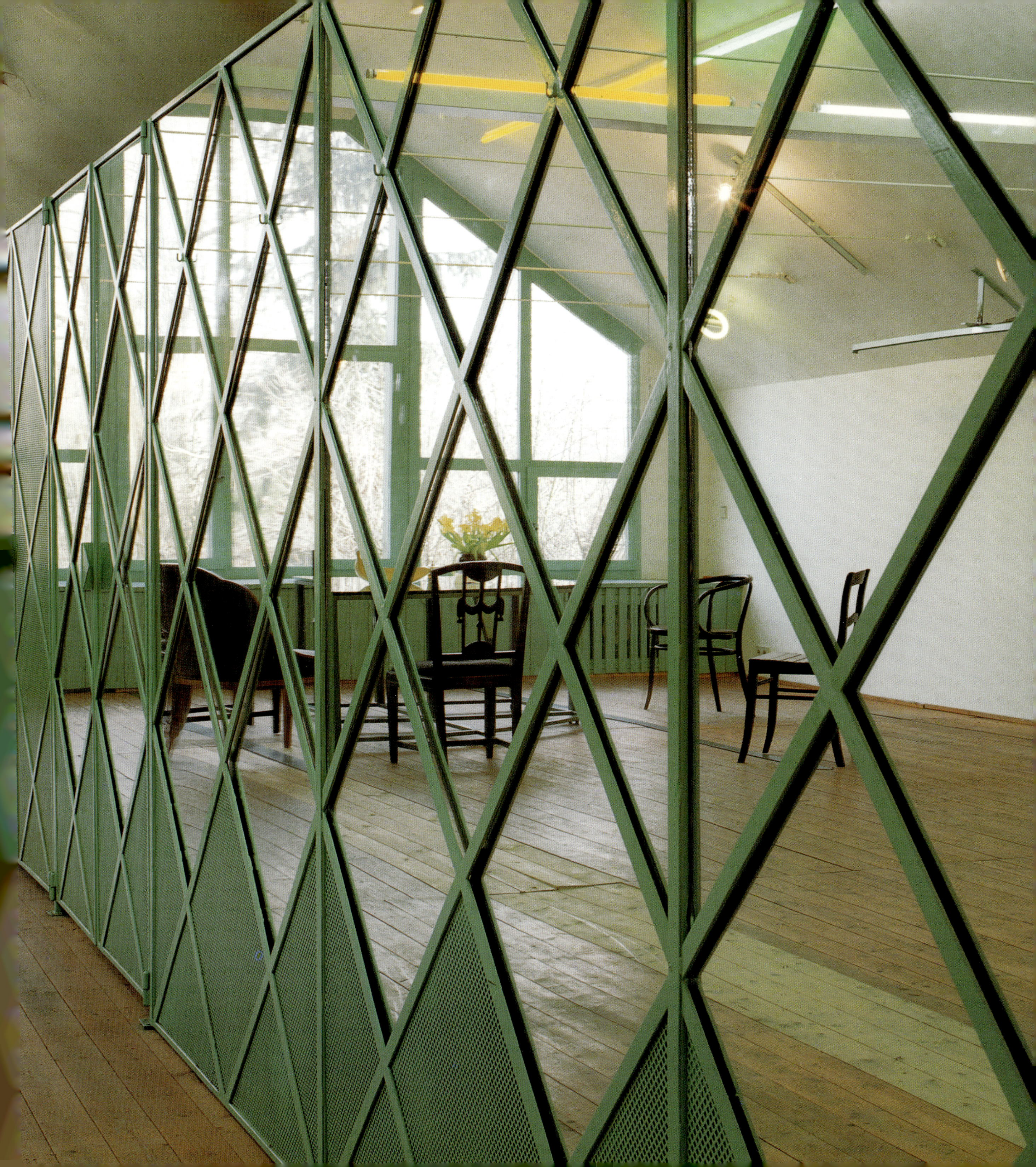

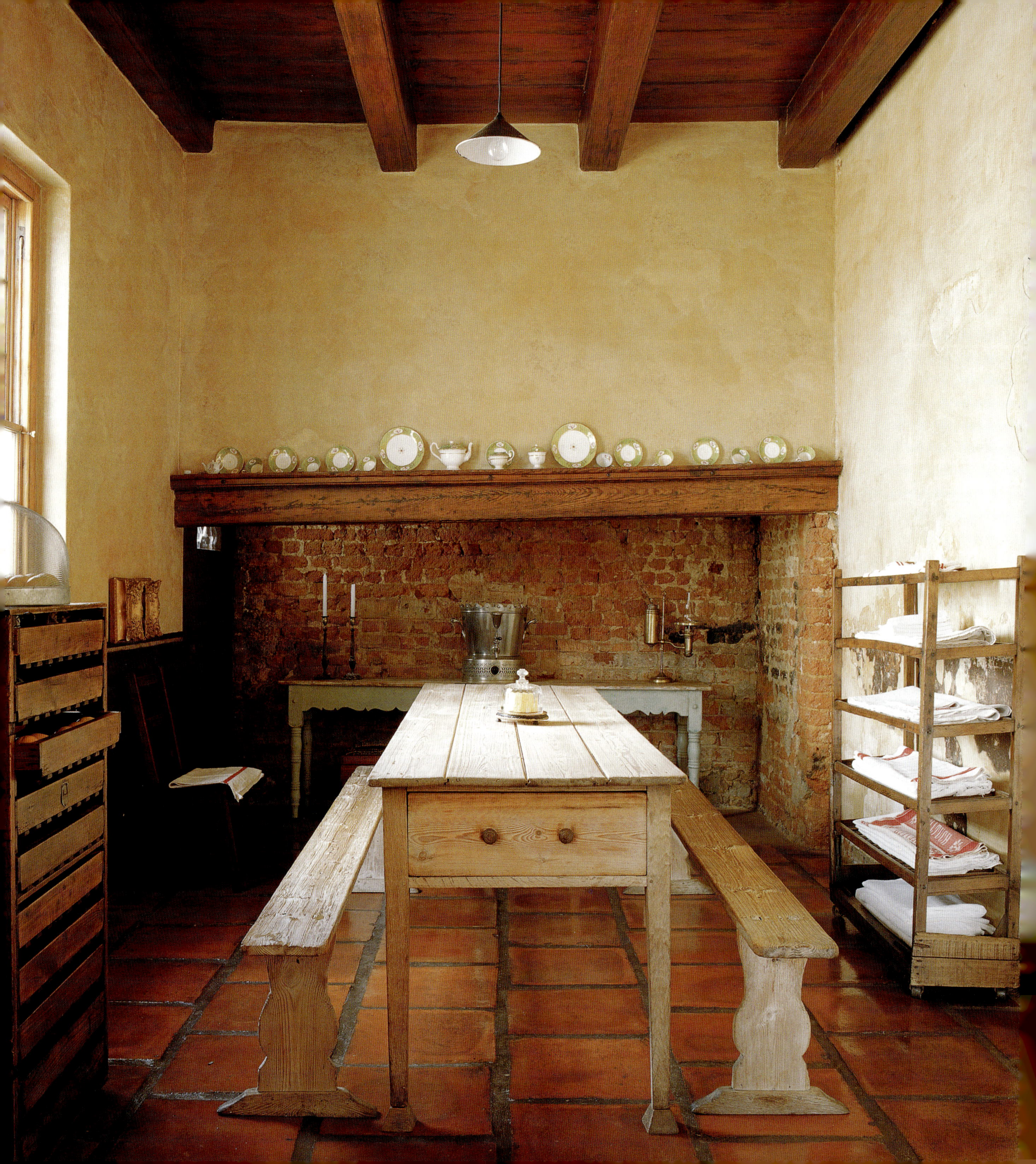

PREVIOUS PAGES The Art Deco-style bathtub and fixtures in this Manhattan bathroom (LEFT) by the late designer Jed Johnson, were shipped over from France to sit against chequered dark green tiles from Pewabic Pottery in Detroit. An entire wall of artist Karl-Heinz Scherer's studio (RIGHT) is lined with mirrored cupboards decorated in a rhythmic pattern of latticed wood.

The placement of the furniture in interior designer Karen Roos's kitchen-dining room in South Africa (OPPOSITE) reinforces the perspective established by the terracotta floor tiles and beamed ceiling, leading the eye towards the fireplace. Italian architect Andrea Taverne creates rhythm in this country kitchen (ABOVE) with a chequerboard tiled floor and floor-to-ceiling glass-fronted cabinets.

'In matters of art, it is not a question of asking what previously known useful things can be brought to the task. Rather a pure idea of the entire formation of the work arises in the soul of the architect. This idea is produced entirely from within himself, quite independently of the existing world. He feels the most profound destiny of the building immediately in his own being.'

KARL FRIEDRICH SCHINKEL, ARCHITECT (1781–1841)

OPPOSITE Marbled columns, interspersed with high-backed wooden pews painted a Neoclassical blue-grey, support a gallery that skirts the interior walls of the restrained 1730s Baroque church of St Gumbertus in Ansbach, Germany.

OVERLEAF Classical marbles, framed by a contemporary marble wall, are the focal point of this staircase, Neoclassically inspired, at the Archaeological Museum in Istanbul (LEFT). The loggia of an Italianate house in southwest France doubles as an outdoor dining room (RIGHT); antique linen sheets have been hung between the stone arches for additional shade.

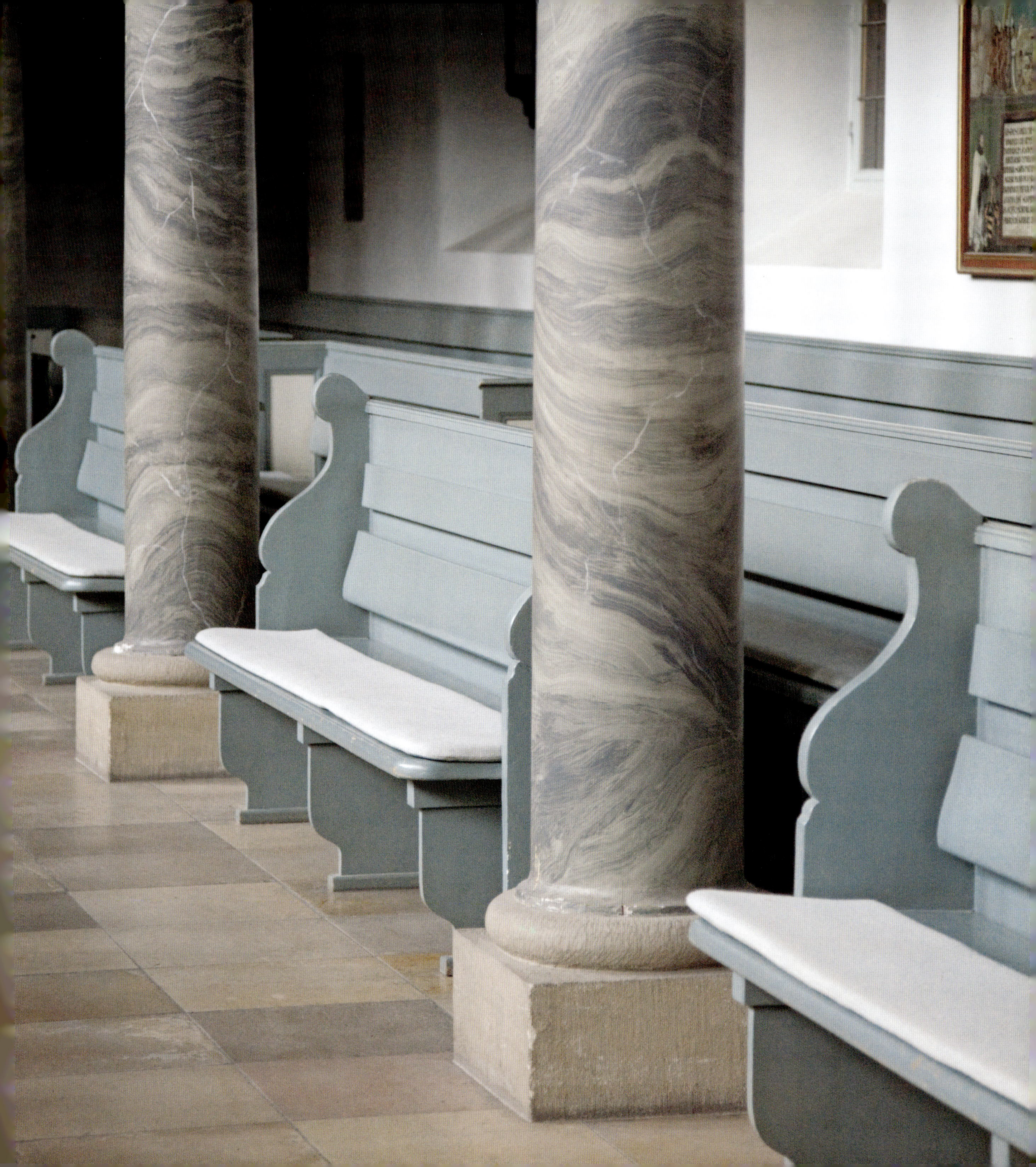

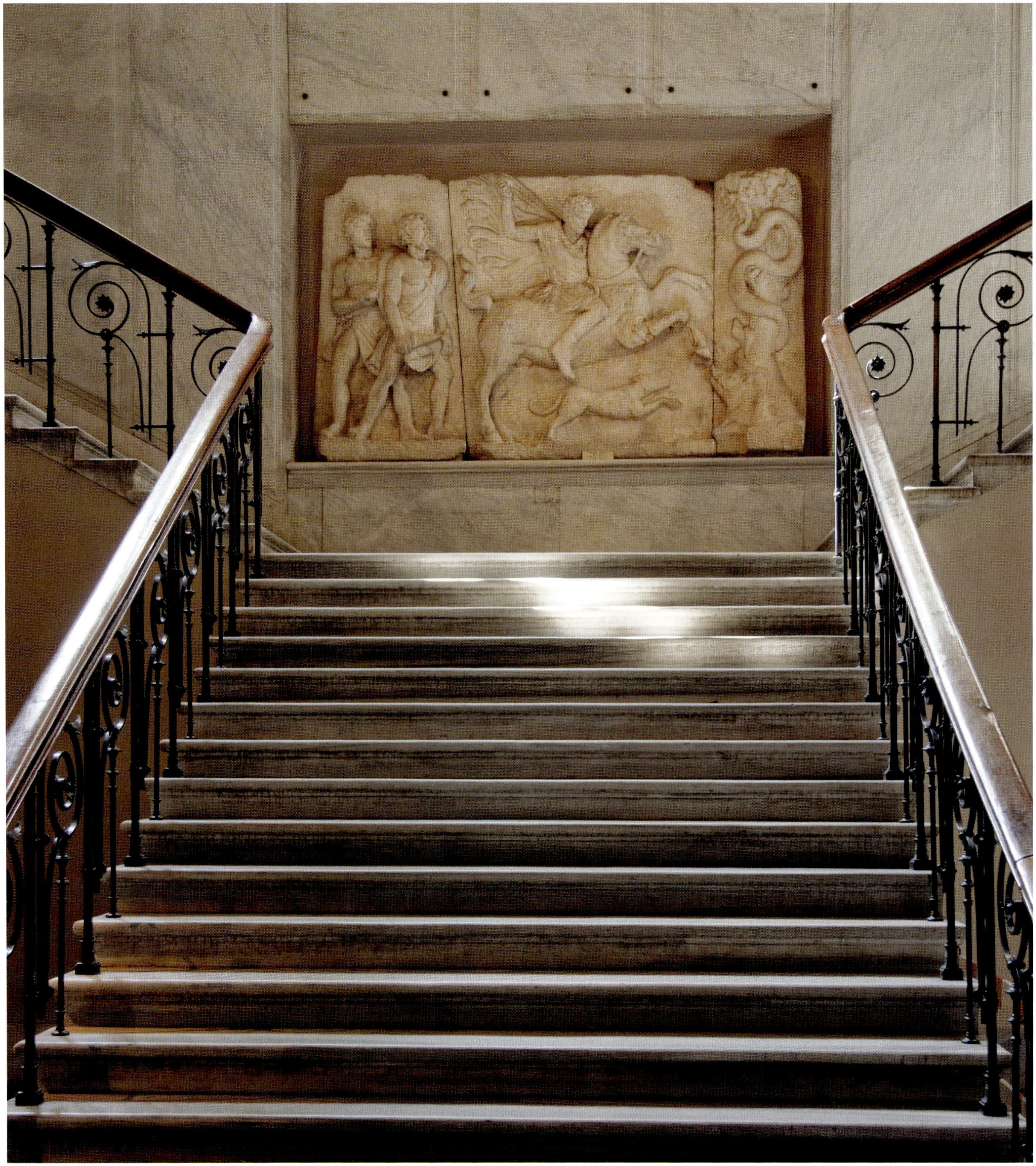

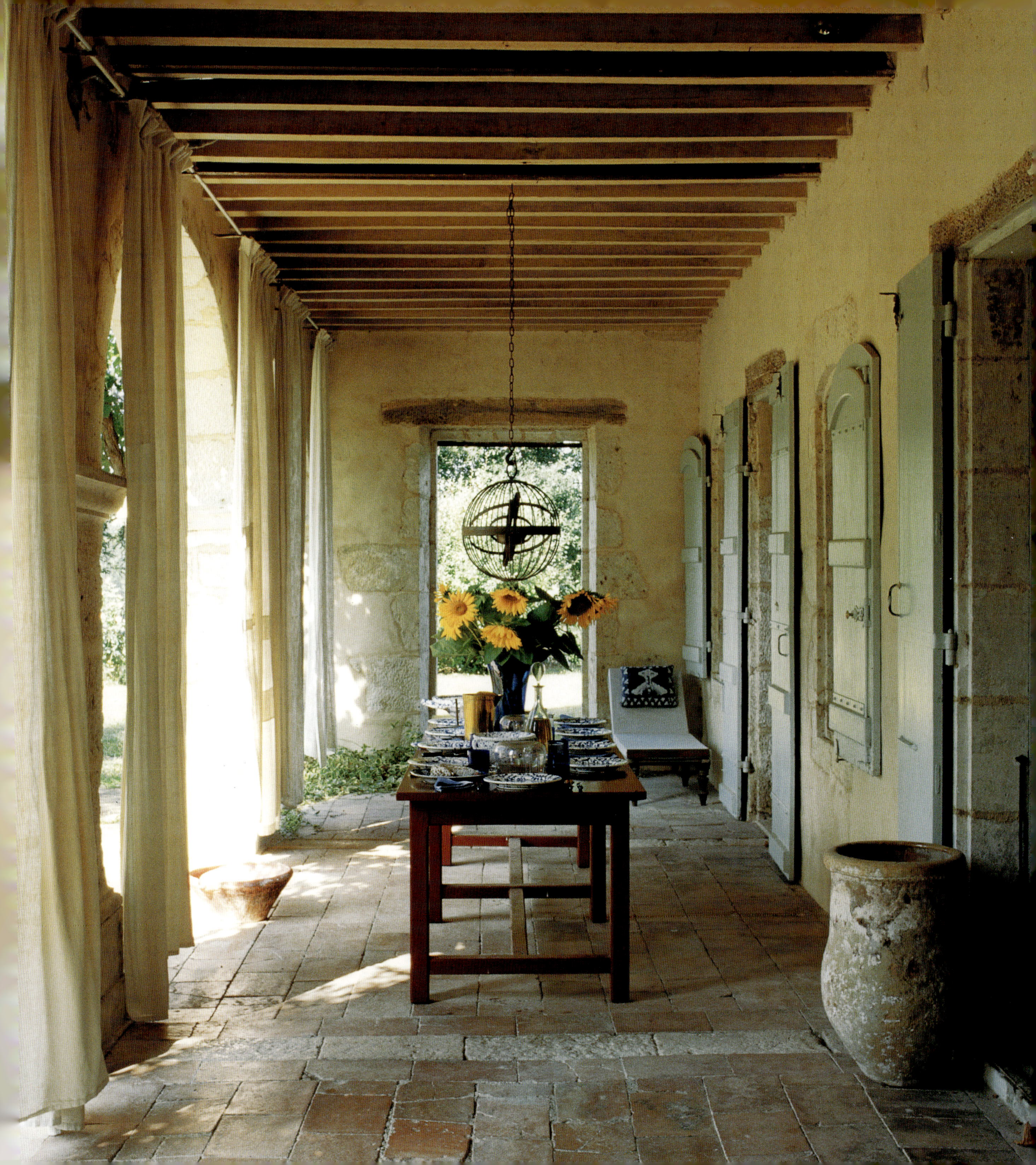

ABOVE Pattern creates rhythm through repetition: the parquet flooring, combined with the hand-painted murals, and punctuated by the orderly row of chairs, gives additional rhythmic emphasis to this Scandinavian Neoclassical anteroom.

ABOVE In South African designer Karen Roos's country home, several patterns work together, from the black and white tiled floor to the antique ceramic tiles that surround the fireplace, while the random shape of a pile of logs adds its own rhythm.

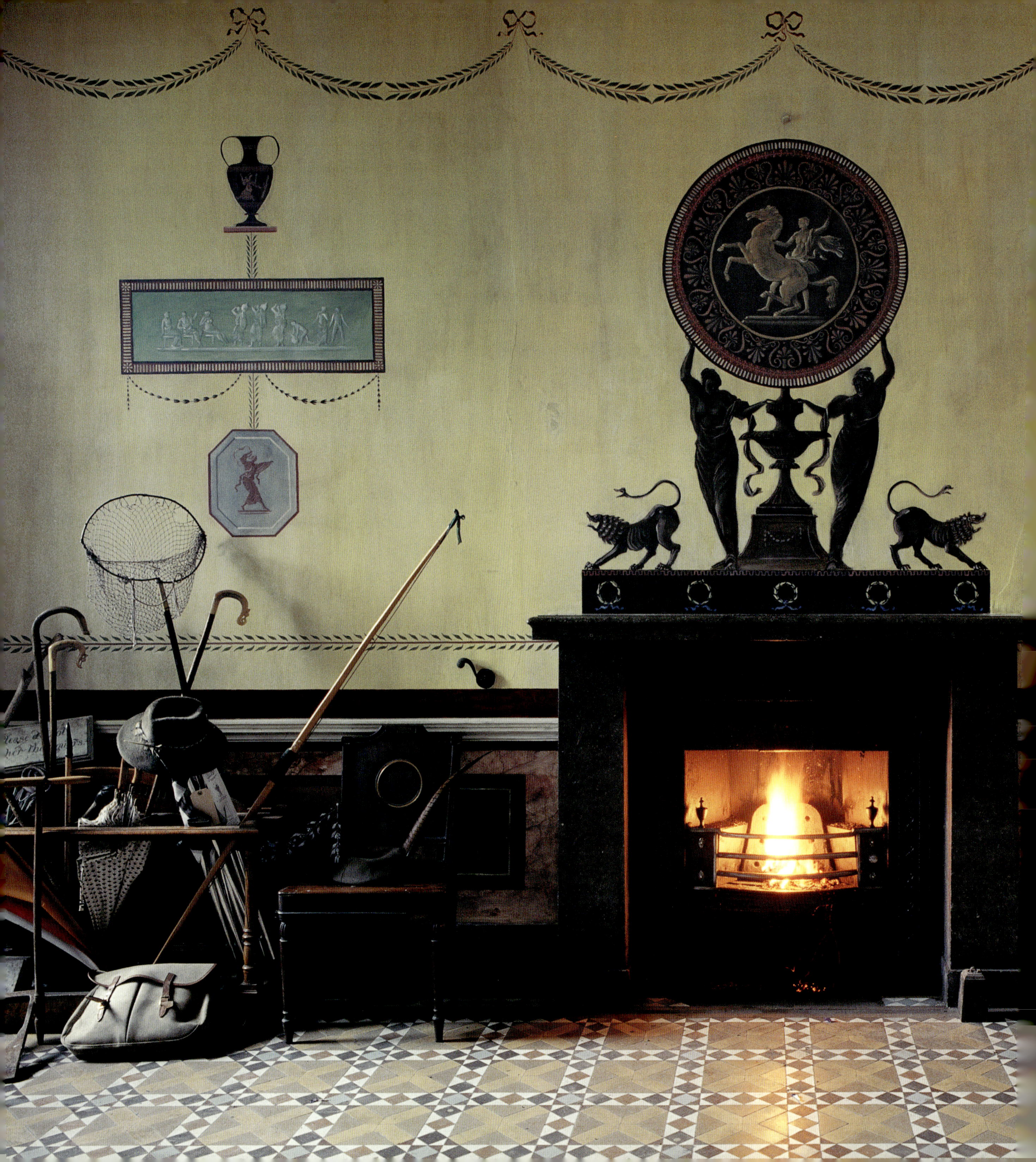

LEFT The entrance hall at Ardgowan House, on the Firth of Clyde in Scotland, combines an original Victorian tiled floor with murals by Alec Cobb, who repainted the swags and border details from original designs discovered beneath the old paint.

COLOUR

Colour is not simply a surface decoration. The way in which it interacts with light, both inside and outside a building, and also with texture and ornamentation, is fundamental to good design. Colour completes the overall composition of a space.

Colour is a personal interpretation – an embellishment – but it adds to the integrity of a building: it complements and highlights the architectural elements; it emphasizes both the ornamentation and detail, and provides the finishing touches to the rhythm.

Leonardo da Vinci established that 'the first of all single colours is white... We shall set down white for the representative of light, without which no colour can be seen; yellow for the earth; green for water; blue for air; red for fire; and black for total darkness.'

Numerous architects and interior designers, in addition to gaining a reputation for designing important and imaginative spaces, are also remembered for their trademark uses of colour. Karl Friedrich Schinkel used intense colours in an almost theatrical fashion, using them to unite the interiors of his Neoclassical designs, such as the summer palace of Charlottenhof and the nearby Roman baths in the Sanssouci Park in Potsdam.

Robert Adam's choice of colour was Neoclassical in influence: he chose pastel-hued blues, greens and pinks with which to apply the concept of movement to his decorative schemes, introducing mythological figures and Classical symmetry.

Others have approached the decoration of a room in much the same way as a painter, juxtaposing colours, pattern and texture with a bold confidence. Picasso is quoted as saying, 'Why do two colours, put one next to the other, sing? Can one really explain this? No. Just as one can never learn how to paint.' Contemporary interior designer John Stefanidis notes, too, that true colours will never clash. He has always approached decoration from a painter's perspective, carrying in his mind's eye nuances of tone and shade.

OPPOSITE A pair of early 19th-century mirrors in distressed, ornately carved wooden frames stands on the concrete floor of Kanaal, the warehouse of antiques dealer Axel Vervoordt, in which he stores his vast collection of art and furniture, near his castle home in Antwerp.

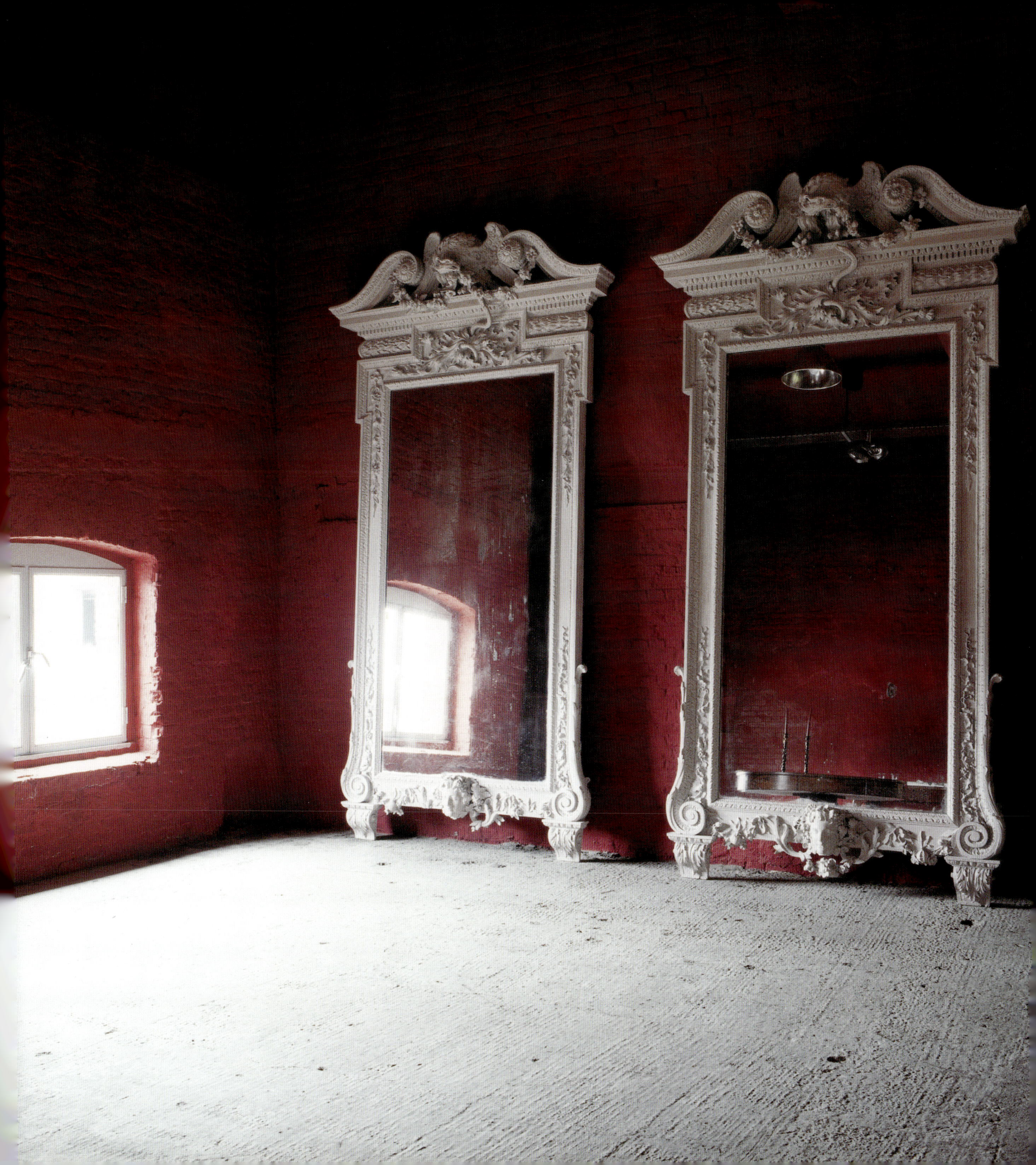

64

Equally at home in grand spaces and simple ski chalets, decorator Nicholas Haslam does not automatically fall into the category of Minimalist in the Grand Style – but he advocates hand-painted walls and pure ranges of colour wherever possible. 'I can't bear murals; and a fresco must be pure fantasy,' he explains. 'I have worked for years with paint specialist Paul Czainski, and will always ask him to paint the walls as if he had his eyes closed!'

Colour in design has seen endless permutations. In the form of paint, it has often been used in plain blocks of colour on walls, against which a collection of artwork is displayed to best advantage; applied in stripes or other geometric patterns it adds rhythm to a space; or in a frieze, murals, papier peint or a trompe-l'oeil scene it allows a more artistic interpretation. The painted canvases that were used as Neoclassical wall decoration were gradually replaced during the Empire period when colour was adapted to fabric. As a result, strong primary colours were chosen for wall coverings and curtains, with geometric patterned carpets and rugs, and silk damask for the furniture.

Today, colourful textiles, wall hangings, carpets, rugs and the wealth of soft furnishings that are intrinsic to the design of a room, continue to contribute to the ultimate composition of its interior an opulence and a grandeur of style.

OPPOSITE An abstract blue and white painting is juxtaposed with a lacquered sculpture of a pair of conjoined chairs, their combination of primary colours the eye-catching focus of a New York loft living room, the former home of architect William Monaghan.

ABOVE The shape of a pair of benches in Kanaal, Axel Vervoordt's converted silo in Antwerp, is emphasized by the use of colour. A simple rustic stool glimpsed through an opening in the warehouse wall (LEFT) is framed with red, while a more ornate Chinese bench (RIGHT) is set against a wall of pale blue.

The mood of a room is directly affected by its colour scheme. While this French dining room (ABOVE) has been painted in a dark and muted palette, conducive to candlelit meals, the tranquillity and empty grandeur of this unfurnished drawing room (OPPOSITE) is enhanced by the Neoclassical blue-green of the paintwork.

66   COLOUR

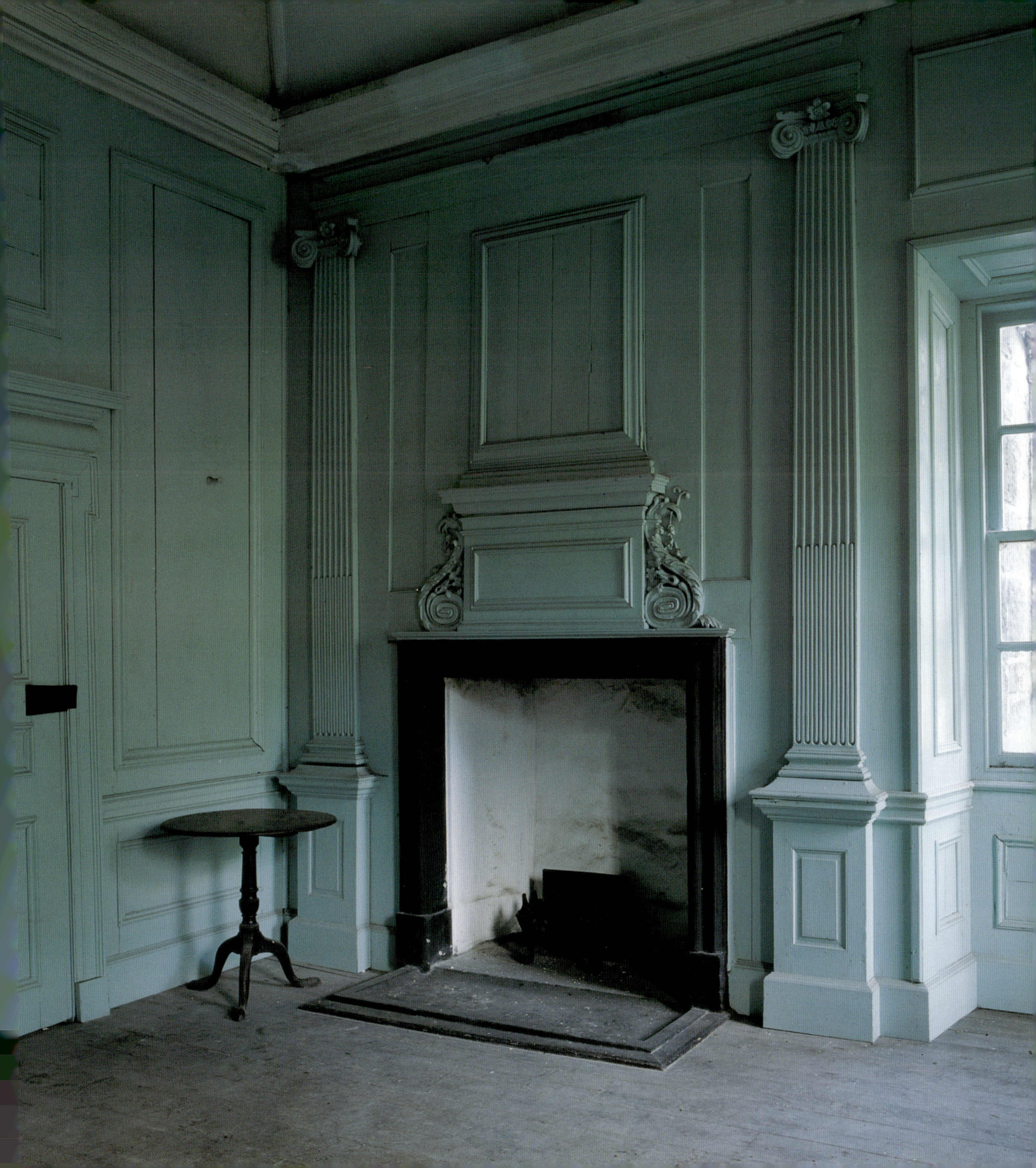

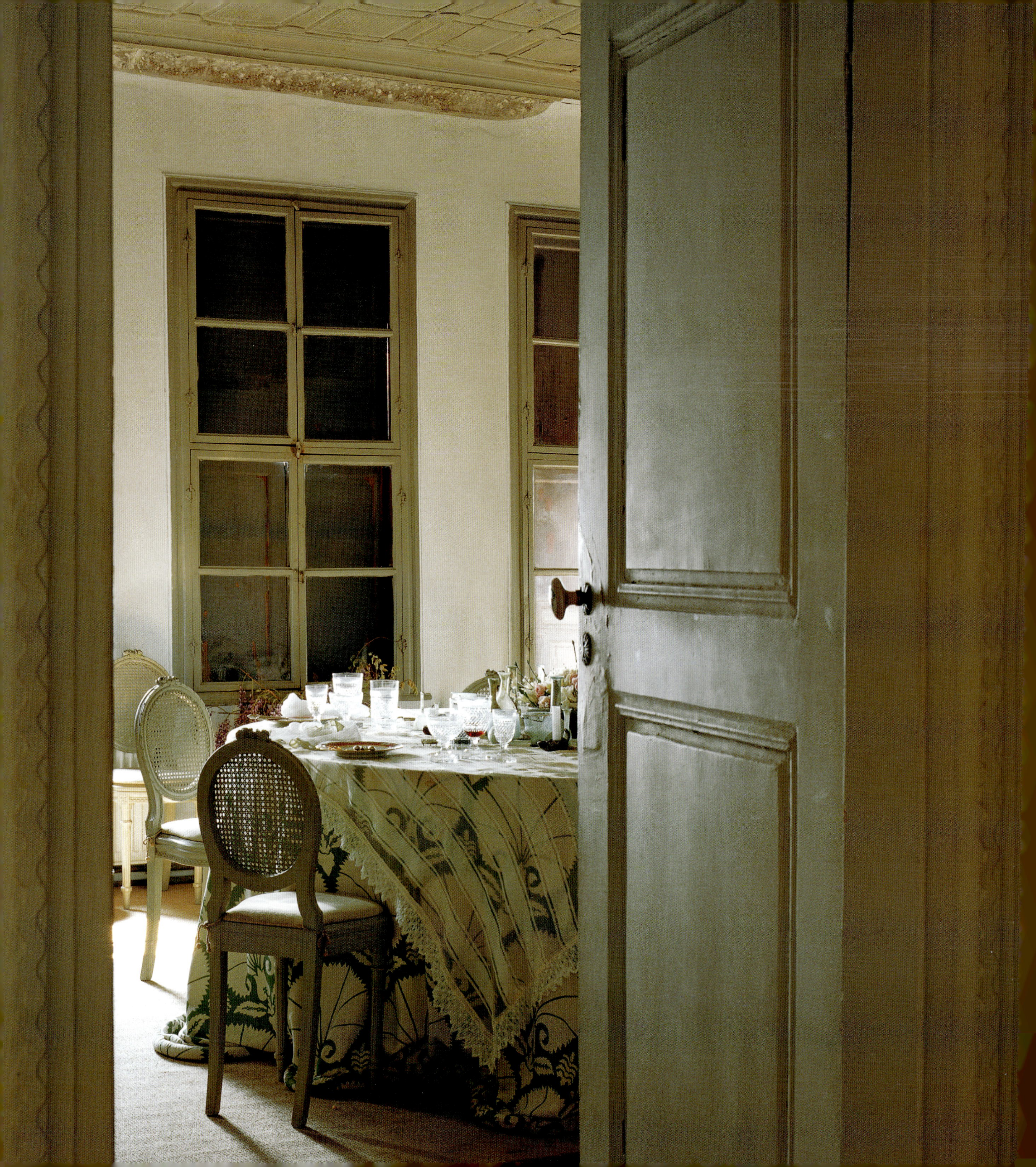

OPPOSITE A glimpse into the first-floor dining room of the Sadullah Pasha Yali, an 18th-century summerhouse named after its first owner and overlooking the Bosphorus river in Istanbul, shows its decoration in muted colours.

ABOVE Artist and interior designer Jean-Louis Germain has used a Neoclassical palette in the restoration of his 18th-century château in southwest France (LEFT). The bold primary colours and furniture of the Arts & Crafts period have been employed by architect Stephen Ibbotson in the restoration of this Queen Anne house (RIGHT) in Covent Garden, London.

COLOUR 69

ABOVE In a small sitting room in a New York townhouse, William Sofield pairs dark, lacquered walls with custom-made silk- and linen-panelled curtains. The generous sofa is upholstered in linen velvet with vintage *obi* pillows, and the gunmetal and bronze demi-lune sconces date from the 1930s.

OPPOSITE Original elements, such as the cornice and windows in the first-floor drawing room of designer John Minshaw's London home, have been restored, and the walls painted in a series of off-whites. Minshaw favours the use of flat oil – an 18th-century technique – which he combines with emulsion and eggshell.

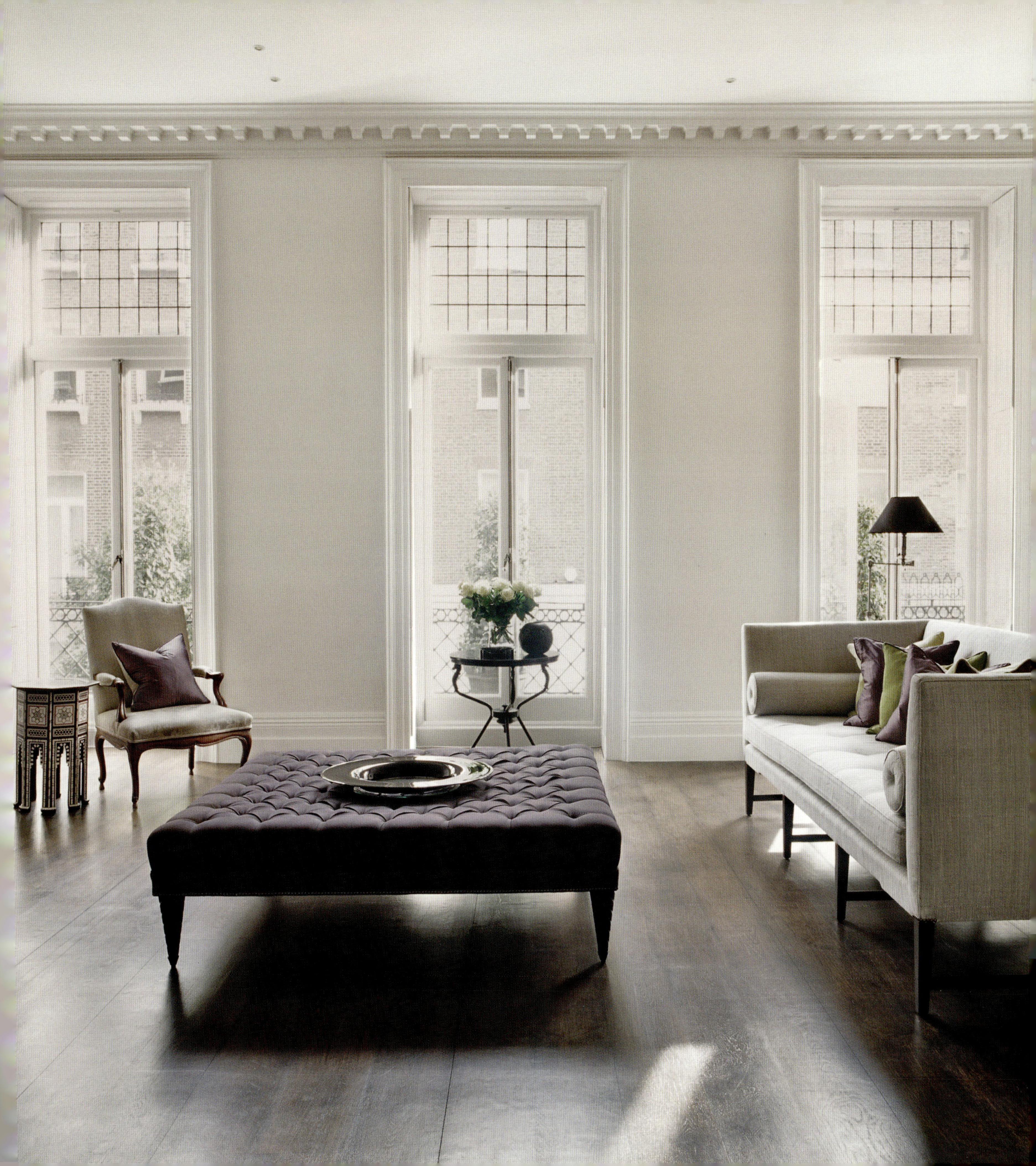

ABOVE LEFT Known for his sumptuous use of colour, interior designer John Stefanidis introduced red-lacquered sliding doors with bronze pulls to separate the living and dining rooms in this Athens penthouse. Sculpted ceramic pots by Paul Philip are displayed on a marble-topped table with brass legs.

Possibly inspired by Neoclassical architect Karl Friedrich Schinkel's use of red felt to line the doors of his pavilion at Charlottenhof (ABOVE RIGHT), German artist Karl-Heinz Scherer reveals a painter's approach to combining colours that lead the eye from one room to another in his rambling country house (OPPOSITE). The open door to the kitchen and the kitchen itself are painted in red lacquer, while the adjacent sitting room is a tranquil dove grey.

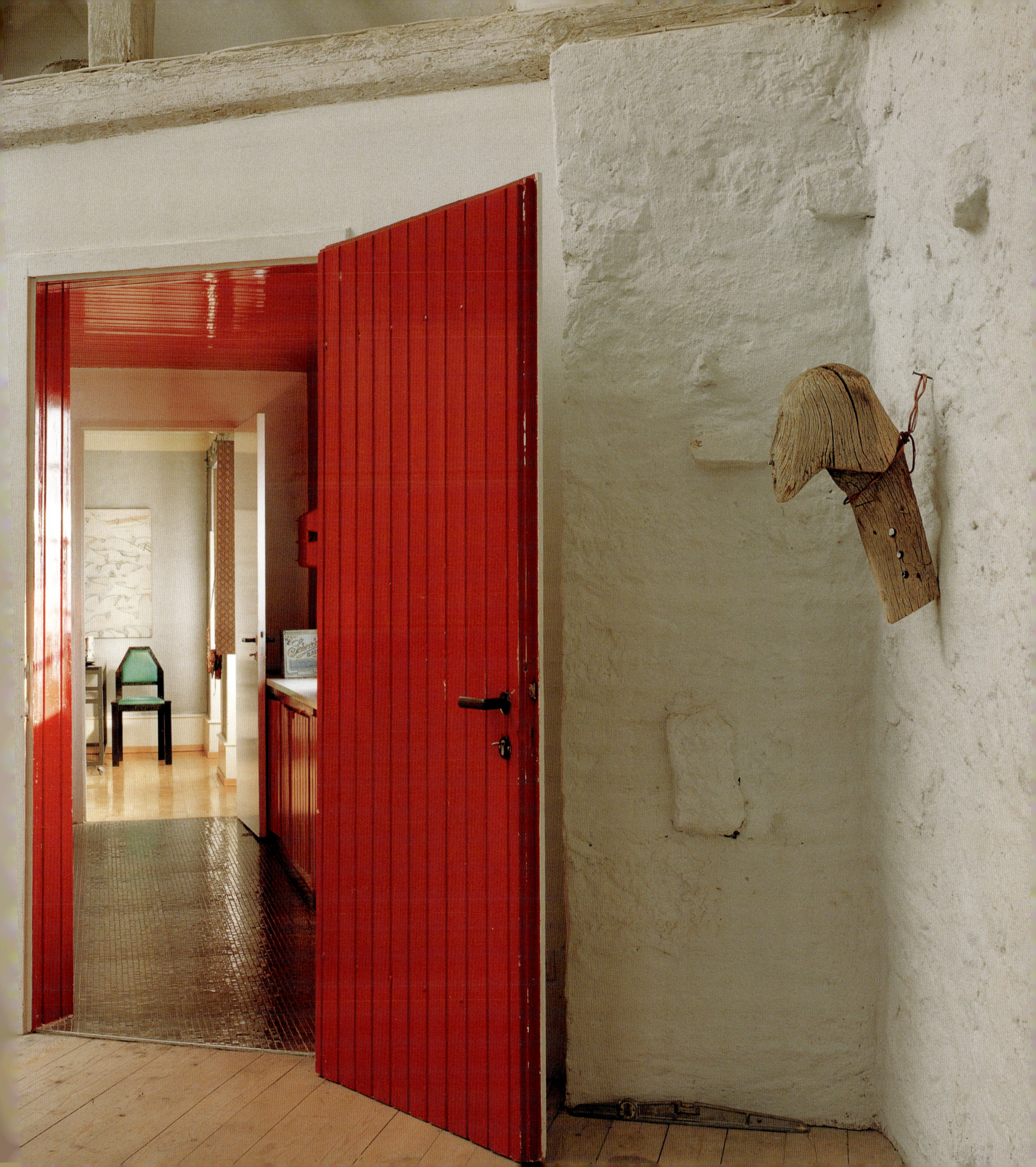

The dark terracotta of the tiles on a flight of steps (ABOVE) is picked out in a cord handrail and painted cupboard door; a contrasting whitewashed wall enhances the simplicity of this Spanish staircase. The use of blue on this spiral staircase in a converted artist's studio (OPPOSITE) accents its shape and the descending size of the treads.

COLOUR 75

Stained glass, combined with a tiled floor, introduces both colour and pattern to the hallway of the Villa Mora (ABOVE), a re-styled 17th-century Italian villa near Cortona. The Long Gallery at Afra (OPPOSITE), described as the most romantic estate on Corfu, is famous for its colourful stained-glass windows and floors of painted tiles.

77

ABOVE Colourful, striped and patterned fabric placed on a daybed emphasizes the use of the stoep, or veranda, as 'a room without walls' for South African interior designer Stephen Falcke, at his garden cottage on the outskirts of Johannesburg.

CLOCKWISE FROM TOP LEFT This blue gate, at John Stefanidis's former country home, leads to the water garden; a classic New England barn is painted ox-blood red; an autumn wreath provides contrast with the blue door of a cottage in California; a weathered iron armillary sphere hangs from the ceiling of Stephen Falcke's stoep.

ABOVE AND OPPOSITE The guest bedrooms in the family wing at Elghammar, a Neoclassical estate southwest of Stockholm, combine the 19th-century campaign beds of its original owner, Count Curt von Stedingk, with Nyköping stoves and Swedish Biedermeier furniture.

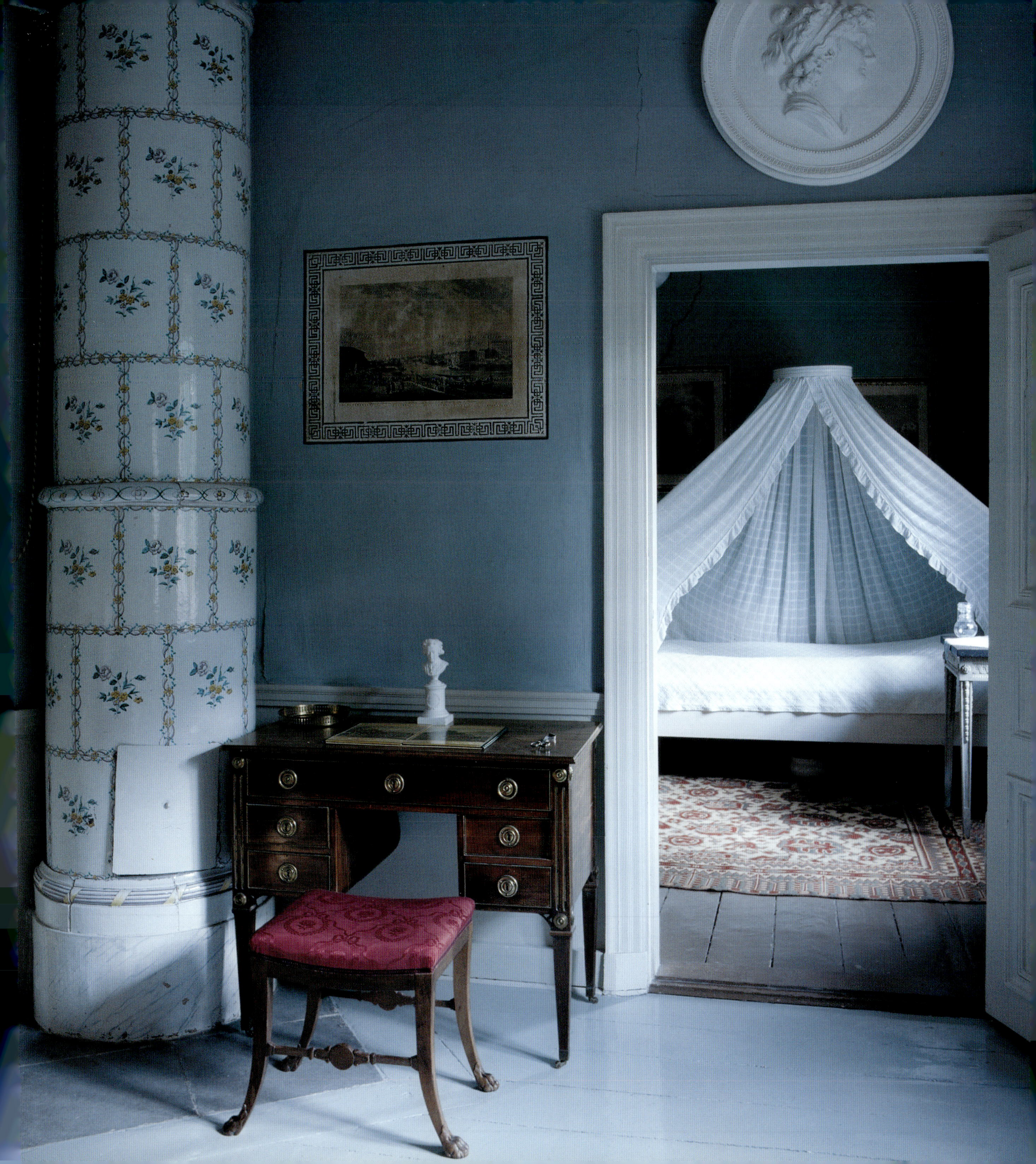

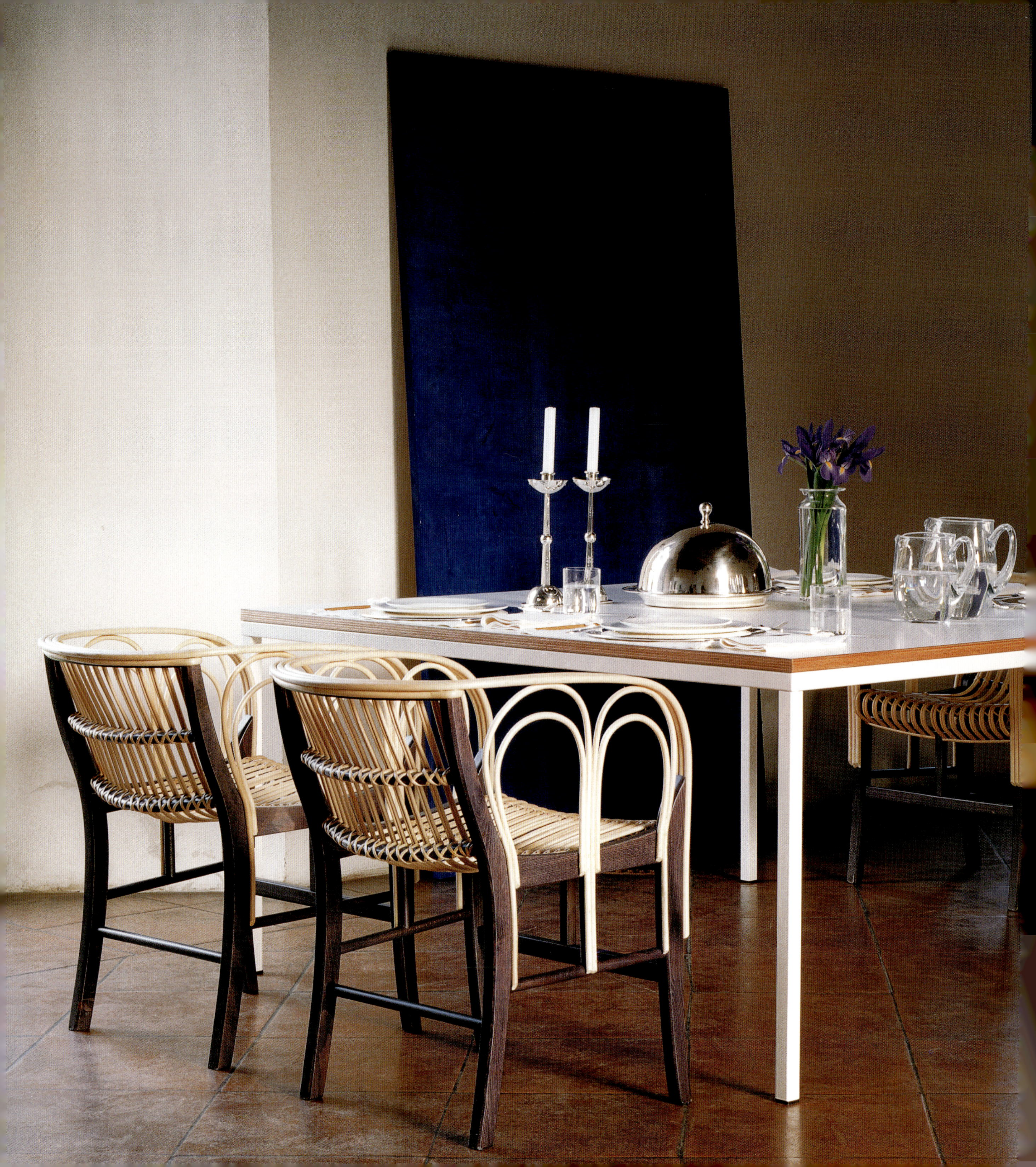

LEFT A dining room in a Piedmontese villa is furnished with contemporary Italian designs from DePadova; the placement of a royal blue painted panel against the wall provides a visual focal point.

IN CONVERSATION WITH JOHN STEFANIDIS

'As a modern-day interpreter of Minimalism in the Grand Style, I don't see myself necessarily as a specialist when it comes to colour, although I would agree that it is one of my strengths. I use colour as a painter would, without inhibition, juxtaposing and combining paint, pattern and textile. There are good and bad reds, any number of blacks, as well as innumerable variations and shades of any colour: but what is the right colour? I carry a colour in my mind's eye and then I try out a series of samples with Tony Allcock, the specialist painter I have worked with for over twenty-five years. We work by osmosis nowadays, and Tony has a wonderful ability to gauge the colour I imagine.

———·———

Colour should introduce an element of surprise, or an accent, into the design of a room. Historically, many houses and palaces were decorated in this way, with unexpected rooms lined in malachite or lapis lazuli; small, unimportant rooms transformed into lacquered boxes; and the stature of others increased by trompe-l'oeil murals or creative paint effects.

———·———

My first house in London, all those years ago, was designed in a palette of browns, whites and beiges, but these became clichés and so I moved on. In my current London house, there are accents of colour everywhere. The use of pillar-box red in the study disguises the smallness of the room. Books fill the downstairs library, in which the shelves are specialist-painted in blue squiggles. Upstairs a wall of books on architecture and design has shelves in aqua green. A narrow linking corridor to the kitchen has sliding cupboards lacquered parakeet green. True colours will never clash.

———·———

Masters of colour, painters like David, Matisse and Picasso, have influenced my sense of composition. Picasso lived in a kind of chaos, but it always composed itself. The same can also be said of Cy Twombly, who has wonderful references to the past – old furniture and Classical busts – juxtaposed with his own canvases. The secret is a combination of objects and paintings, which are best changed and juxtaposed. This keeps a room vibrant.

———·———

In a Modernist context, references to the past influence composition. I never considered incorporating Louis XV furniture into my designs at the start of my life of toil, but I am always learning and adapting and in essence contemporizing. Each piece of furniture occupies a space, so Minimalism and Grand Style are compatible: the 16th century with Mies van der Rohe or Oscar Niemeyer.

———·———

Minimalism in the Grand Style was exemplified by Karl Friedrich Schinkel, who would have welcomed the best of 20th- and 21st-century design.

———·———

It is a paring down of all the non-essential elements in a room. It is about space. How you use that space is what defines you as an architect or as an interior designer. Initially you have to create the space, and if that space has structure, it possesses an architectural integrity. Structure comes from a self-imposed discipline. Good design, irrespective of the period, radiates a sense of repose.

———·———

Interior space can always be enhanced and redefined.

———·———

Accomplished architects throughout history have revealed a Minimalist approach to their buildings. Andrea Palladio, with his innate sense of volume and light, is a perfect example, and although it might be stretching a point to suggest that they were Minimalist, even Baroque architects, such as Francesco Borromini and Donato Bramante, built with a pared-down discipline that epitomizes Grand Style. The empty spaces are as important as the Baroque column, entablatures, ceilings and plaster decoration. Incorporating Classical conceits, even putti, first sculpted by the Greeks without sentimentality, are acceptable in a Minimalist ethic.

———

Aestheticism can be the enemy of creation. Too much aesthetic means getting lost in the details, as many a painter would agree. Some designers, because they concentrate on the trimmings and frills, lose the point of a room, which is the volume, the emptiness.

———

When you create a design, you must first consider the country and climate in which the existing building or the new house is. Weather and available natural light influence the architecture. Whatever the style, a building needs a coherence achieved with the use of imaginative space, light and colour.

———

It is only because I live in England that I have adopted a succession of 'funny' houses: the converted cowsheds in the country and, more recently, the London terraced houses of Cheyne Walk and Ebury Street. It is an accident of chance that my island house on Patmos in Greece is an old house. Originally of the 16th century, it is neither cute nor folkloric, despite the use of local designs and objects from the Eastern Mediterranean.

———

If you inherit an old property, then inevitably its unique architectural integrity will influence the design you wish to impose. Natural light, particularly its direction and influence on an interior space, is very important. I have never been over-fond of curtains, but we design them when appropriate and they can be very elaborate and fun. A grand 18th-century house needs curtains. Closed shutters at night are sparse and monastic, and sometimes appropriate. Louvred shutters in hot climates work well in cities.

———

If you design and build your own house, then the design can be anything you choose. I would love to build my next house in concrete and glass. I admire Philip Johnson's Glass House, but I would do things differently. It would be furnished extremely sparsely, as it is, but with areas of sublime comfort – the ultimate solace for the mind and body!

———

In Europe, there are so many period houses and it is rare to build new properties, but the plains of the American Northwest, Brazil and Australia beckon with opportunities to build from scratch.'

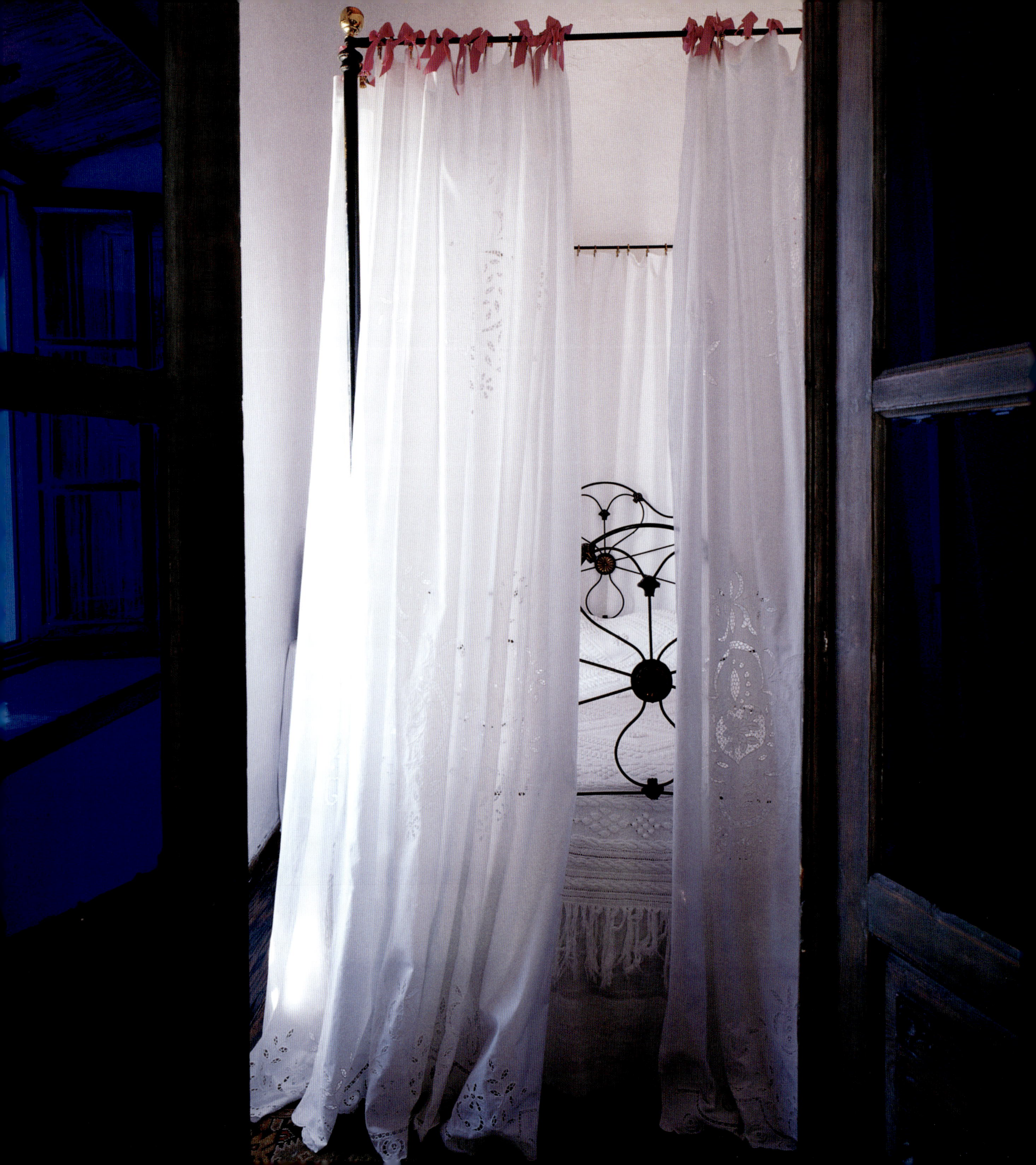

OPPOSITE Interior designer John Stefanidis's holiday home on the Greek island of Patmos is a symphony of colour. This simple guest bedroom, viewed through the blue-paned glass door of the adjoining bathroom, contains a wrought-iron bed with hand-embroidered bed hangings tied with pink grosgrain ribbons.

ABOVE Johnny Stuart, the antiques dealer and expert on Russian history, fulfilled a long-held ambition by renovating a derelict apartment in the heart of St Petersburg. In the house where playwright Ivan Turgenev once lived, Stuart created a 19th-century palatial residence, his pale yellow bedroom filled with original Neoclassical furniture and accessories.

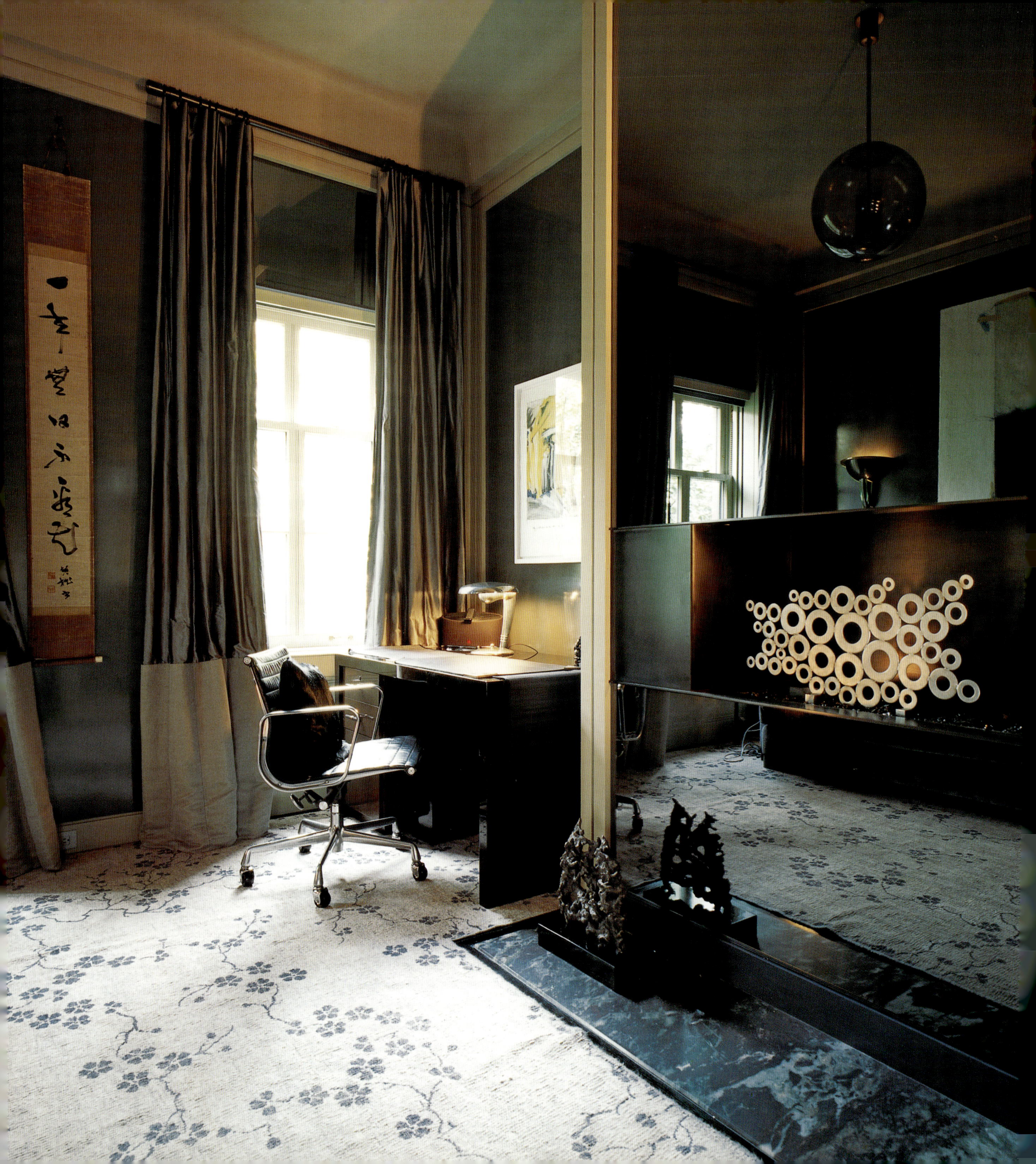

OPPOSITE A custom-made silk and wool carpet in a Japanese poppy pattern enhances the contrasting dark lacquer walls of this intimate sitting room in a New York townhouse designed by William Sofield.

ABOVE Designer John Minshaw's drawing room has a dark, ebonized oak floor that provides tonal contrast to the pale English Regency fireplace and the linen upholstery of a lone armchair that furnishes this part of the room.

ABOVE The red and white colour scheme predominant in interior designer Karen Roos's country home in South Africa is emphasized by a homemade sculpture: a tower of magazines and books in coordinating colours.

ABOVE It is thought that the Shakers draped fabric around the walls of their rooms to provide insulation, as illustrated in this bedroom in the Hancock Shaker Village in Massachusetts.

Hand-painted ceramic tiles have been laid to create a series of coloured patterns in this Spanish country kitchen (ABOVE). The rustic kitchen of an early 19th-century Danish fisherman's cottage on the Baltic Sea (OPPOSITE) has been painted a uniform and practical colour, in contrast to the naïve floral designs that decorate the cupboard and door.

COLOUR

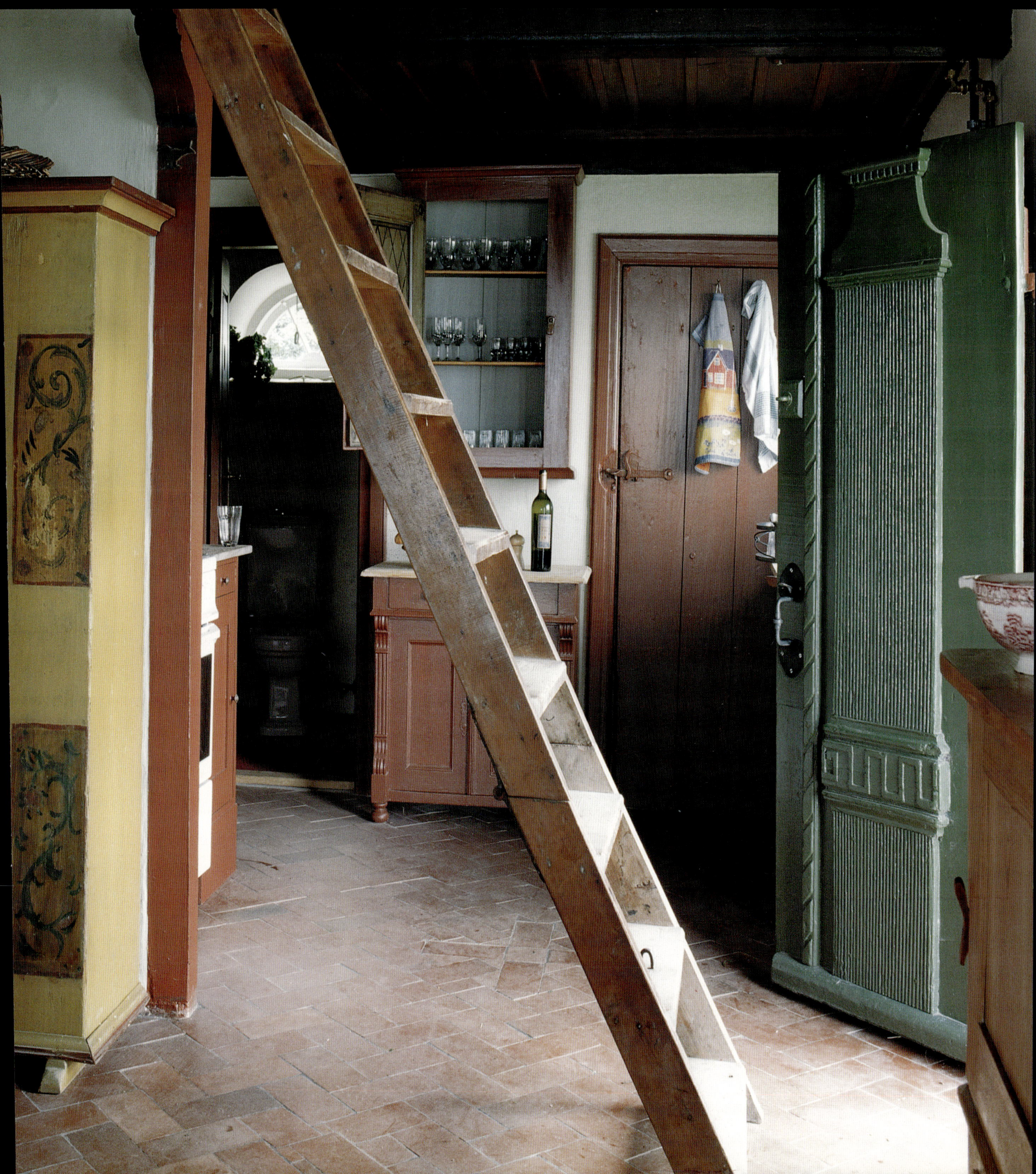

ABOVE The walls of the music room in designer David Collins's London apartment are clad in silk, which is said to aid acoustics. The room is furnished with a navy and purple daybed and a 1960s bar trolley made of glass and bronze, used as a coffee table.

ABOVE In his drawing room, David Collins's own designs include the Venetian travertine fireplace with bronze trim and black painted-glass surround, a pair of leather sofas upholstered in lavender ribbed silk, and a Nepalese silk and wool rug with sculpted inset.

ABOVE Antiquarian Axel Vervoordt displays an eclectic collection, gathered over the last thirty years and including a life-size Dvaravati sculpture, against walls washed in ox-blood red paint.

OPPOSITE The photo studio at Axel Vervoordt's Kanaal building is painted a dramatic matt black, and in this corner is furnished with a pair of modern paintings and an André Turpin armchair dating from *c.* 1925.

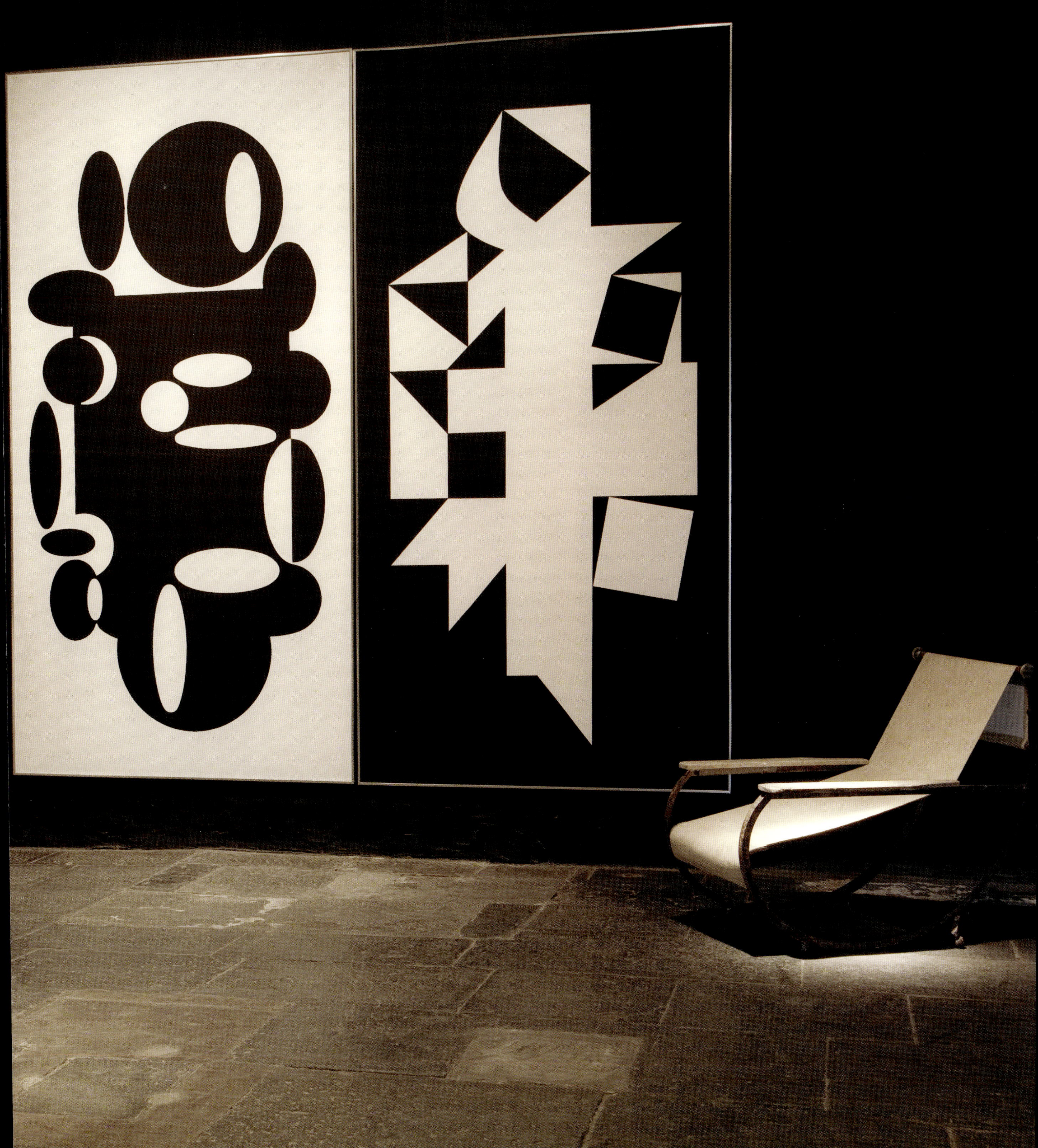

The Pompeiian decoration in Queen Charlotte's dressing room at Rosersberg (ABOVE), one of Sweden's best-preserved Neoclassical palaces, was designed by Gustaf af Sillén in 1812. The faded pink of the wall fabric and soft furnishings in this Neoclassical drawing room (OPPOSITE), combined with eau de nil wood panelling and window surround, lends it an air of unmistakable grandeur.

COLOUR

An accent of colour can provide the focal point of a room: an 18th-century monogrammed hall chair, contemporized in a shade of emerald green, in this Neoclassical-grey kitchen (TOP); the coral pink upholstery of a small chair in a black and white marble bathroom, designed by John Stefanidis (ABOVE); royal blue seat cushions, dominating a Swedish country living room (RIGHT).

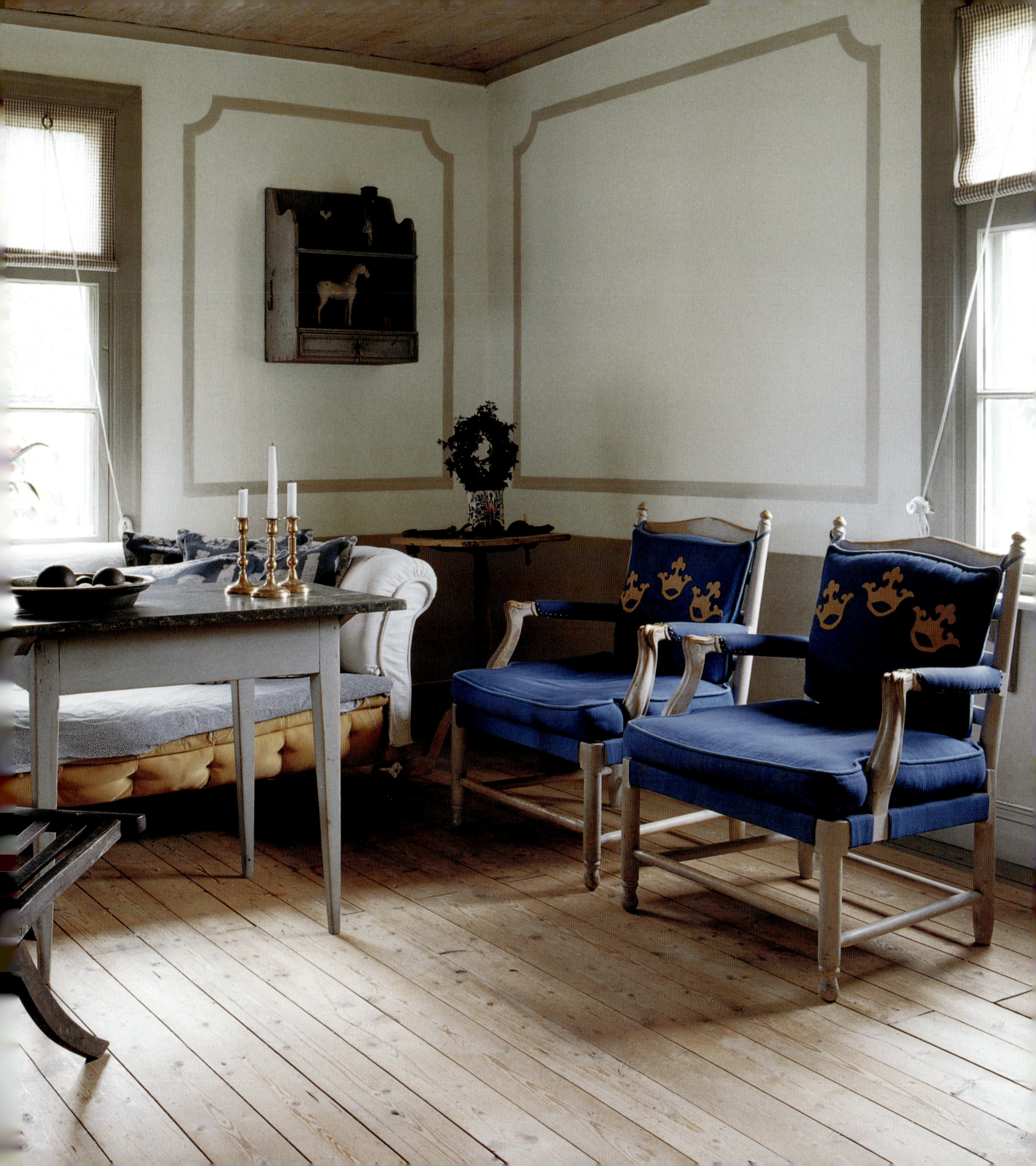

'You can never judge a paint hue by the liquid colour in the paint pot. You must apply it to a wall, wait for the paint to dry, then decide.'

DOROTHY DRAPER, INTERIOR DECORATOR (1889–1969)

OPPOSITE Baroness Ottiliana Liljencrantz's dressing room at Sturehof, an estate south of Stockholm, is connected to her bedroom by a jib door. The panelled wall decoration recreates a style that was fashionable in Sweden in the 1780s.

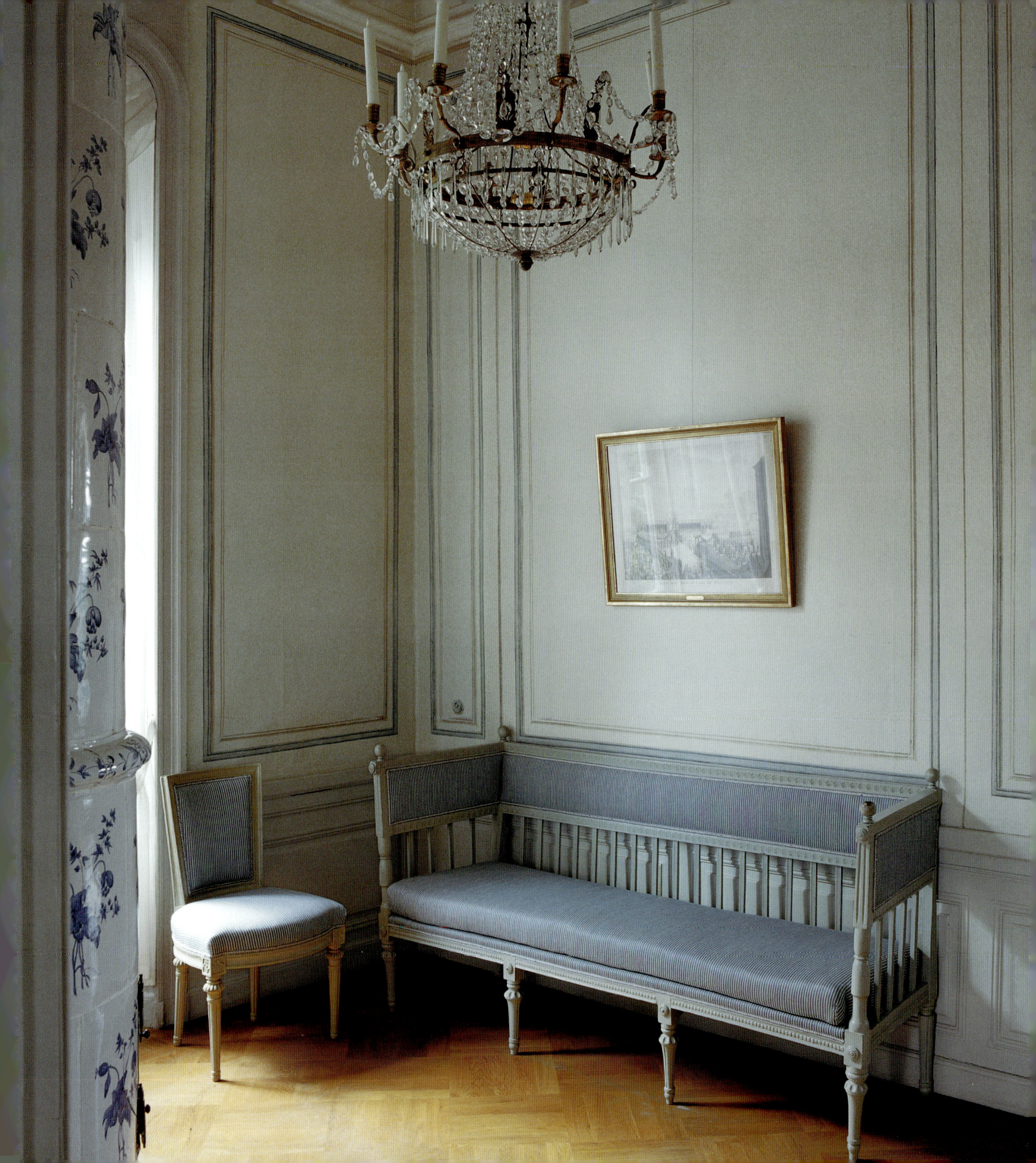

The choice of upholstery adds to the mood of a room. Empire sofas in different styles and colours are displayed against a variety of wall treatments (ABOVE). The formality of the lit bateau, or boat bed, in this French country bedroom (OPPOSITE) is softened by the red and white patchwork quilt and a blue striped rug.

COLOUR 105

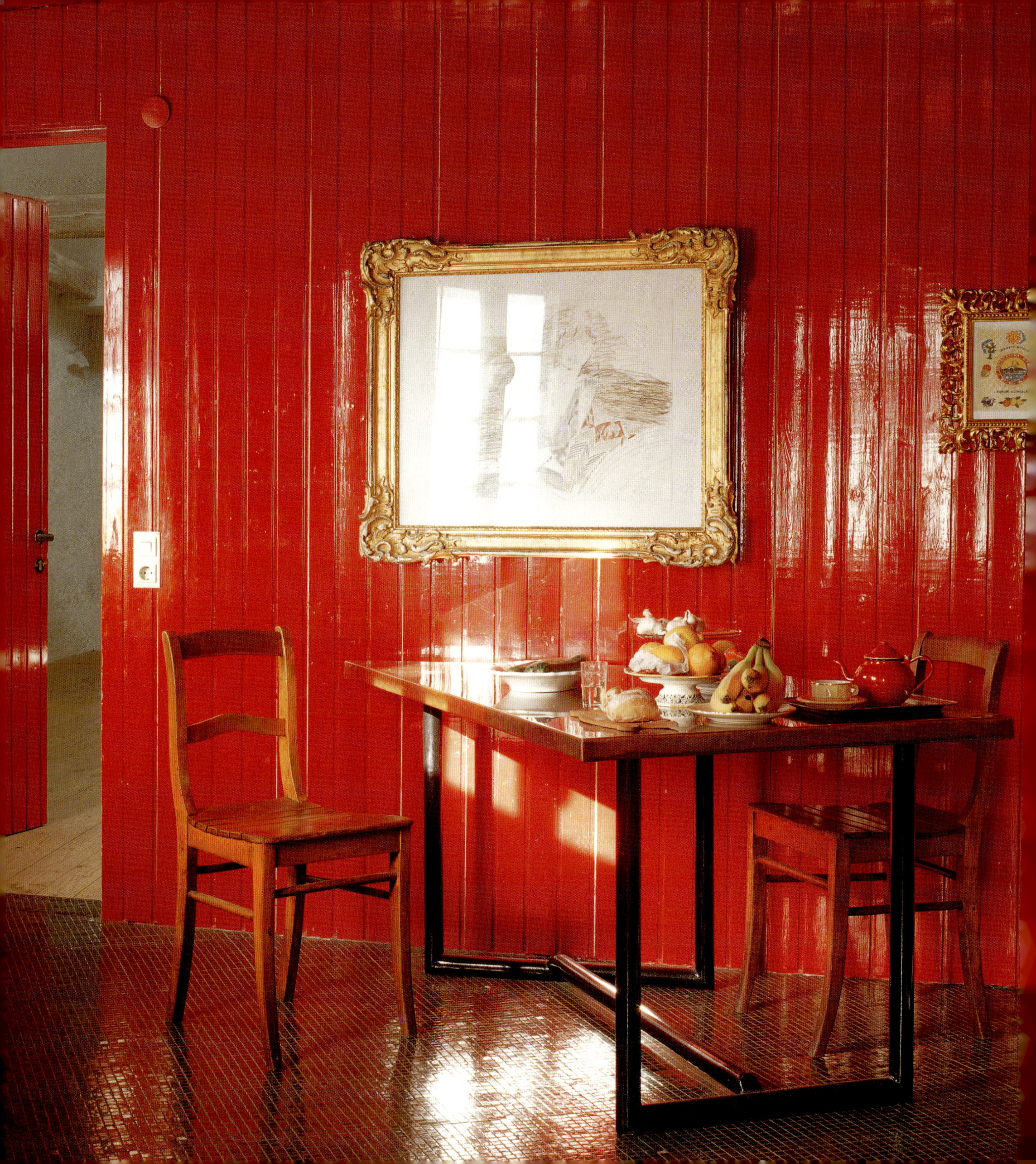

Red lacquer walls are combined with a copper-topped table and a metallic mosaic floor in artist Karl-Heinz Scherer's eye-catching kitchen (OPPOSITE). An antique bathtub (ABOVE) has been spray-painted ox-blood red and placed beneath a collection of black and white engravings of Scottish castles in this French country bathroom.

COLOUR 107

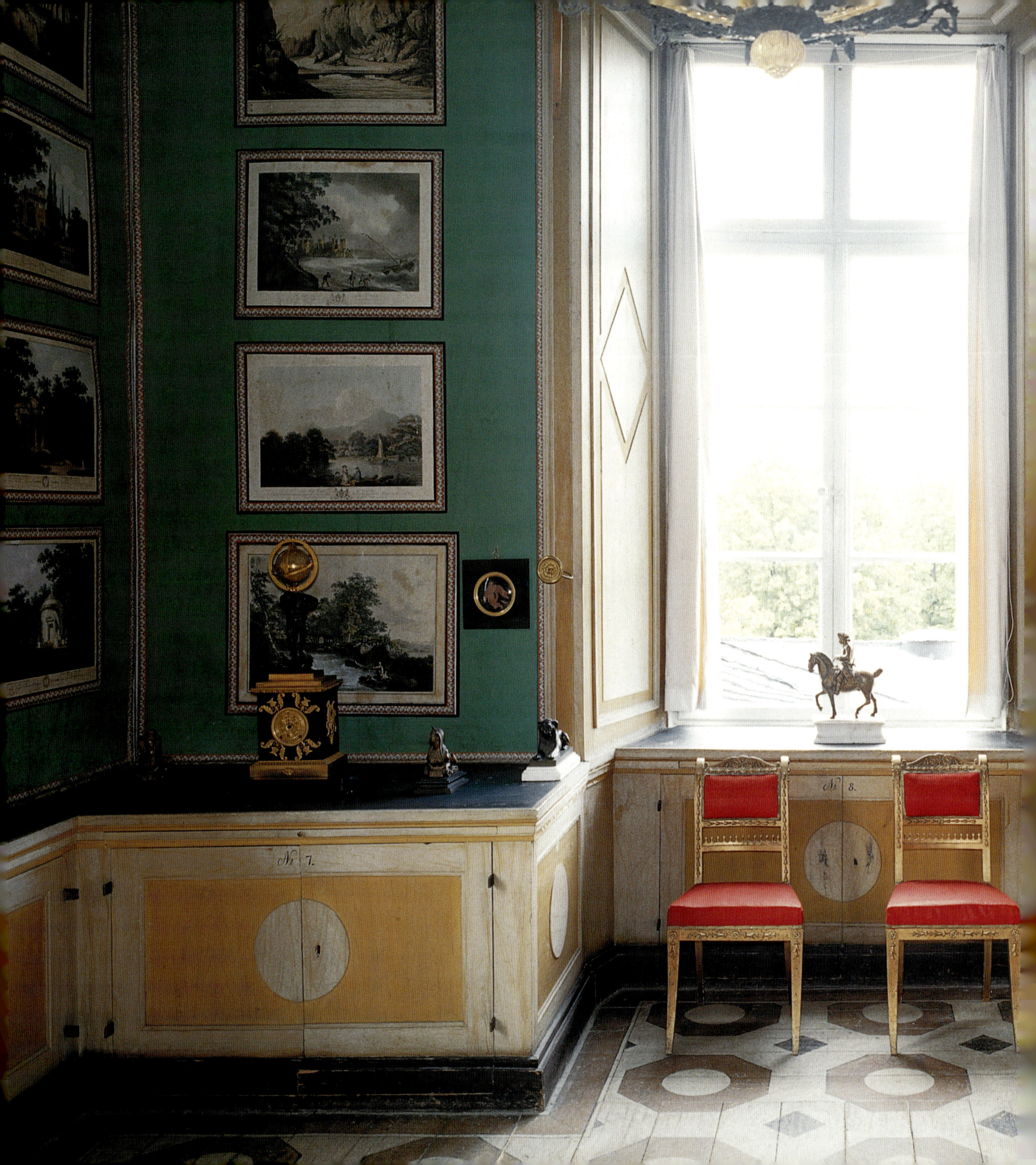
№ 7.
№ 8.

LEFT Known as the 'Green Cabinet', King Karl XIII's study at Rosersberg, near Stockholm, was decorated as a print room, with coloured engravings pasted directly onto the wall. The wooden floor was painted in a trompe-l'oeil effect to resemble marble.

COLOUR 109

LIGHT

Light has an extraordinary diversity, which can be used to create mood and atmosphere, drama, contrast and emphasis. Light transforms the spatial context of a building, enlarging or diminishing it, highlighting key architectural details, while casting others into shadow.

Le Corbusier is quoted as saying that 'architecture is the wise, correct and magnificent play of volumes collected together under the light'.

Light gives context to form and shape, as well as to colour and texture; it enables us to define what is around us and to appreciate changes in our perception of objects and the space that contains them. The lack of light, perhaps more than its presence, continually transforms a space. Anthony Collett, of Collett-Zarzycki, considers light to be extremely important in design and yet is not afraid to play with darkness. Nicholas Haslam shares this sentiment: his approach to a dark room is to make it even darker and more dramatic, by introducing layers of colour, texture and lacquered paint effects.

Architects use natural light to dramatize a structure. Minimalist John Pawson has proved that removing superfluity from an interior greatly improves our appreciation of its quality of light and proportion. The size of windows, as well as their position in a room, influences the intensity of light in a space, while structural elements, such as skylights and ceilings of frosted glass, direct and diffuse any available natural light. Shutters and blinds ensure constancy, allowing a designer to articulate and control the levels of light. Robert Kime believes that light in an interior should be made lighter, and the effect emphasized by avoiding strong colours.

One of the most significant developments in architecture and interior design in recent years has been the technological improvements in artificial lighting and the resulting plethora of lighting effects that are now achievable. Designer John Minshaw rejoices that he is now able to light the inside of a drawer with a pin light. Good lighting

OPPOSITE Light filters into the tranquil interior of this 300-year-old hammam, or bathhouse, in Konya, Turkey, through holes in the cupola, which would once have been filled with glass. Now damaged, many of the tiles are missing from its decoration.

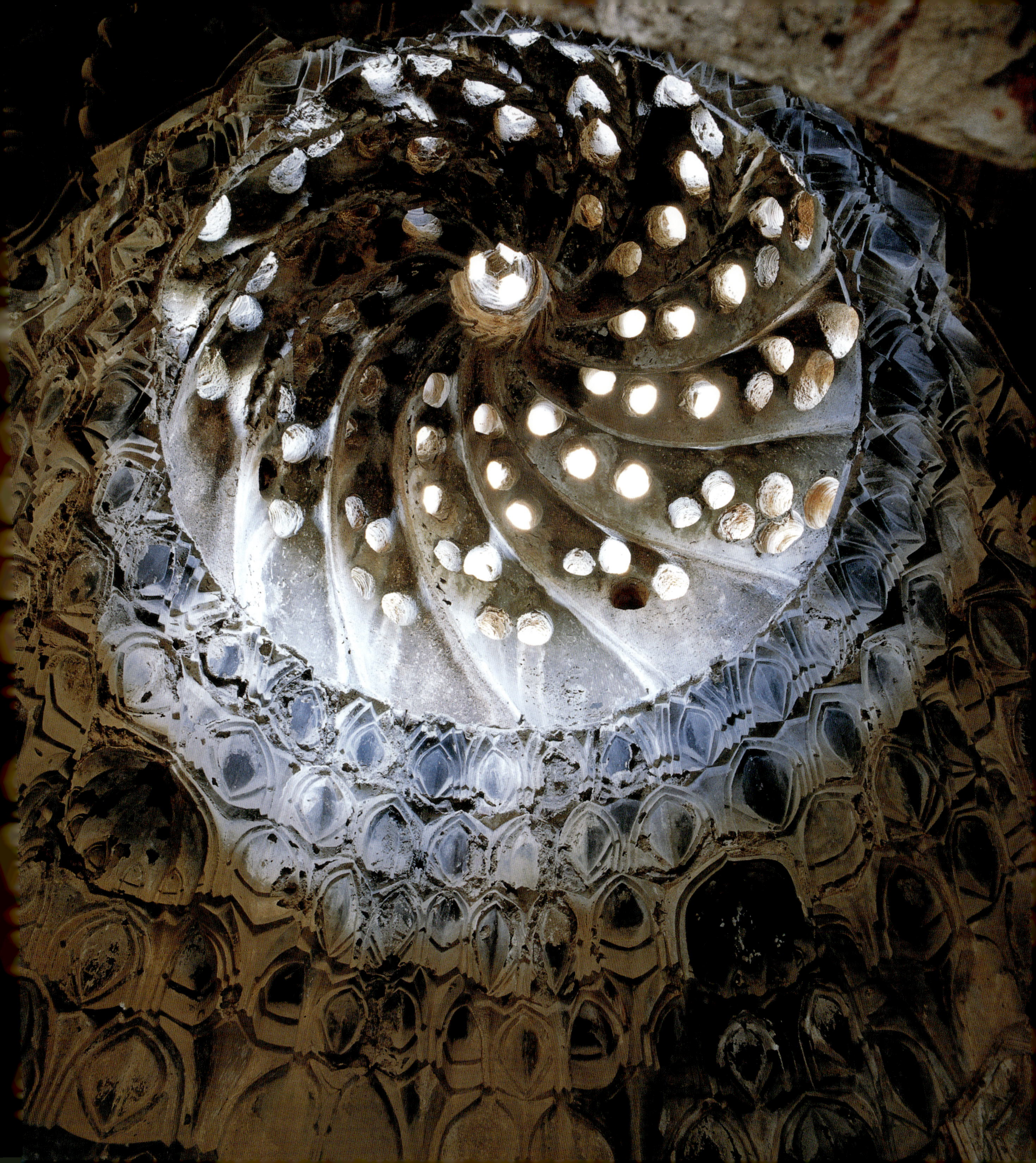

112

illuminates and clarifies; bad lighting confuses and blinds; while the correct balance of light enhances and improves a space, defining and expanding areas and accentuating and delineating rooms.

According to contemporary lighting designer Sally Storey, the balance of light must be adjusted to set a series of different moods, creating layers: it is important to consider rooms as single spaces, and not to blanket-light the whole of an interior. She advocates the use of ambient lighting, such as downlights and wall-mounted up-lights, to provide the background; the focal light should come from a chandelier or pendant light, as well as strategically placed table lamps. Then there is task lighting, over a kitchen worktop or a desk; while accent lighting adds a touch of interest and glamour to a space, be it a dramatic beam of light on a sculpture or a painting, or an emphasis on an attractive architectural detail.

Reflected light is also an important trick in any designer's repertoire and the use of mirrors, mirrored walls and ceilings, and even mirrored furniture helps to bounce light around a room. Wall treatments including lacquer and wax, as favoured by designer William Sofield, as well as metal cladding in copper and stainless steel, and other shiny, reflective materials such as mica, marble and Corian are also effective light enhancements when introduced to small, dark interiors.

OPPOSITE A glimpse into the Small Salon at Östenå on the coast of Sweden reveals its Pompeiian–style decoration, executed during the 1790s, and late Gustavian furniture.

ABOVE An Empire chair (LEFT) is silhouetted against the light filtering in through the half-closed shutters in the late Bill Blass's New York apartment, while an uncurtained window in interior designer Karen Roos's home in South Africa (RIGHT) allows the sunlight to fall where it will.

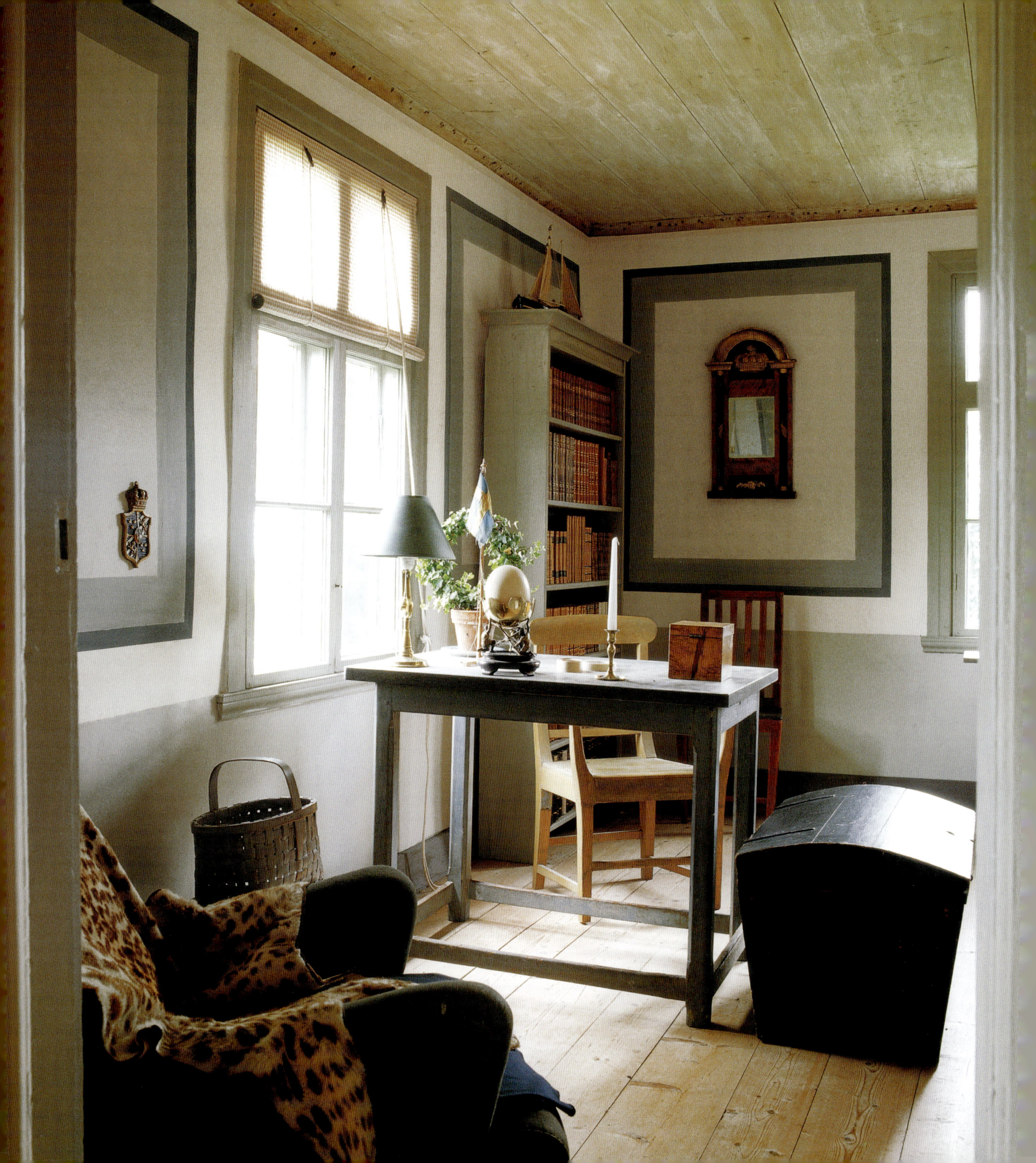

The Neoclassical colour scheme of this living room in a simple country house in Sweden (OPPOSITE) is enhanced by the soft northern light from windows on two sides. Daylight from tall double windows combines with artificial spots (ABOVE) to highlight the books on the wide first-floor landing of this French manor house.

'Good lighting is about creating layers, and it is important to consider how a space is used.'

SALLY STOREY, DESIGN DIRECTOR, LIGHTING DESIGN INTERNATIONAL

OPPOSITE Built between 1720 and 1727 by the Frenchman Joseph Gabriel Destain, Tullgarn in Sweden was purchased in 1772 as a summer residence for Prince Fredrik Adolf, who was personally involved in the redecoration of its interior. The dining room – the largest room in the house – is bathed in light shafting in through unshuttered windows. The walls are decorated in varying shades of Neoclassical grey and blue, with a Wedgwood-style frieze depicting a festive procession in honour of Bacchus.

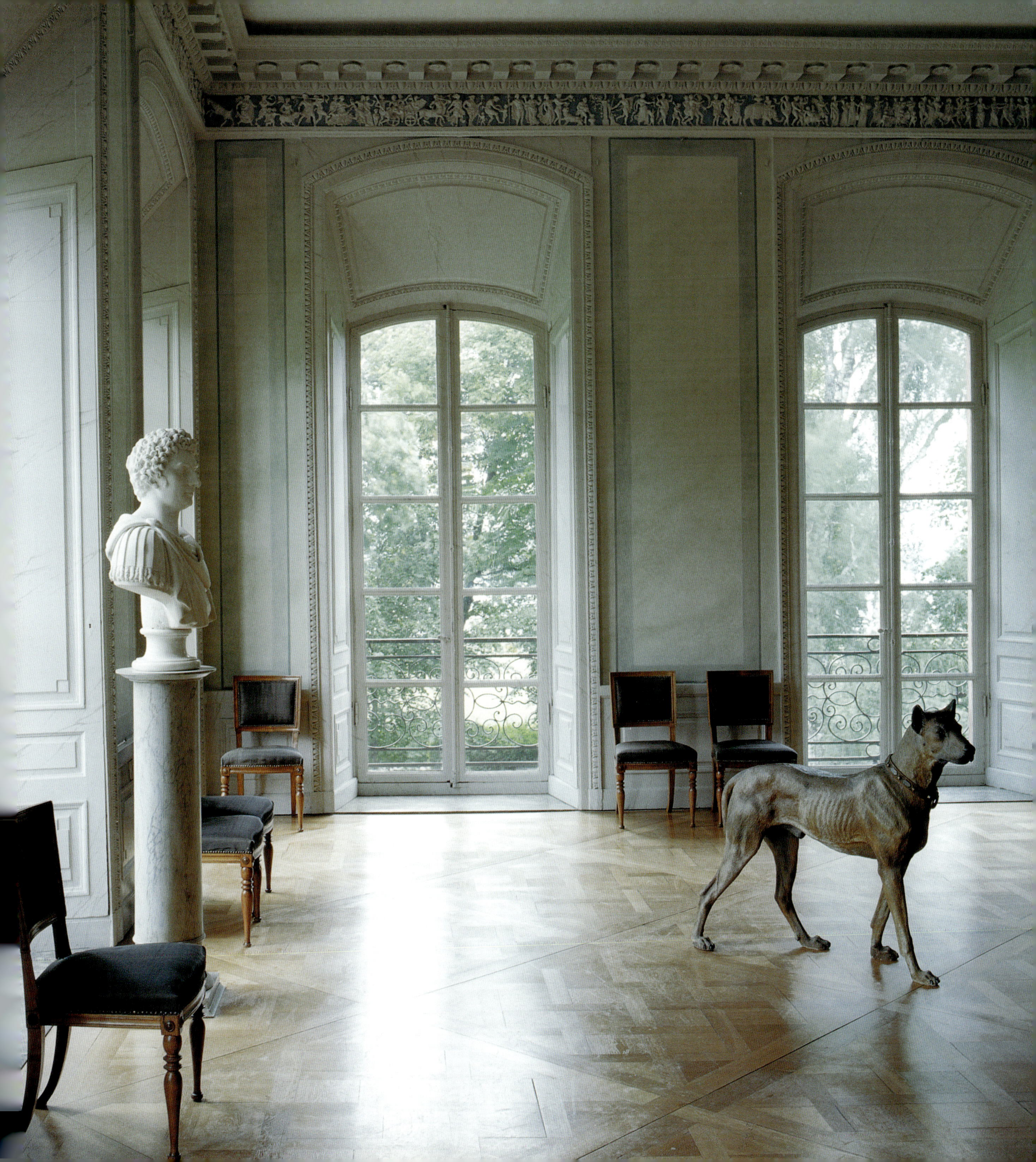

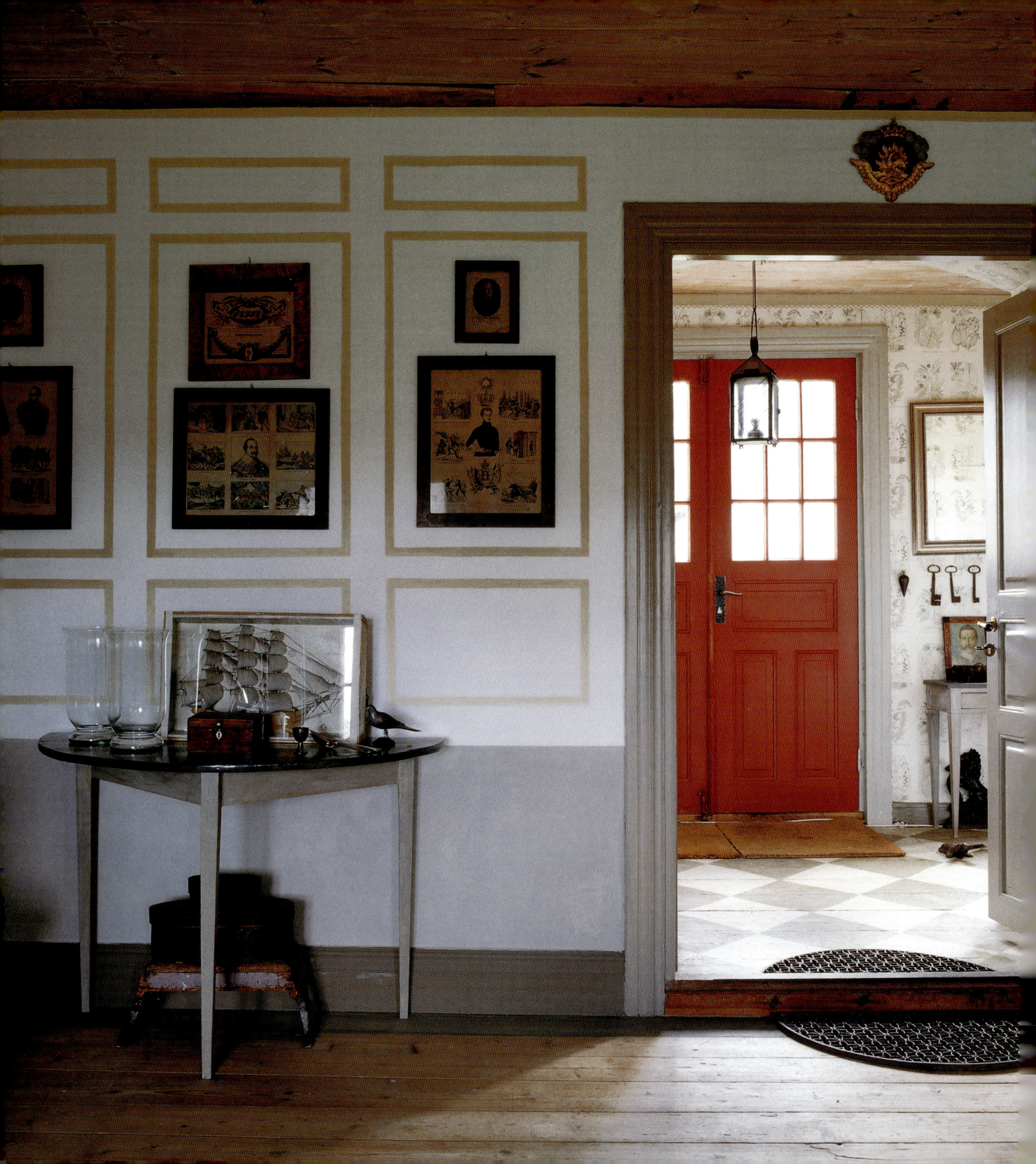

OPPOSITE AND ABOVE This sparsely furnished Swedish country house benefits from many windows, some softened with fabric blinds, which allow a great deal of daylight to enter the rooms and highlight the colour and pattern of its interior decoration.

LIGHT 119

This beach house on Fire Island (ABOVE LEFT), a short distance from Manhattan, was once the home of architect Alan Wanzenberg and interior designer Jed Johnson. Simply furnished with a pair of 1940s beach chairs, this room (ABOVE RIGHT) is bathed in a pure light reflected off the waters of the Great South Bay.

OPPOSITE This ground-floor dining area, within artists' studios, is lit by a row of sash windows and simply furnished with a scrubbed wood table, flanked by a pair of simple benches. The late children's book publisher Sebastian Walker lived within this community in the heart of London's Kensington.

LIGHT 121

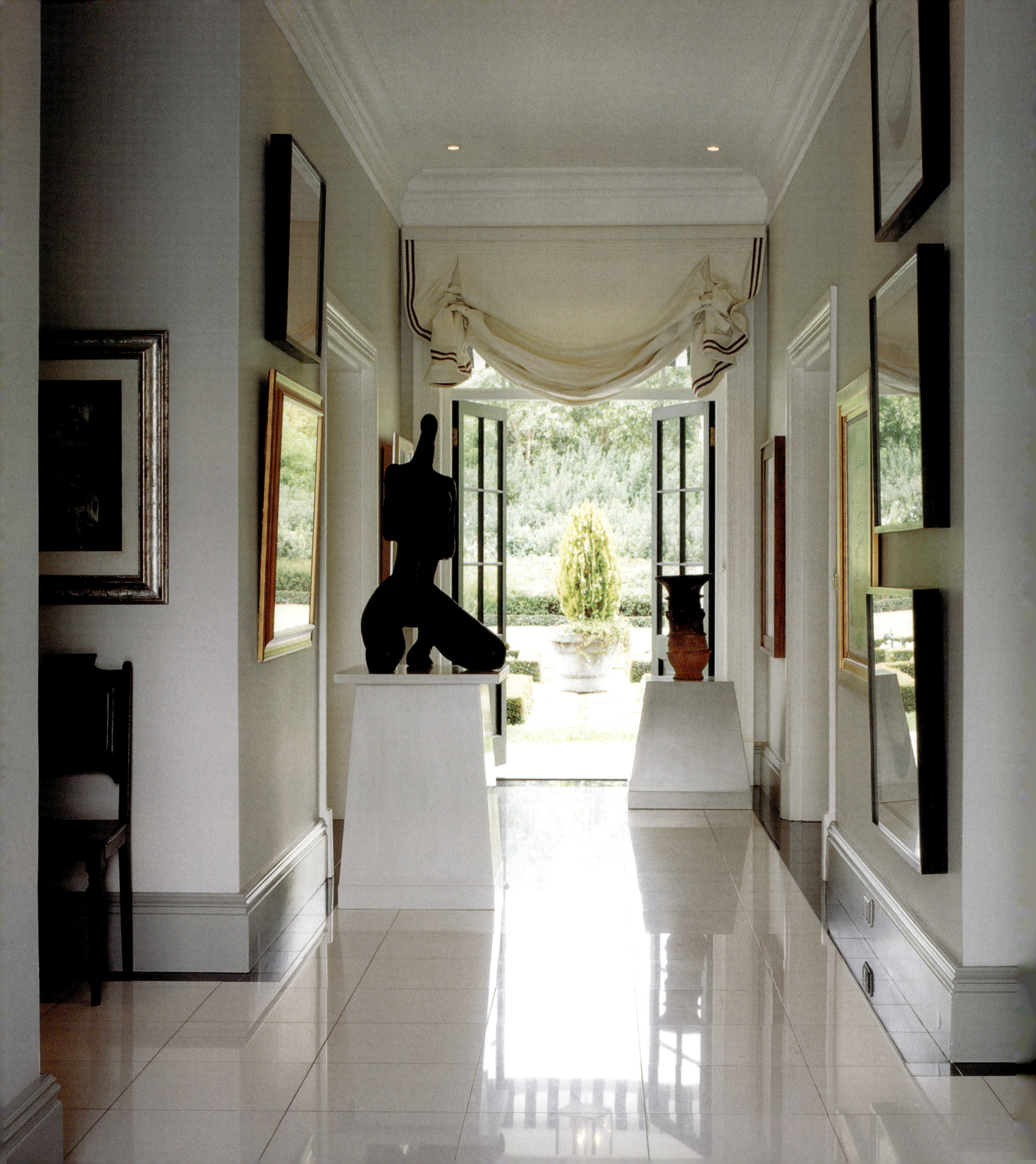

OPPOSITE The polished white marble floor of the hallway in this contemporary villa in South Africa, designed by Boyd Ferguson, reflects the light through double-glazed doors, which open onto the garden.

ABOVE This graceful, marble-floored vestibule at the Palais Sursock in Beirut has classic, triple-arched, fifteen-foot-high French windows in intricate wrought-iron frames, which lead onto a balcony.

IN CONVERSATION WITH DAVID COLLINS

'When it comes to light, I tend to start off with darkness and then shine light on to it.

Colour is extraordinarily important to me. I like to wear blue and see endless possibilities in the array of blue sweaters that I favour! For me, blue is the colour more influenced by light than any other: I cannot think of another colour that reflects light in the same way as blue. Colour subtly changes with distance, creating rhythm, harmony and pattern – and I like that.

Time and space are the great luxuries of the 21st century, and the concept of Minimalism, as I understand it, presents us with an opportunity to enjoy and luxuriate in a space. However, I see myself more as a perfectionist than a Minimalist. My designs require perfect editing and a perfect sense of proportion, confidence, simplicity and a focus on the detail.

In aspiring for perfection in my buildings, first of all I need to be able to picture the empty space. After that, I may fill a room with anything I like, from Biedermeier to Art Deco. I can paint the walls, lacquer them or cover them with texture, whatever I wish, but from an architectural point of view I need to start by visualizing the elegance and light, as well as the detailing. When rooms are over-decorated and heavily ornate, it may be more diverting but it is certainly less focused. So for me, what entails a good project is a simple idea combined with clarity of execution.

The first building you study, as an aspiring architect, is the Parthenon in the Acropolis. If you were to try to encapsulate the essence of Minimalist architecture, a good example would be the Doric column. The Greeks had the ability to design the Corinthian column with its acanthus leaves, and the Ionic column with its scrolls, yet settled for the simplicity of the Doric column for the greatest Classical monument of all time. This surely is a reflection of the confidence of great architects – that although you can do more, you will always do less.

Although I struggled with mathematics at school, I nevertheless have a mathematical brain. I love symmetry – for example, my favourite number is 3 – and I like things that are balanced, such as weighing scales or an abacus. As an architecture student, my hero was Mies van der Rohe, even if he was then out of fashion; I was obsessed with the bronze Seagram Building and his Barcelona Pavilion. When I finished college, I became more aware of the work of Eileen Gray, again a Modernist and a fellow countrywoman, and then I became interested in Jean-Michel Frank, whose work was extensive in France and Argentina. Frank's rooms were geometrical essays. His sense of luxury was in the simplicity of his designs and in the combination of materials, such as straw and vellum with bronze and copper. He used doors to make a room symmetrical. So too did Robert Adam, who as an architect was something of a Minimalist, but as a decorator liked to embellish his rooms.

Few rooms are truly square, so I manipulate the focal point, just as a set designer would, by adding an interesting painting or a piece of furniture, or by realigning the elements of the room. In almost every project I do, you will find yourself entering a room off-centre, or through the back or the side of the room.

The focus is predictably at the front in the shape of the fireplace or chimneybreast and, just like Robert Adam, I use visual tricks, such as the design of the floor, as well as carpets and pattern, to pull the eye in one direction or another and create rhythm.

———

Even if I don't start from scratch, then the renovation of an existing building will still be quite radical. The Connaught Bar was formerly the hotel's water storage area and not some long-forgotten apartment vacated by a dowager duchess in the 1920s. Yet for its decoration I was inspired by English Cubist and Irish 1920s art and, echoing the period, the walls are covered in platinum silver leaf overlaid with dusty pink, pistachio and lilac. The design of the bar came to me when I was flying over the west of Ireland – the sky was an incredible blue and the inspiration for the wall panelling came from that moment. A great deal went into the design of this room, very little of which is obvious to the untrained eye. There are a lot of hidden elements in its structure and patterns within patterns that create the overall vision. The original design was developed using just hard materials, such as glass, marble and mirrors, yet the undersides of all the tables, the chairs and the leather banquettes are lined with baize to absorb the sound and, more recently, I have added linen and velvet curtains in an abstract pattern to make the acoustics of the room even better.

———

I try to be controlled in the way that I work. I understand the need to change the sense of space, provided the balance and proportion of a room stay the same, but I do not necessarily agree with embellishments for their own sake. I believe that to be a great designer your inner confidence needs to be counterbalanced by an insecurity, which makes you constantly question and push the boundaries. The sign of a great project for me is that it is never absolutely finished and that a door has been left open to do one more thing.

———

Like other architects and designers before me, I have ended up developing my own range of furniture because I could not always find those rare and beautiful designer pieces that I was looking for. I have designed furniture to fit a specific setting only to find that a client has moved it to another room and given it a new and quite different interpretation from the one I had intended. I have learned a great deal from this!

———

I feel what I am doing now is really Modern, because it is of the moment. While I am aware that some might be dismissive of my style because it reflects my passion for Art Deco, I believe that it is my own up-to-the-minute interpretation of this hugely influential period, and one that allows me to continue to experiment with form, function, scale, colour and composition.

———

Although it is not necessarily something that has struck me before, some of the people I most admire, such as Sir John Soane, Schinkel, Mies van der Rohe, Le Corbusier and Frank Lloyd Wright, were all experimenting with space and the early concepts of Minimalism. You can even go back as far as the Renaissance and Reformation and still further to the pre-Romanesque periods, where there was simplicity of style, consciously influenced by scale, proportion and light. Napoleon III in my view was the precursor to what we call Minimalism, a style that Jean-Michel Frank reinterpreted for the 20th century, and 1927 is contemporary now.'

ABOVE The bedroom in designer David Collins's London apartment is carpeted in white linen. He designed the lacquer furniture and leather screen around the bed, while the blue blinds, which filter the light so beautifully, are made of fringing in homage to a Missoni installation in Milan. The leather ottoman is by Christian Liaigre.

ABOVE John Stefanidis painted the window shutters and walls of this guest bedroom a pale blue. His 'Rothschild' armchair occupies a quiet corner of the room.

LIGHT 127

ABOVE An eclectic composition that includes a Mexican mud pot and a Peruvian top hat is backlit by a simple lead-paned window in this English country cottage.

OPPOSITE This monastic tower room in antiquarian Axel Vervoordt's Belgian castle, with its narrow double-height shuttered windows, is sparsely furnished with a 16th-century Italian sculpted table with a new top and a found stone, yet exemplifies Vervoordt's talent for composition.

OVERLEAF Silhouetted against an arched window with views over the garden, an ornate urn and pedestal are flanked by a pair of Gustavian stools (LEFT). The airy Classical-style porch of antiques dealer Keith Skeel's Edwardian property is bathed in the reflected light from the waters of False Bay on the Cape Peninsula (RIGHT).

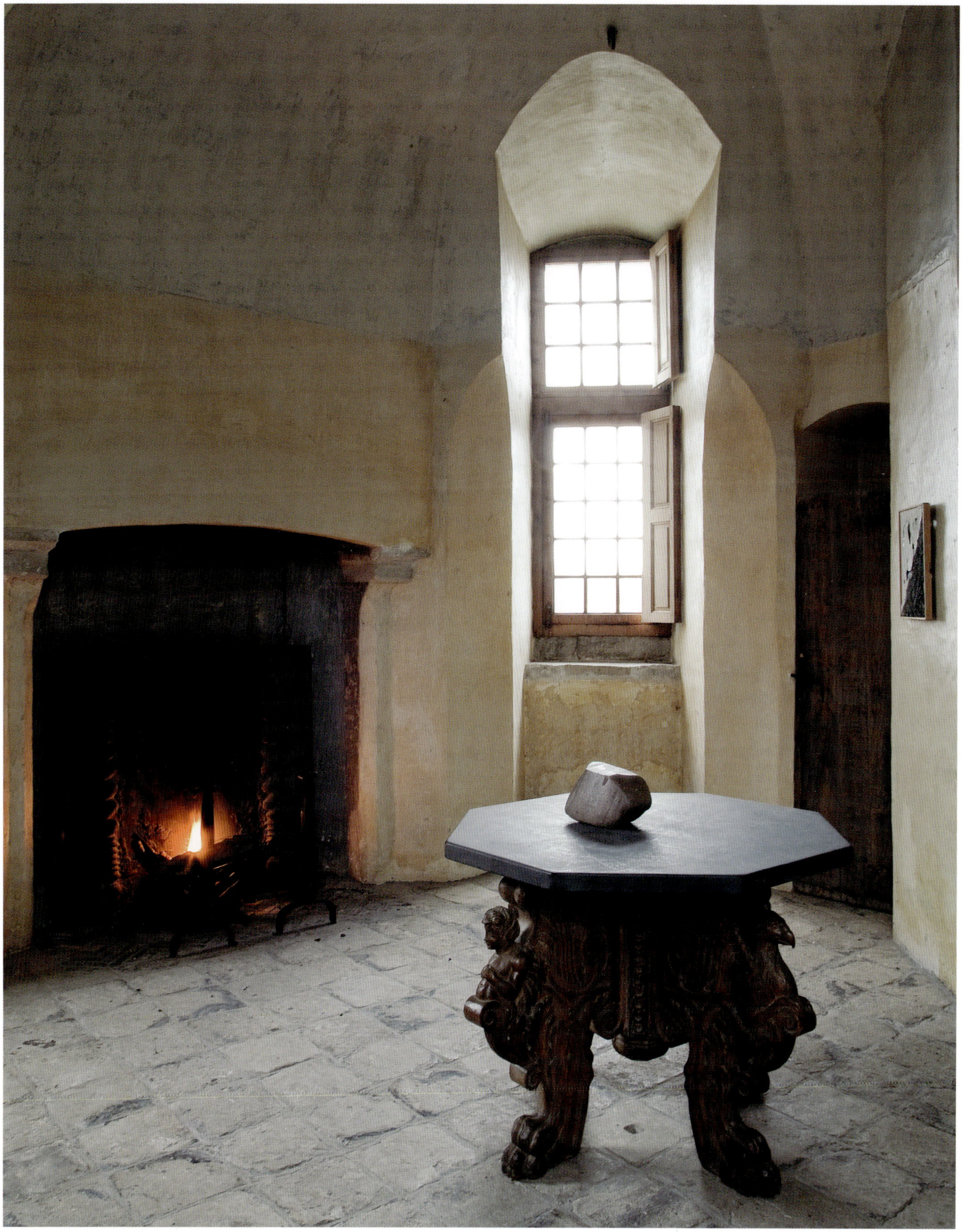

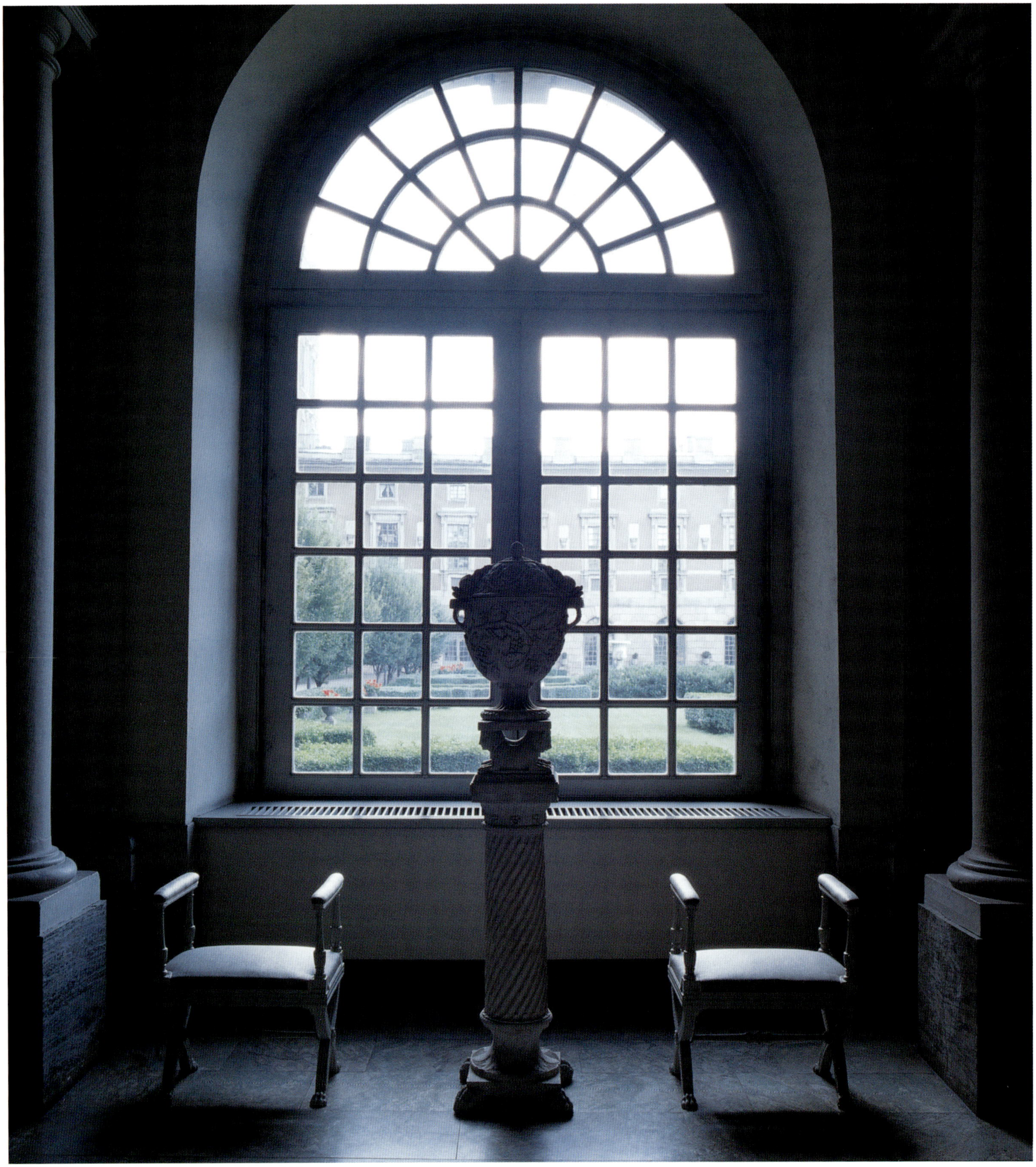

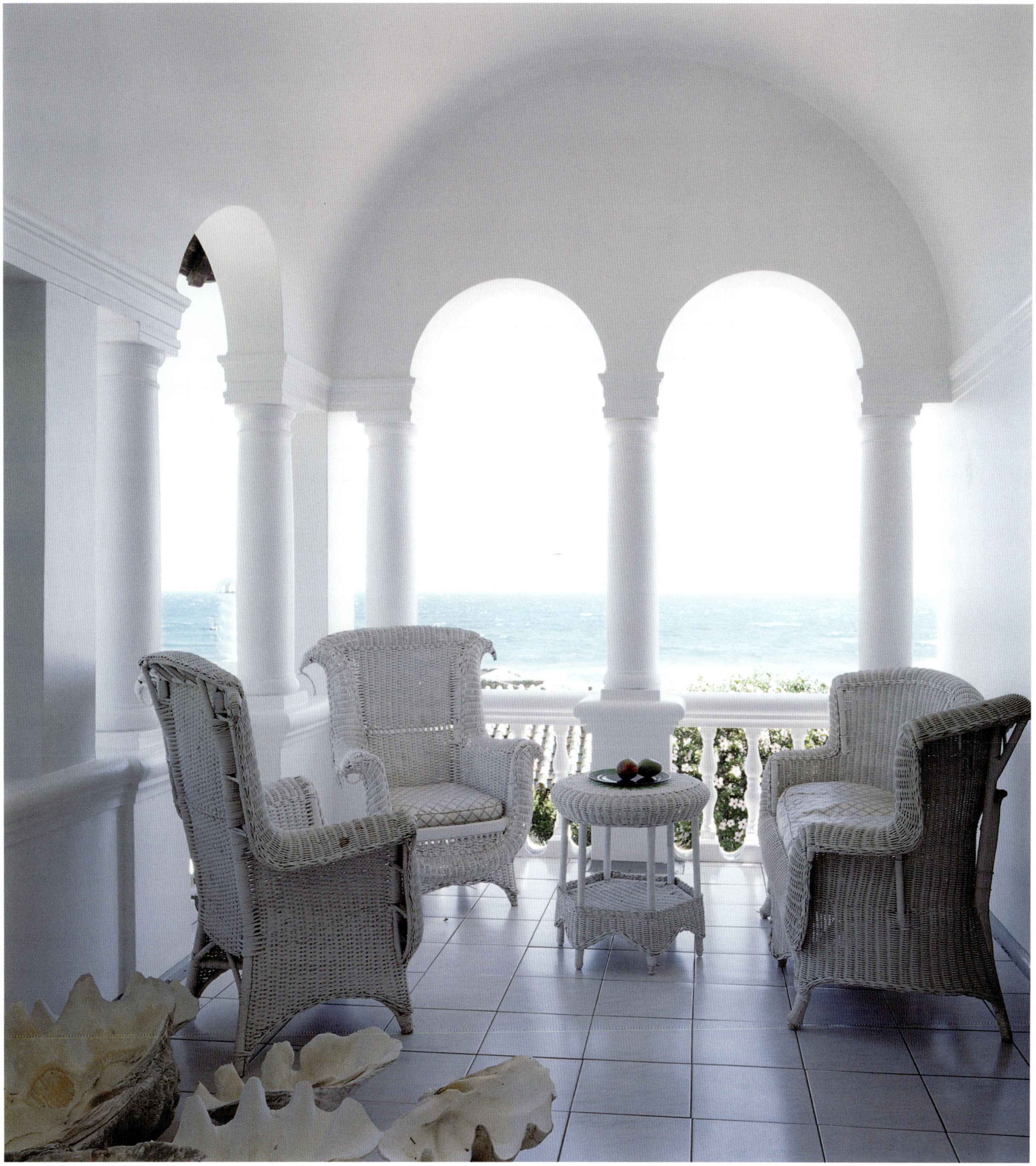

Light enhances colour in decoration, as illustrated in this blue and white Mediterranean sitting room by designer Mimmi O'Connell (ABOVE LEFT). It also creates interesting areas of shadow (ABOVE RIGHT), as well as pattern by the use of louvred shutters, which also ensure privacy in this bedroom in couturier Jasper Conran's London apartment (OPPOSITE).

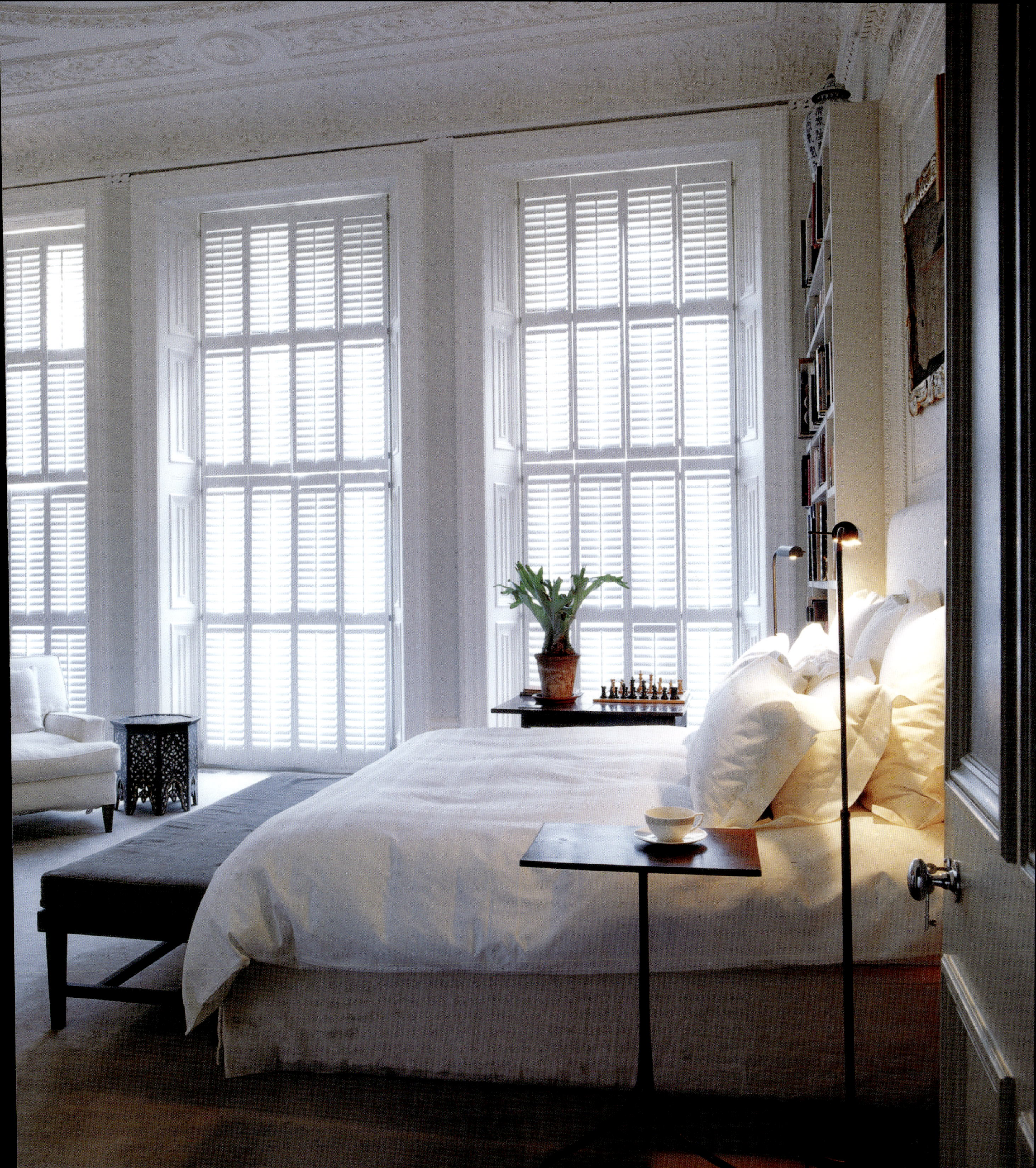

ABOVE Attic rooms often have small windows and are poorly lit, so designer Mimmi O'Connell has kept the decoration and furnishing of this bedroom simple.

ABOVE Shafts of sunlight infuse a corridor in the late Bill Blass's country house in Connecticut with a warm glow.

RIGHT This contemporary loft space was created in the attic of a 19th-century villa and used by its owner, a Belgian antiques dealer, as a gallery for his collection of art and sculpture. A-frame-shaped windows at either end flood the room with natural light.

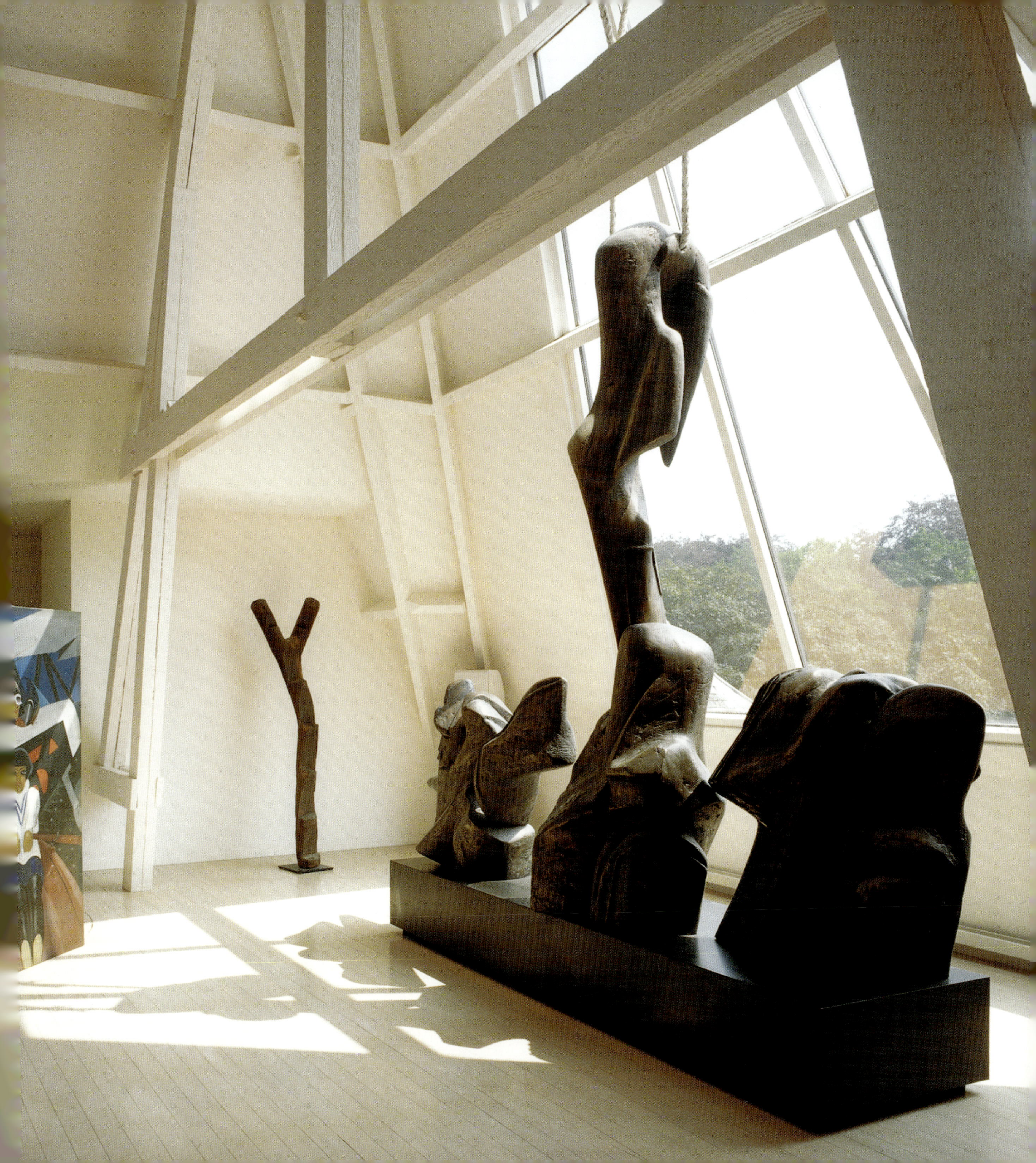

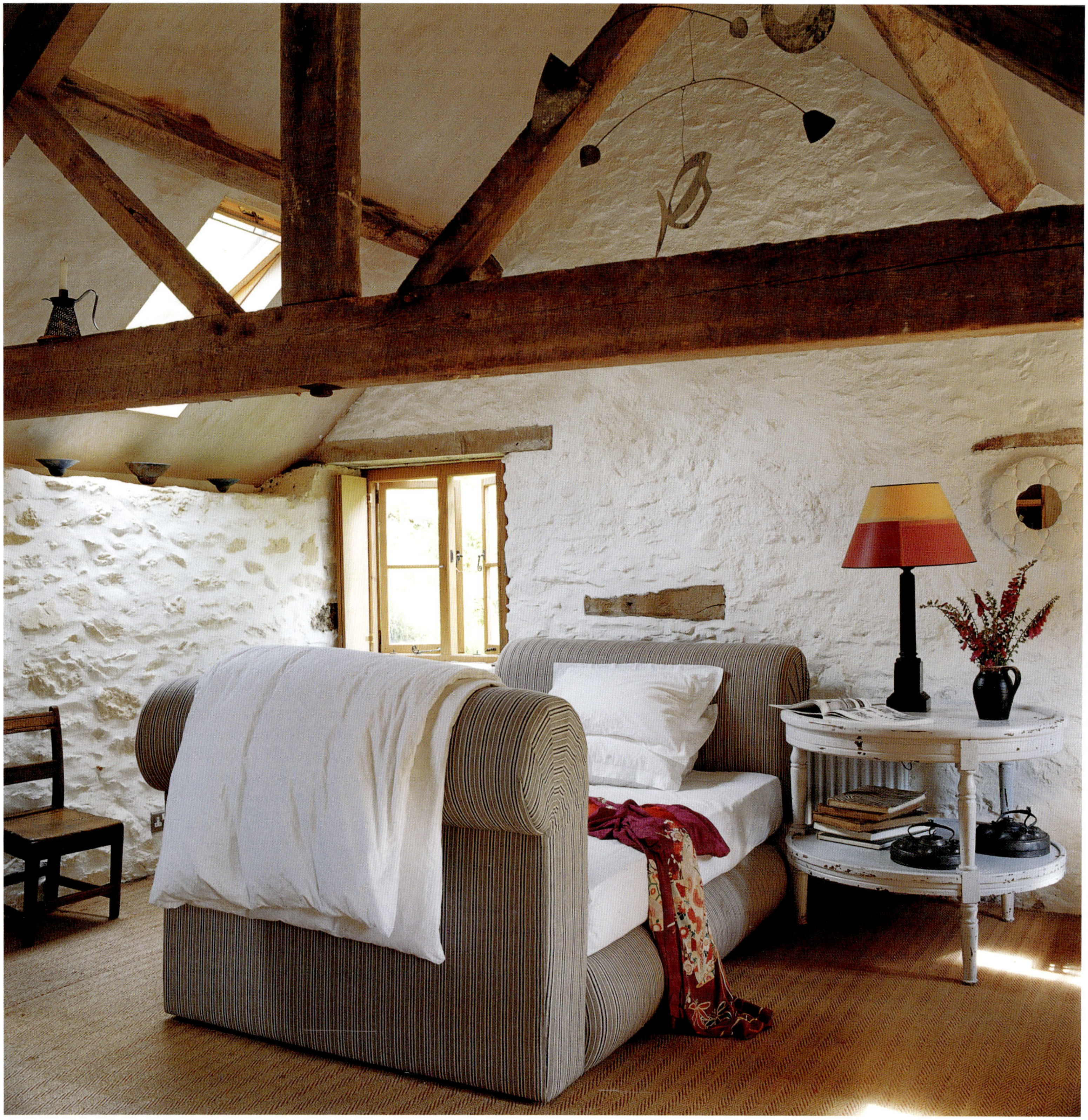

OPPOSITE A former sheep stall in the grounds of a Welsh longhouse has been transformed into an 'outhouse guesthouse'. The addition of a skylight above the bed directs daylight where it is needed.

ABOVE Daylight floods this country living room through an uncurtained window, highlighting a Chinese sideboard and whipping stool, flanked by a pair of 18th-century English chairs.

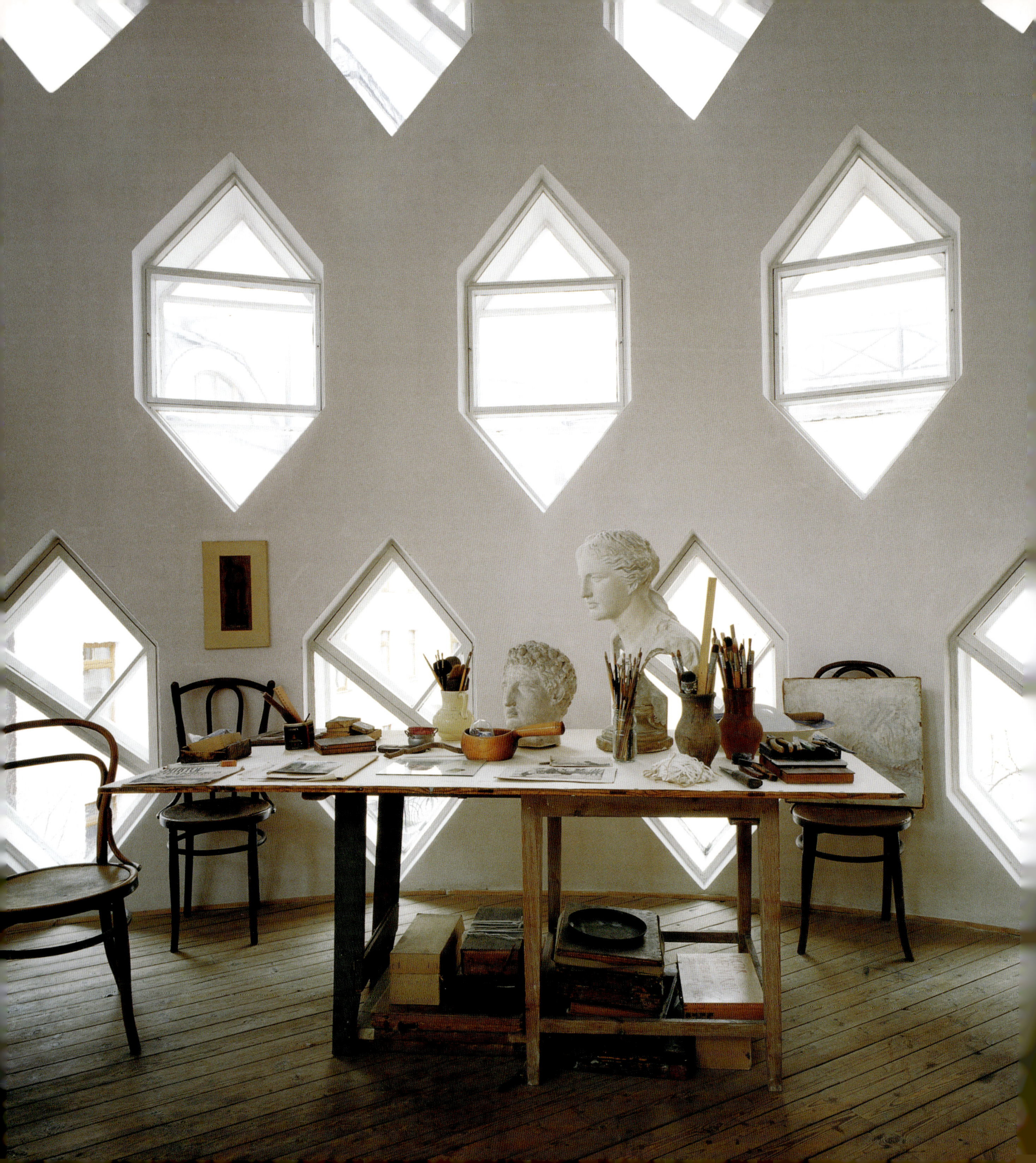

OPPOSITE AND ABOVE Architect Konstantin Melnikov built this extraordinary house in Moscow in 1929. Unique in its design and sculptural quality, the property has 36 hexagonal windows cut into the wall of a vertical cylinder: Melnikov's workshop benefits from three rows of these windows and is subsequently bathed in light.

ABOVE Designer John Stefanidis created this long skylight in the study of a London house, enhancing the rhythmic effect of the Neoclassical-style columns.

ABOVE A 'Chatsworth' bench dominates this garden room with a small arched window that opens onto Table Mountain in South Africa.

LIGHT 143

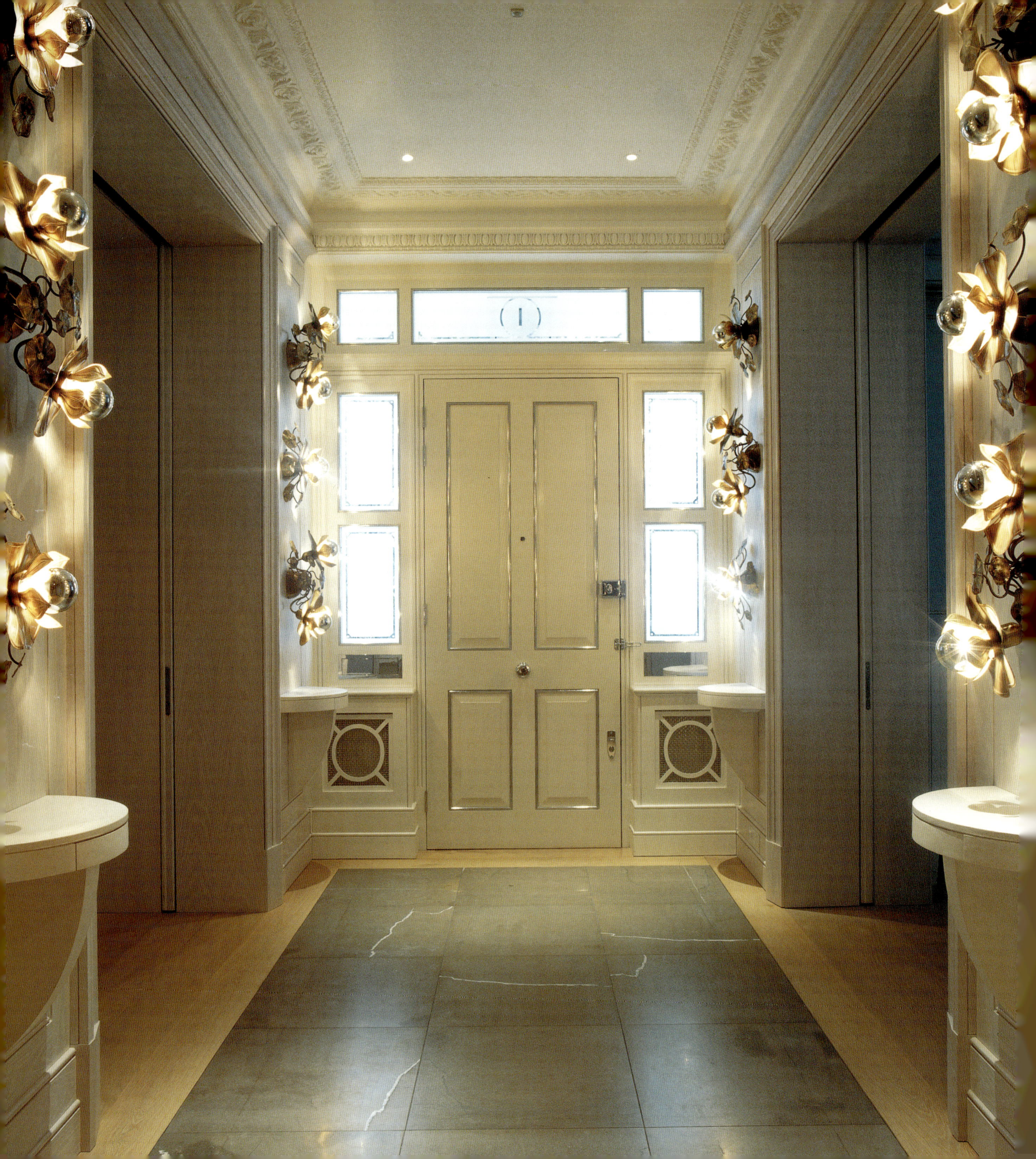

OPPOSITE This entrance hall designed by Collett-Zarzycki combines a Neoclassical colour scheme with a series of decorative light fixtures.

ABOVE A pair of Italian 1840s ironwork armchairs occupies a small stone-flagged landing on the original Georgian staircase which ascends five floors in designer John Minshaw's London house.

ABOVE Three evenly spaced, uncurtained windows in interior designer Karen Roos's South African home flood the living room with sunlight.

OPPOSITE Artist Karl-Heinz Scherer's studio benefits from a vast window at one end. In this space natural and artificial light are deliberately combined, with the introduction of neon tubes of different colours.

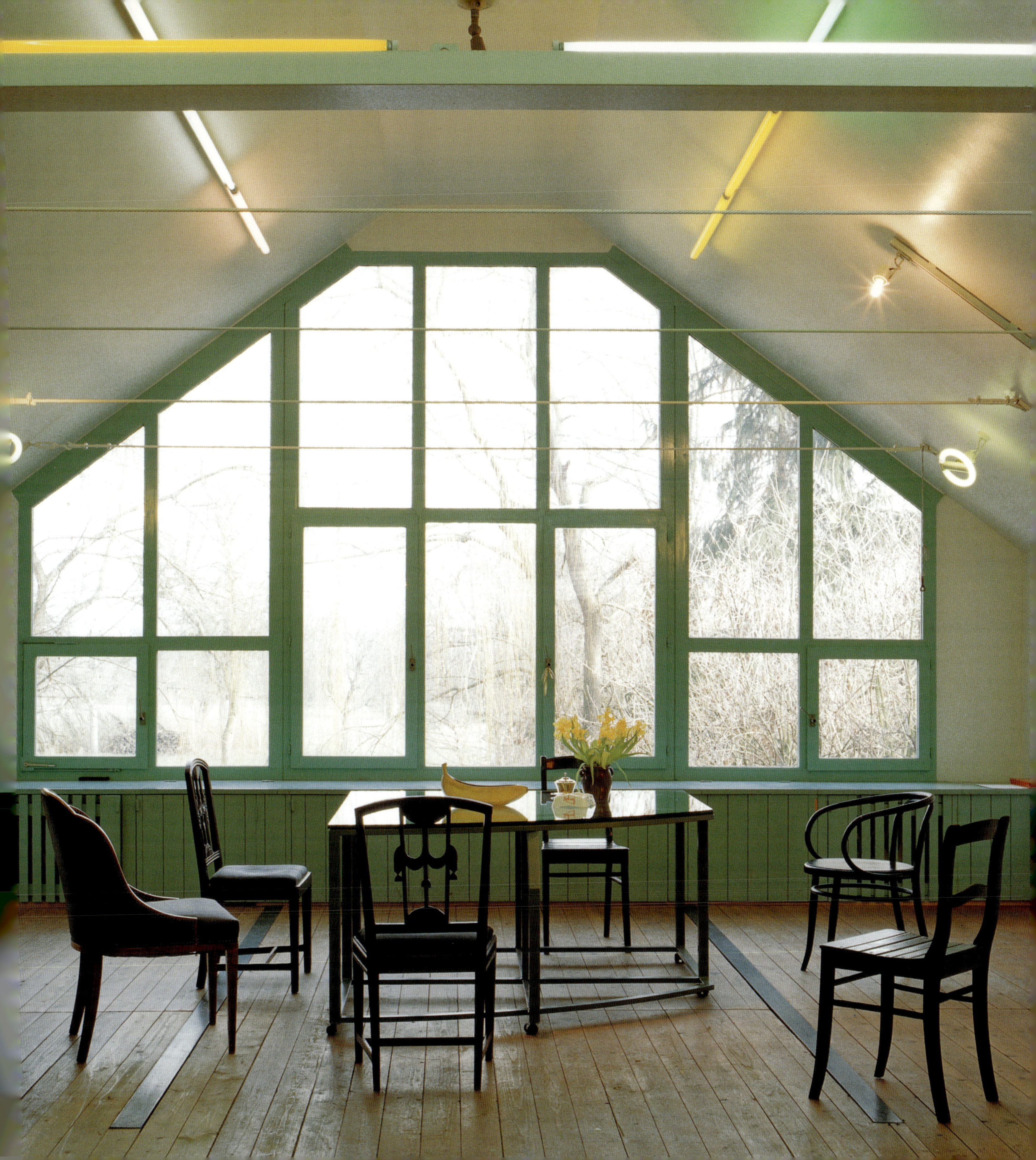

CLOCKWISE FROM ABOVE In the music room in designer David Collins's London apartment, chairs by Jean Royère found in a Paris flea market are grouped around a 1955 blue plastic table which reflects the natural light flooding the room; a 'Spider Sconce' by Serge Mouille is silhouetted against a modern artwork on the blue silk-upholstered wall of the music room; a contemporary chair in an Art Deco style designed by Collins has been placed against the drawing-room wall, made of canvas panels with cracked gesso on a copper leaf base.

OPPOSITE The contrast created by South African designer Stephen Falcke between the dark mahogany furniture and crisp white bed linen in this bedroom is softened by the diffused light from the louvred windows.

OVERLEAF At the centre of the couturier Bill Blass's mahogany-floored bedroom-cum-sitting room-cum-library is a solid Edwardian library table on which is displayed a collection of model staircases and a bronze copy of the column in the Place Vendôme in Paris. Permanently closed shutters on either side of the fireplace mask an unappealing view and double as hanging space for pictures.

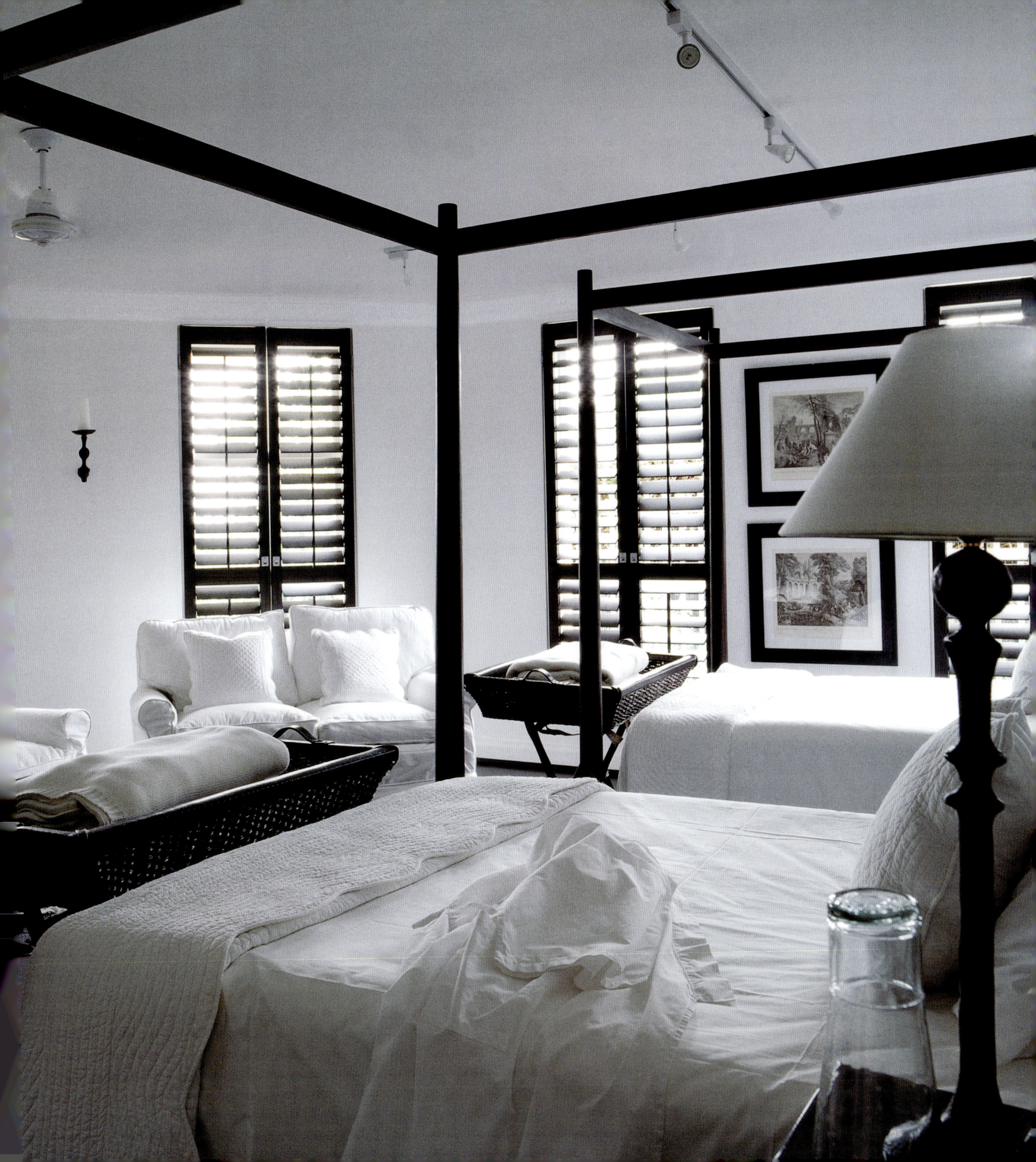

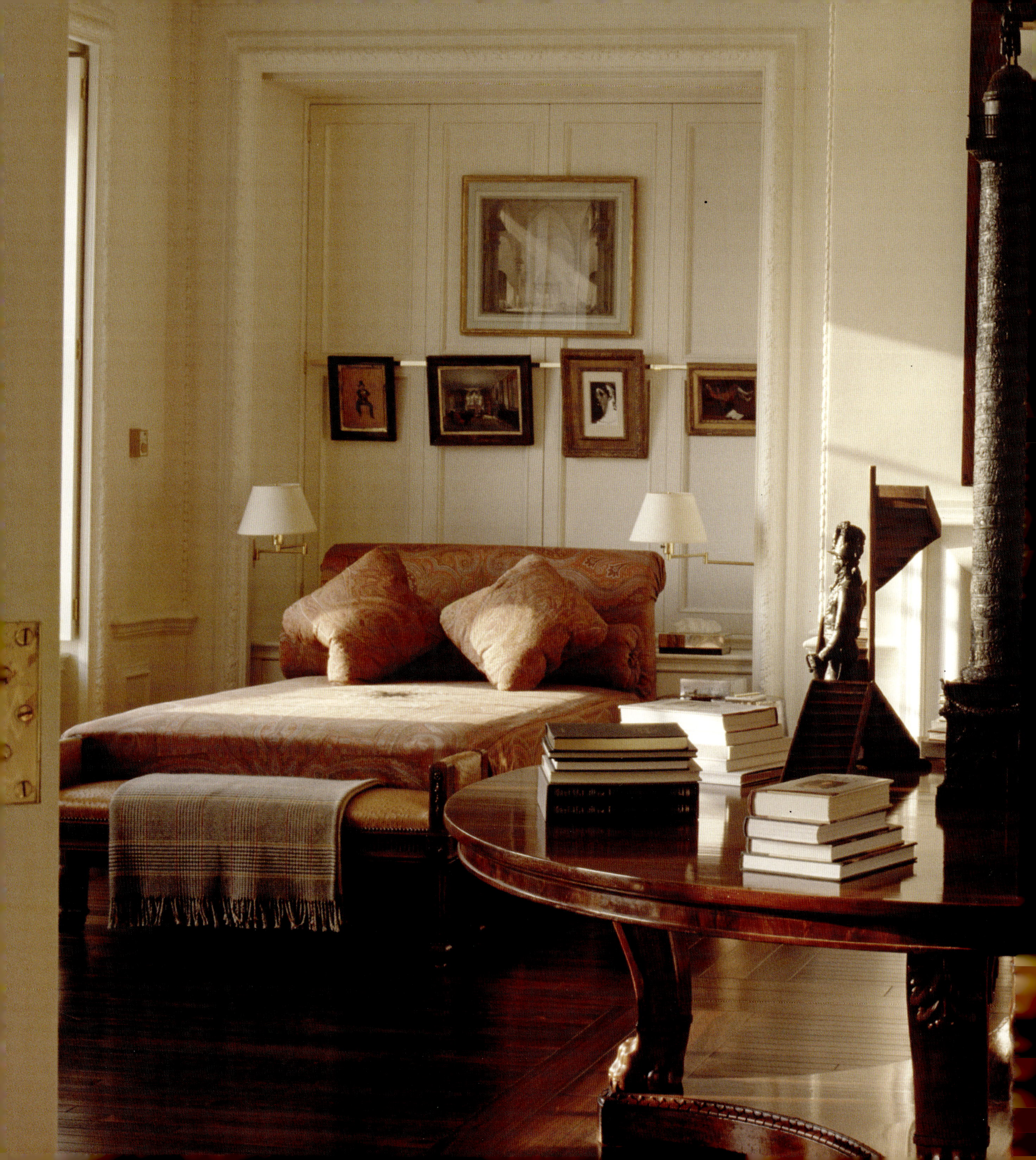

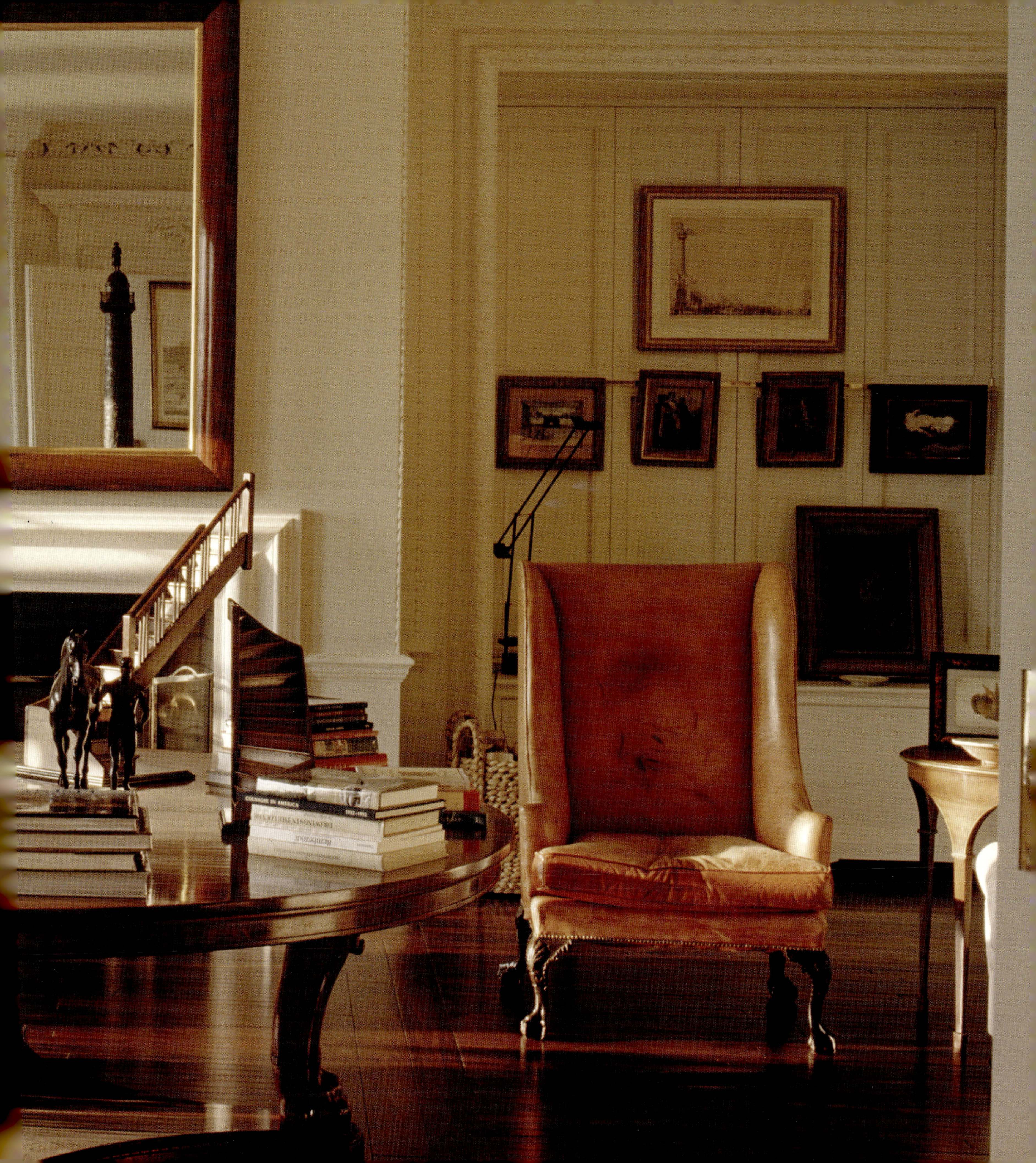

SPACE

Space is fundamental to our understanding and enjoyment of architecture and interior design. Of the six identified elements within Minimalism in the Grand Style, none would appear to be more important a reference than the sense of space, its interpretation and context.

According to the early Chinese philosopher Lao-Tse, 'architecture is not four walls and a roof; it is also, and above all, the air that remains within, the space that these enclose'. Surely every architect must identify with this philosophy: that the space between the ground, the walls and the ceiling does not represent a void, but the fundamental context of a building.

Aristotle defined space as a container of things, a succession of all-inclusive envelopes, rather like a succession of rooms, an enfilade. He suggested that there is no such thing as empty space, rather that everything is positioned and placed within space. If his view is applied to architecture and interior design, then space is the way in which we see a room in terms of volume, proportion, orientation and distance. It is the interpretation of space that defines an architect or an interior designer.

The introduction of shape into a space, such as twisted columns, grand stairways and high domes; a sense of perspective; application of colour to exaggerate architectural form and symmetry: all represent acknowledged and recognizable signatures, in both historical and contemporary architecture.

Space is born from the relationship between objects and their boundaries. It is sometimes said that space is suggested by a painter, filled by a sculptor and contained by an architect. As if to illustrate the point, sculptor Andy Goldsworthy created a series of simple rectangular, square and circular sheepfolds out of stone. As outdoor sculptures, these were essentially empty structures, which suggested a need to enclose something – balancing on the boundary between sculpture and architecture. The 19th-century art historian August

OPPOSITE The Sharon Temple in southern Ontario was built by the Children of Peace, a breakaway group of American Quakers, between 1825 and 1831, and is considered to be the most remarkable religious building in Canada. The square wooden structure rises over three storeys that represent the Trinity. Inside, a gently curving wooden staircase painted a deep green leads up to the musicians' gallery.

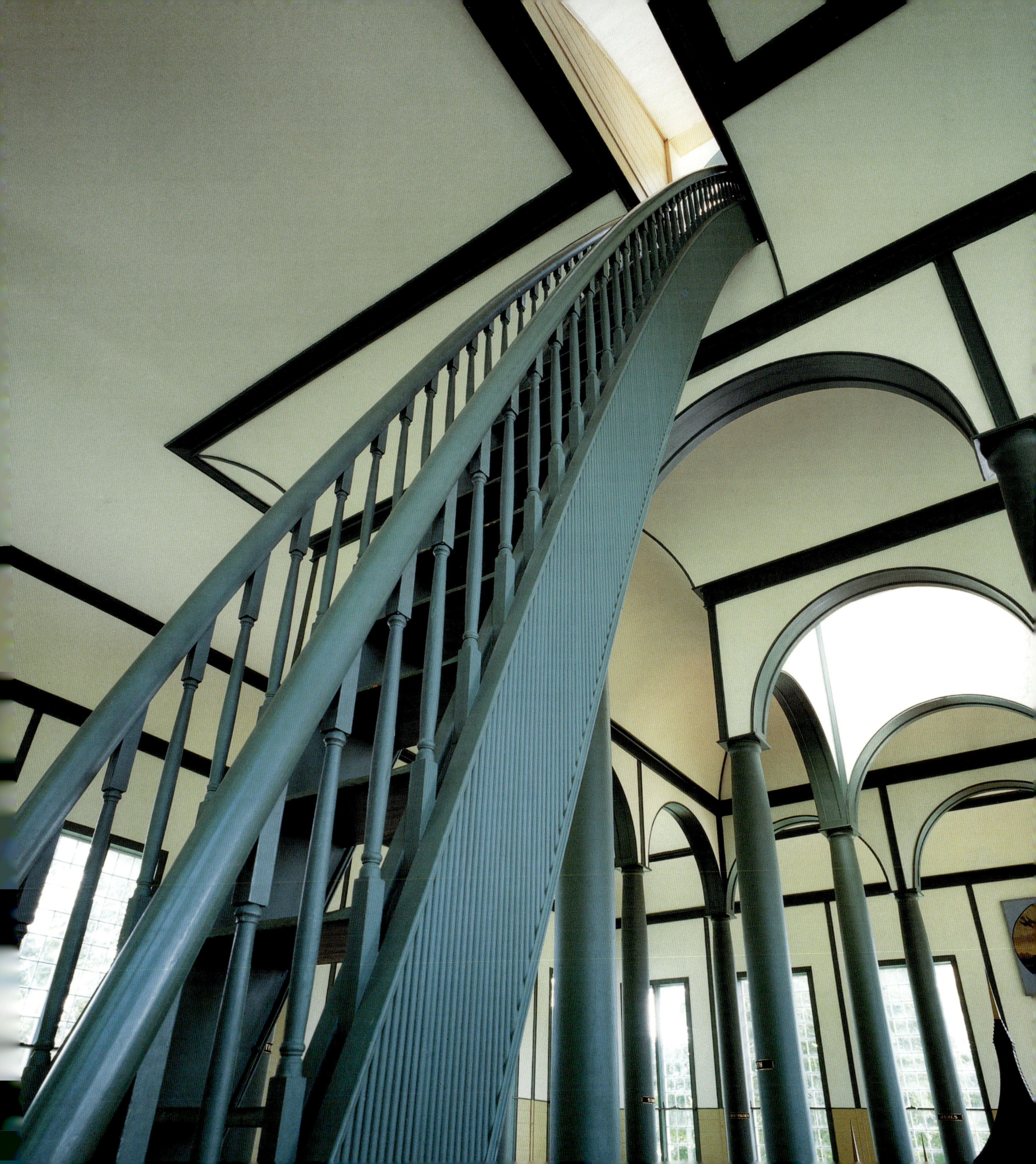

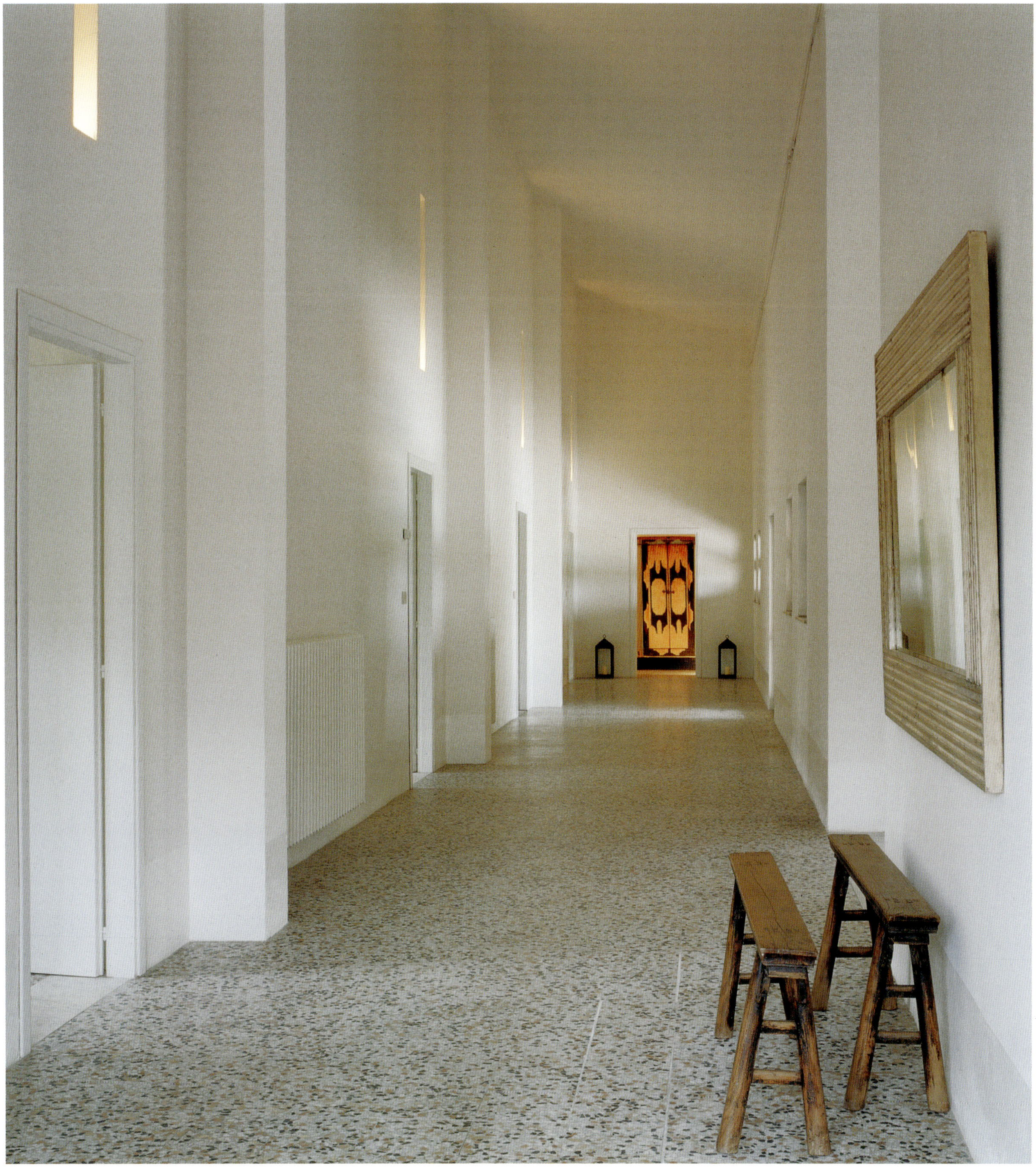

Schmarsow, addressing this threshold from the other side, wrote that 'architecture is art when the design of space clearly takes precedence over the design of the object. Spatial intention is the living soul of architectural creation.'

In one of several books that antiquarian Axel Vervoordt has produced over the last decade, he describes the influence of Oriental art, and the importance it places on a life of meditation, on his own practice. In an architectural context, Vervoordt sees meditation as an empty space, which represents proportion, balance and harmony. When restoring a building, he will always allow the space to inspire him and, more than his ability to think and analyze, it is of paramount importance to him simply to spend time in rooms that he has designed in a deliberately sparse and pared-down fashion.

Whether it's the beauty of the air between two adjoining rooms decorated by Nancy Lancaster, or the breath between objects juxtaposed in a room setting, our sense and appreciation of space is strongly influenced by light. The diversity of light – natural and artificial – in an interior affects the perceived size and the context of a room, as well as its shape and definition. The perception of a space is directly connected to its interplay with light: depending on how it is used, qualities of light will always transform space.

OPPOSITE The corridor of designer Mimmi O'Connell's converted schoolhouse in Tuscany benefits from a double-height ceiling. The original 1960s terrazzo floor tiling enhances the sense of space and leads the eye to an Indonesian door at the far end.

ABOVE A guest bedroom in the vaulted basement of Yasnaya Polyana, the 19th-century former country residence of the Russian author Leo Tolstoy, located in the Tula region, about three hours from Moscow (LEFT). The vaulted ceiling above the bed in this bedroom at Hill House outside Glasgow (RIGHT), designed by Charles Rennie Mackintosh, echoes the shape of the Art Nouveau dressing table.

ABOVE The massive double-height kitchens at the Vila Viçosa in Portugal are punctuated with great stone arches, and are renowned for the collection of copper pots and pans that occupies every cupboard and flat surface.

OPPOSITE A glimpse through an arched doorway into the dining room of a private guesthouse in the grounds of the Palais Sursock in Beirut, furnished with a set of Queen Anne chairs and a Regency table. The window is decorated with ornate tracery.

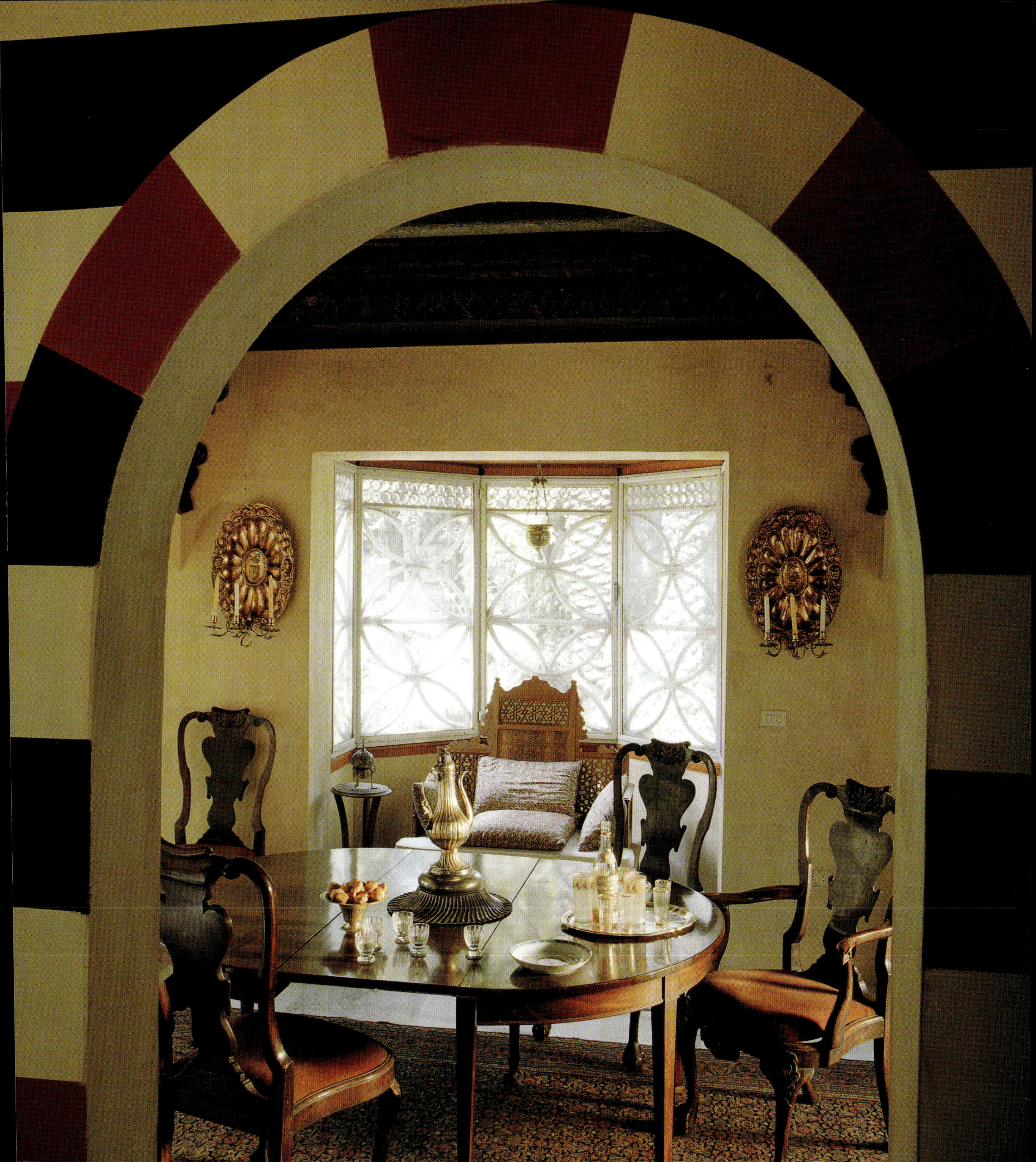

RIGHT One of Axel Vervoordt's favourite rooms, with plain walls and a stripped wooden floor, is dominated by large-scale pieces of contemporary art.

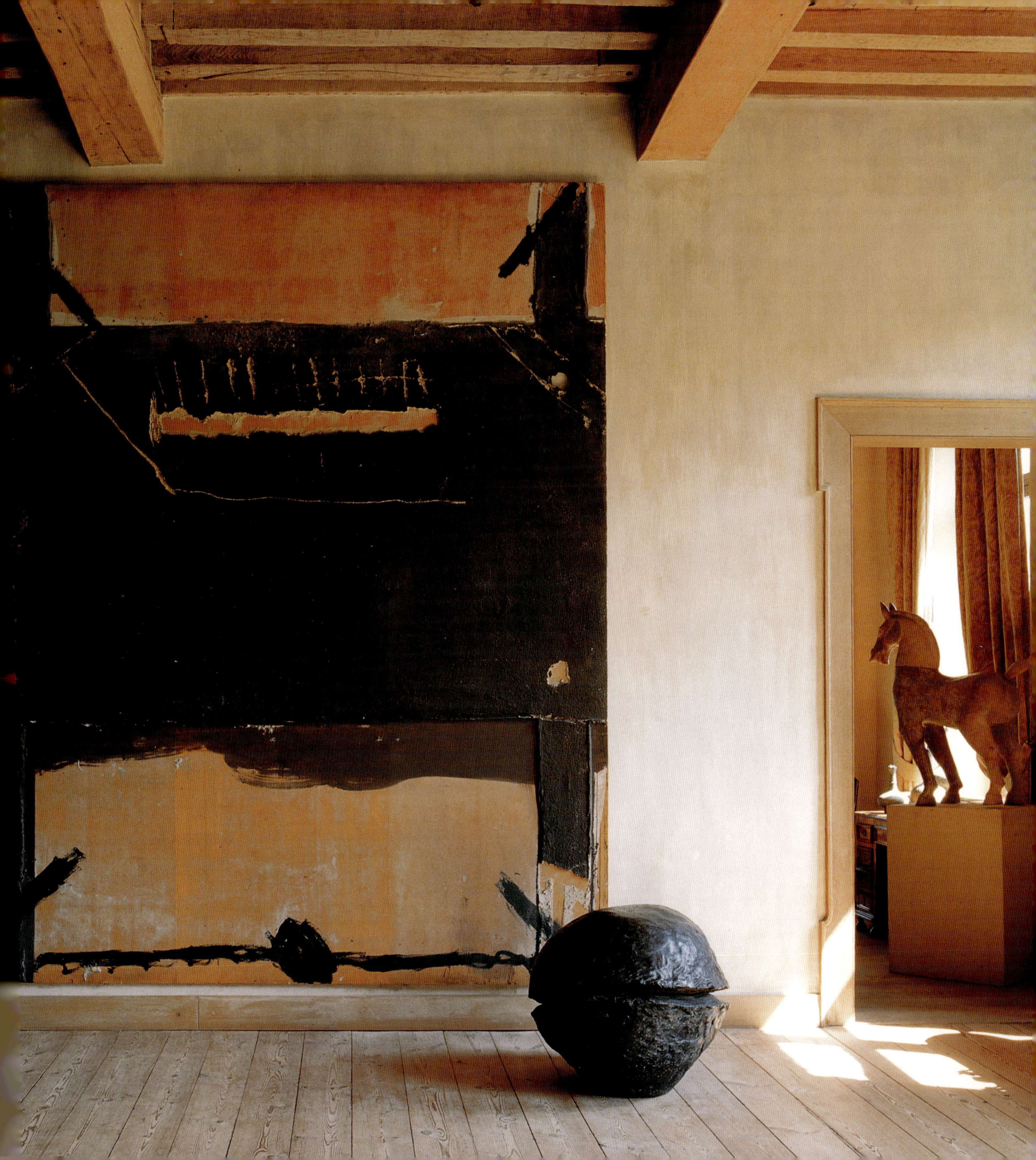

ABOVE A group of distinctive asymmetrical black and yellow 'Torso' chairs by Paolo Deganello nestle beneath the overwhelming height of this gallery loft space.

ABOVE A contemporary sitting room has been created beneath a magnificent beamed ceiling in the attic of a French château.

ABOVE The vaulted ceiling at the top of this spiral staircase enhances the sense of space in the stairwell.

OPPOSITE The architectural centrepiece at the Palais Sursock in Beirut is a dramatic double staircase, which is supported by slender pillars and curves upwards on either side of a central well.

OVERLEAF A sense of height has been achieved in the narrow entrance hall to a loft apartment, designed by Italian architect Paola Navone, by incorporating into its design an industrial-style staircase and a tiered chandelier of coloured tea-lights (LEFT). Light falls from the top of this sensuous contemporary staircase, which echoes the shape of the 18th-century sleigh in the hall below (RIGHT).

SPACE

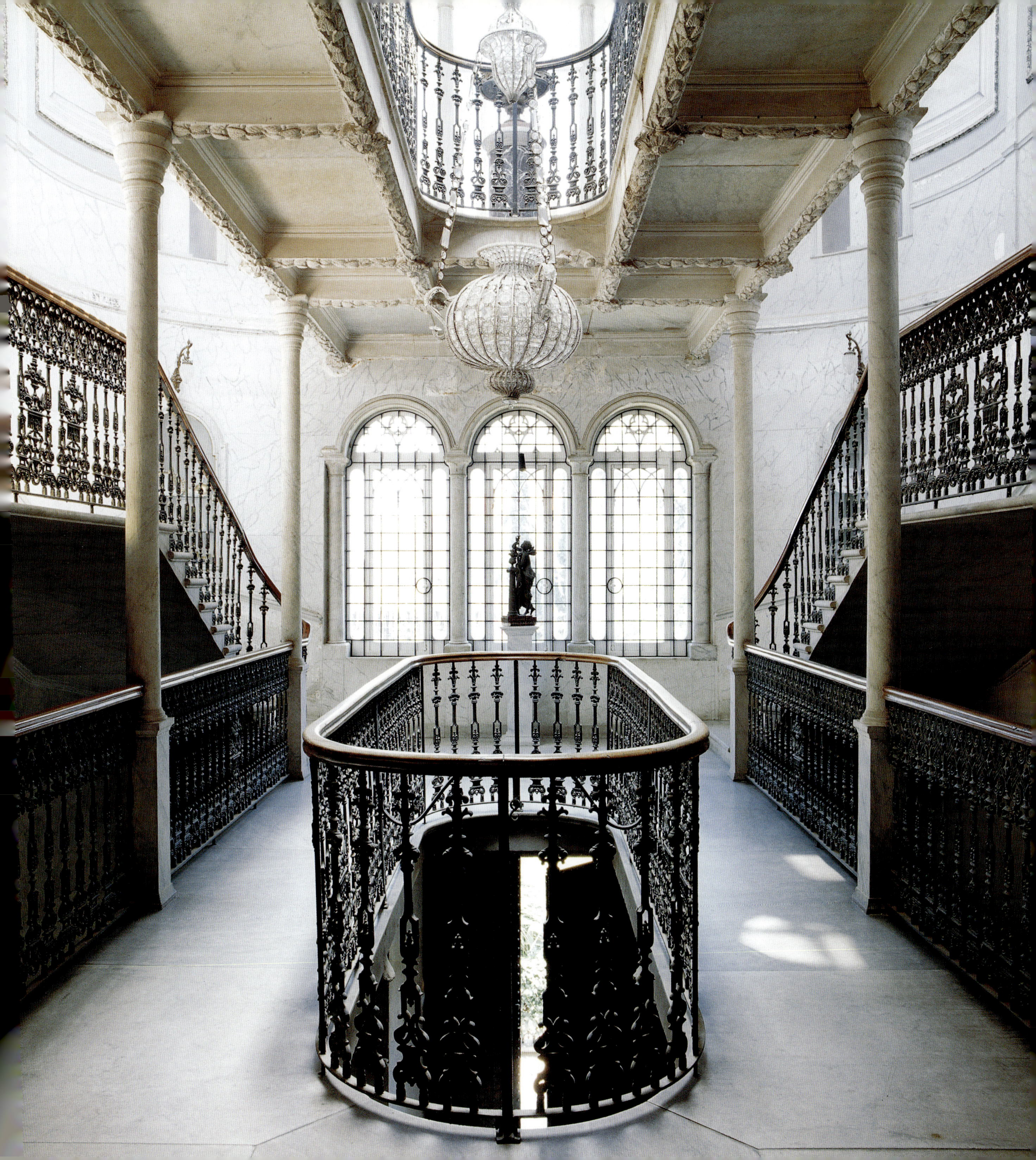

164

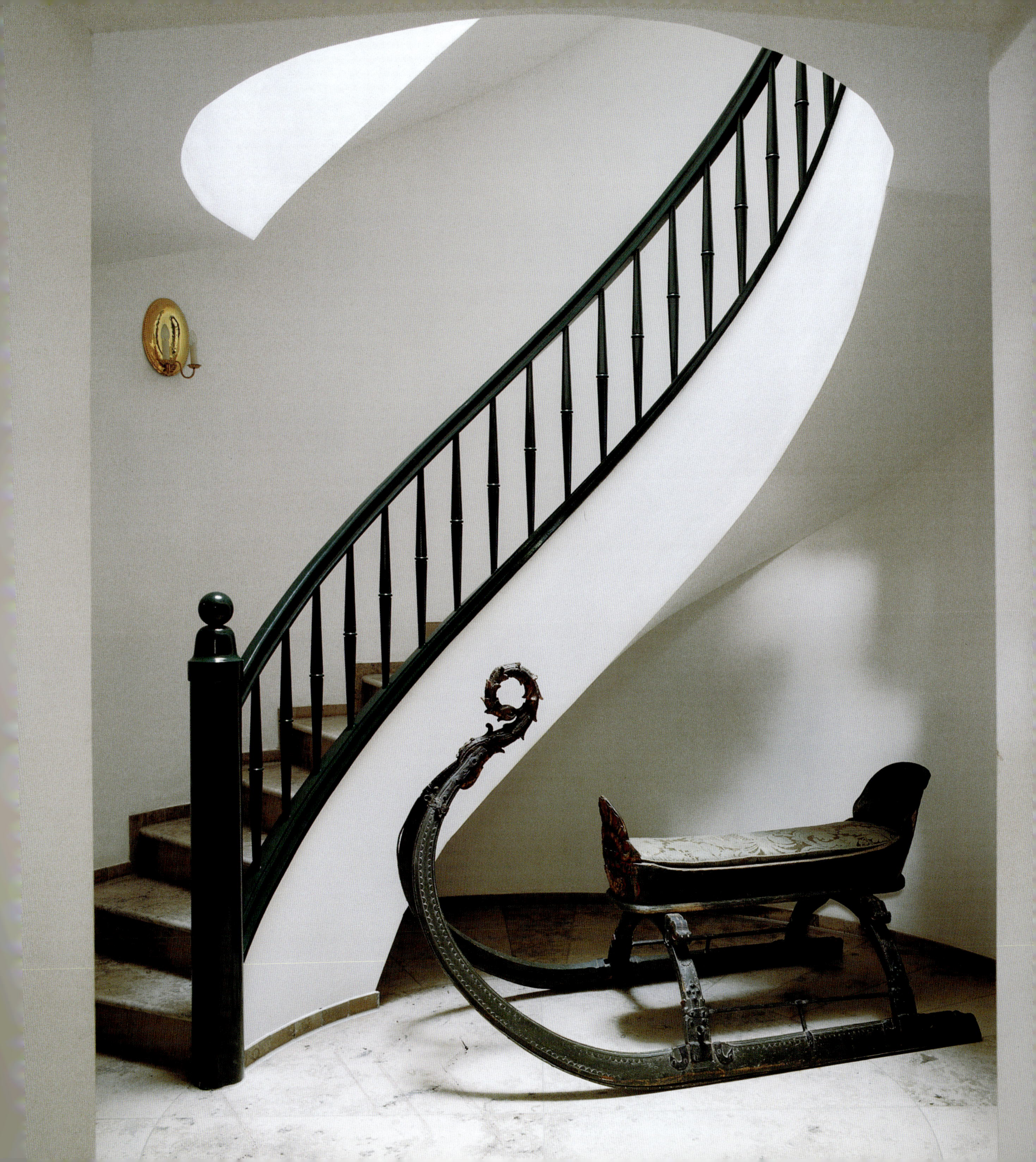

IN CONVERSATION WITH ANTHONY COLLETT

' Collett-Zarzycki's Classical references are to Ancient Greece, in particular to the formality and to the construction of space.

———

As a partnership, the core of our design stems from Classicism, so our approach to Minimalism is to go back beyond the architectural milestone represented by Palladio, to an even more distilled form of Classicism.

———

It is rare for Andrzej and me to take on a decorating project without first becoming involved with the architecture, since structure and geometry are intrinsic to our principles of design. However, by virtue of the fact that we operate out of London, the majority of our work inevitably involves the refurbishment of existing buildings. Many properties will have been subjected to bad restoration, resulting in the loss of original cornice and plasterwork, period windows and doors, and sometimes even the staircase. We believe that re-establishing or recreating the integral structure of a property is fundamental to the success of any good design.

———

Stripping a property back to its bones enables us to understand its original geography as well as the idiosyncrasies of its particular period. From this base we then create an overlay that covers all the elements of the new design, from lighting to soft furnishings. These are always hand-drawn and help a client to visualize the entire scheme.

———

Coincidentally, Andrzej and I were both born in Zambia and draw on our African background, even if at times I like to think it is done subconsciously. Everything in Africa is so open, not just in the great expanse of nature, but also in the way in which people have adapted to the climate. The inside/outside fad that obsessed designers some ten years ago is how people lived and still live in Africa today. The veranda was the living room and led out to the garden, and the garden in turn linked back to the veranda, so inside and outside were intrinsically linked. One of my earliest childhood memories is of crossing a courtyard via the veranda to reach the bathroom. The veranda was the main artery of every house.

———

My approach to colour is greatly influenced by my African upbringing. Combining colours can be very intimidating but by drawing on my background I found I was able to trust my instinct. Good colours, like good art, always work well together. Over the years I have acquired a large collection of Arts & Crafts vases, which are displayed around the walls of my London living room. In arranging this collection, I recognized that a good turquoise can live happily next to a good mustard, which in turn can sit beside a good terracotta; and you can hang a Léger or a Giorgio de Chirico anywhere.

———

Oddly, my favourite colour is magenta – a shade I associate with my mother and which holds a particular magic for me. Magenta is a true colour and very powerful. Then there is monochrome, in which I include grey, black, taupe and cream – Minimal, Neoclassical colours that work better if they are layered.

———

From an artistic perspective, colour is not just a detail of the decoration, but is foremost in the design and often shapes an interior. I tend to push the boundaries when it comes to the form and shape of the furniture I design, and then will exaggerate the fact in the texture and colour I choose for the upholstery. John Stefanidis has also influenced my approach to colour. Not only is he a great inspiration, he also opened my eyes to the possibilities in great design. His sense of colour is unerring, and he taught me to be bold and to have the courage of my convictions.

Light is extremely important in design and yet I am not afraid to play with darkness. I went through a stage during which I insisted that there should be one room in every house we worked on which was dark. I'm not sure we do this any more. It wasn't supposed to be a signature; I was simply fascinated by polar opposites. We once did a house for a client in which there were two interconnecting rooms, one dark and the other light. The white room we filled with dark furniture, and the walls of the second room we covered in a deep bronze fabric, while the furniture was white. It was yin and yang. I have always been intrigued by the differences you get when you show white against black, and vice versa. The form and shape of each piece of furniture is exaggerated and transformed into sculpture.

I have no desire to shut out the light but find controlling it through filters, such as blinds and shutters, intriguing as a point of design. A client's house featured in this book illustrates the point beautifully. The kitchen is the piano nobile of the house, a fabulous first-floor room with floor-to-ceiling windows on two sides, for which we created beautiful shutters covered in linen. While reinterpreting the original Victorian shutters is not a new idea, our treatment gave the room a contemporary, Minimalist touch. The shutters are in wooden rather than steel frames and the shutter boxes are grandiose and monumental. Instead of acknowledging the traditional panelling of the period, we chose to introduce something foreign and glamorous to the kitchen, and imposed the mirrored wall of units, instantly introducing a touch of theatre.

The Arts & Crafts movement was a unique period in design, a period in which architects were responsible for designing much of the furniture. It is equally important to me that Andrzej and I are largely responsible for the design of the furniture, the choice of fabric and textiles, and in many cases also the artwork for an interior, as well as the structure of the house. I don't differentiate between the lampshade and the structural column; a beam will influence where a curtain is placed and so the two are co-dependent.

Because our initial plans are so detailed, we have already established at an early stage the placement of the furniture, the lights and the artwork. But things don't always go to plan, so the composition of a room must be flexible if a painting does not look right in its predestined position on a particular wall. If a grouping of furniture does not work, it's like putting a tie with the wrong suit – it must be changed instantly!

How it all comes together is somehow intuitive. Again, Andrzej and I share a similar approach. I can only compare it to cooking: you have the same ingredients as any other designer, yet the last final tweak, which you will never find in a recipe book, is what makes the dish wholly your own.'

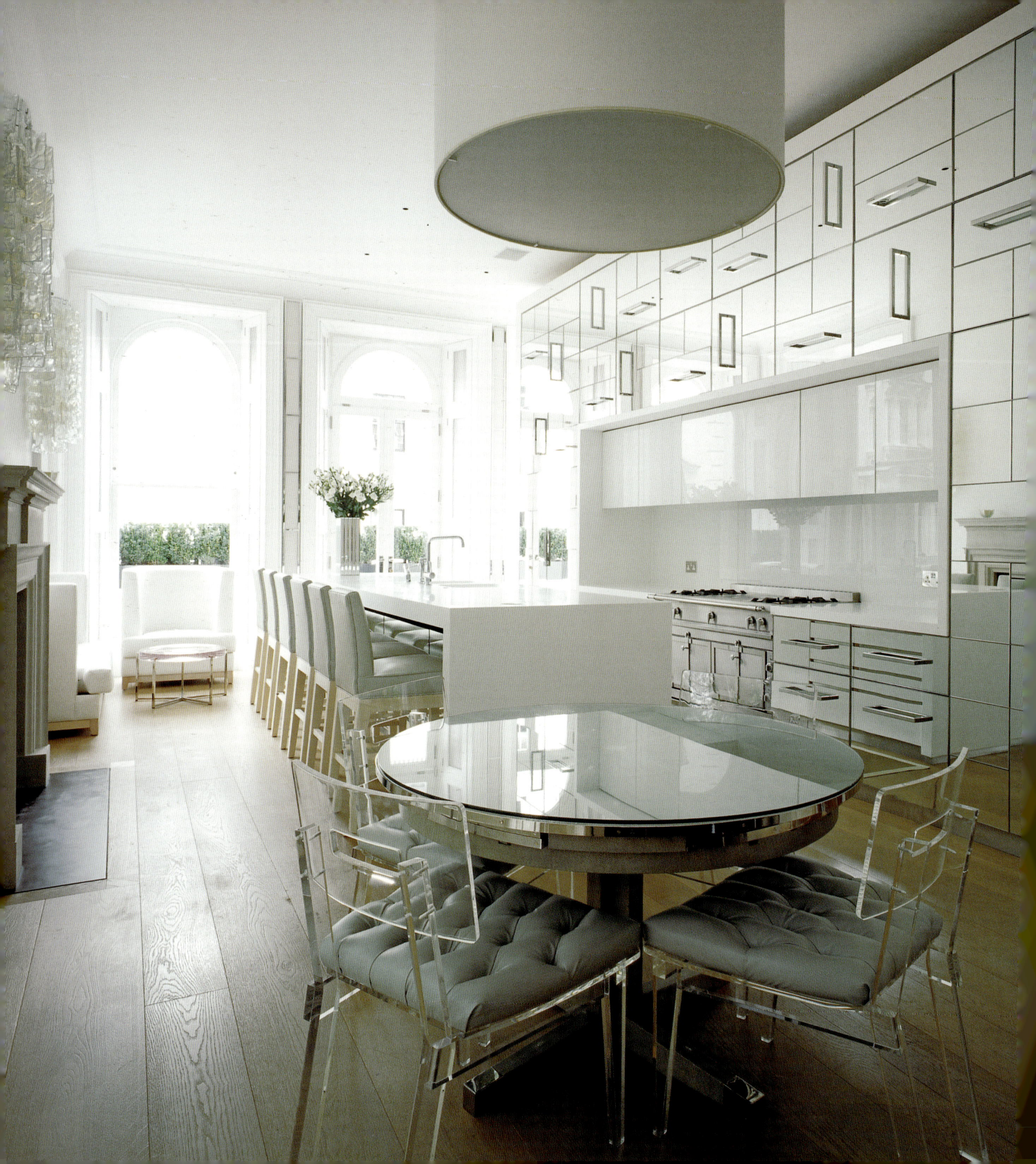

OPPOSITE A kitchen-cum-family room has been created by Collett-Zarzycki on the first floor of a Victorian house in London, in which the light from windows on two sides is reflected in the stunning mirrored wall of kitchen units.

ABOVE Mirrored wardrobes engraved with a floral design preface the entrance to the master bathroom, designed by Collett-Zarzycki.

SPACE 169

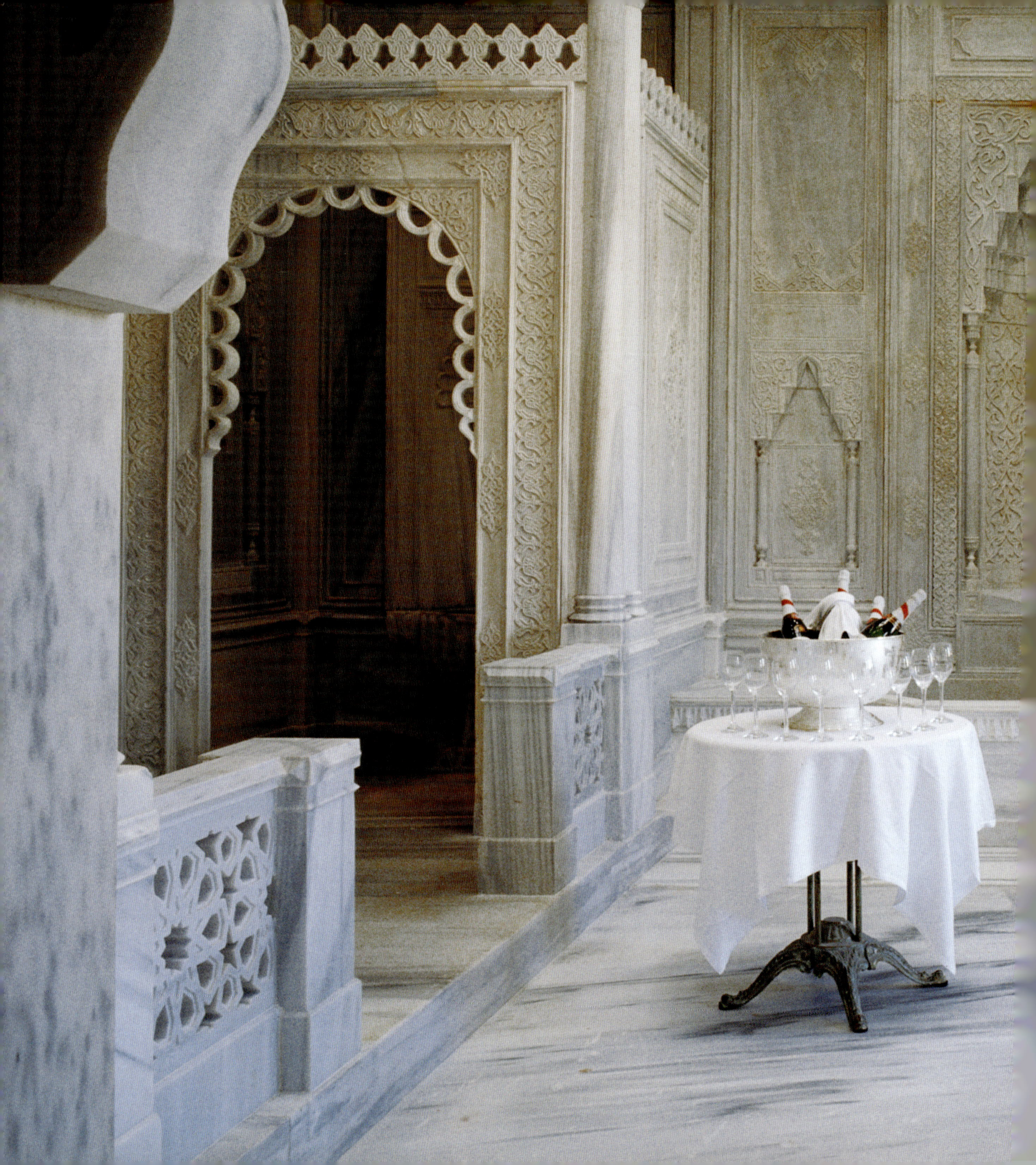

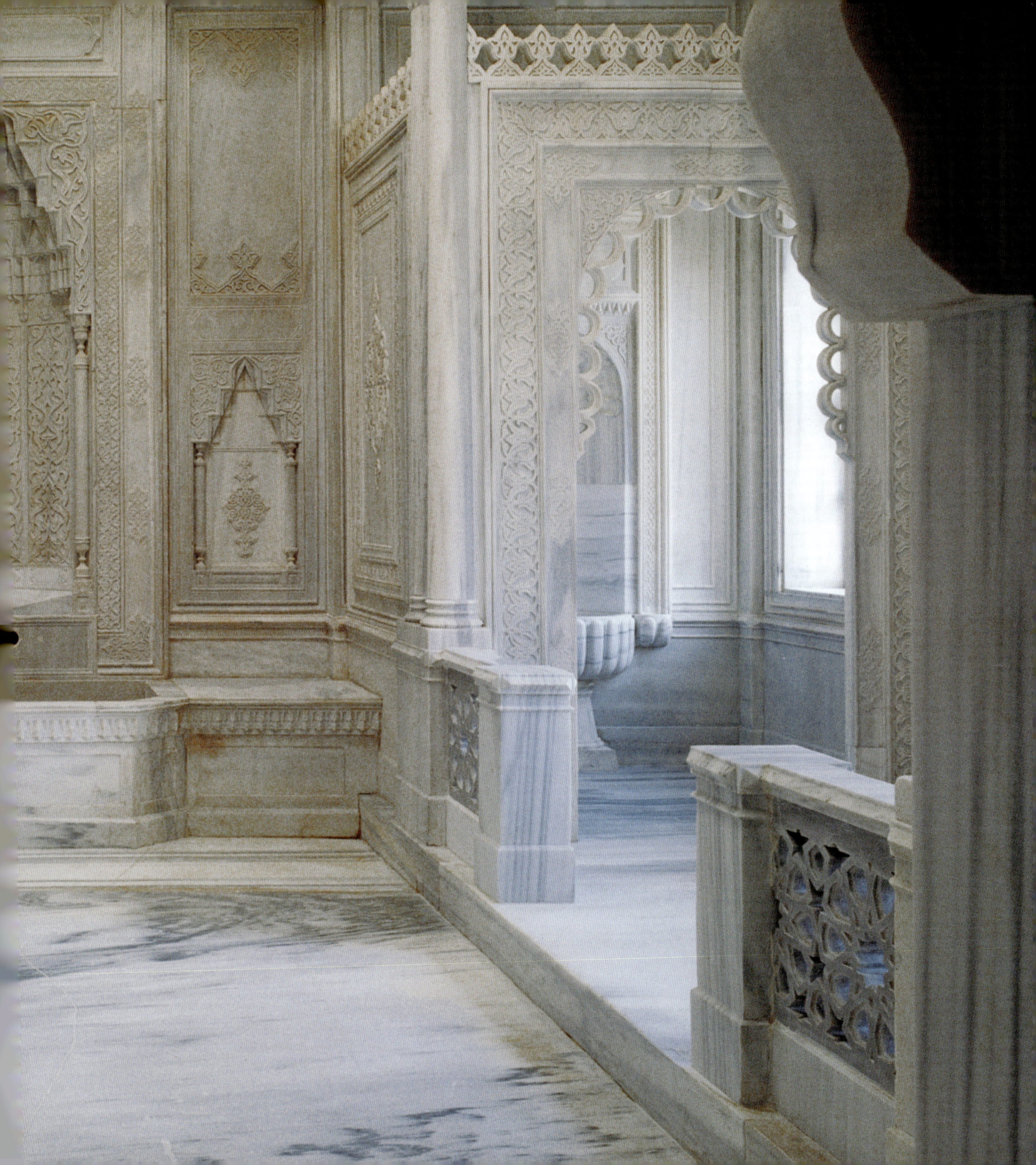

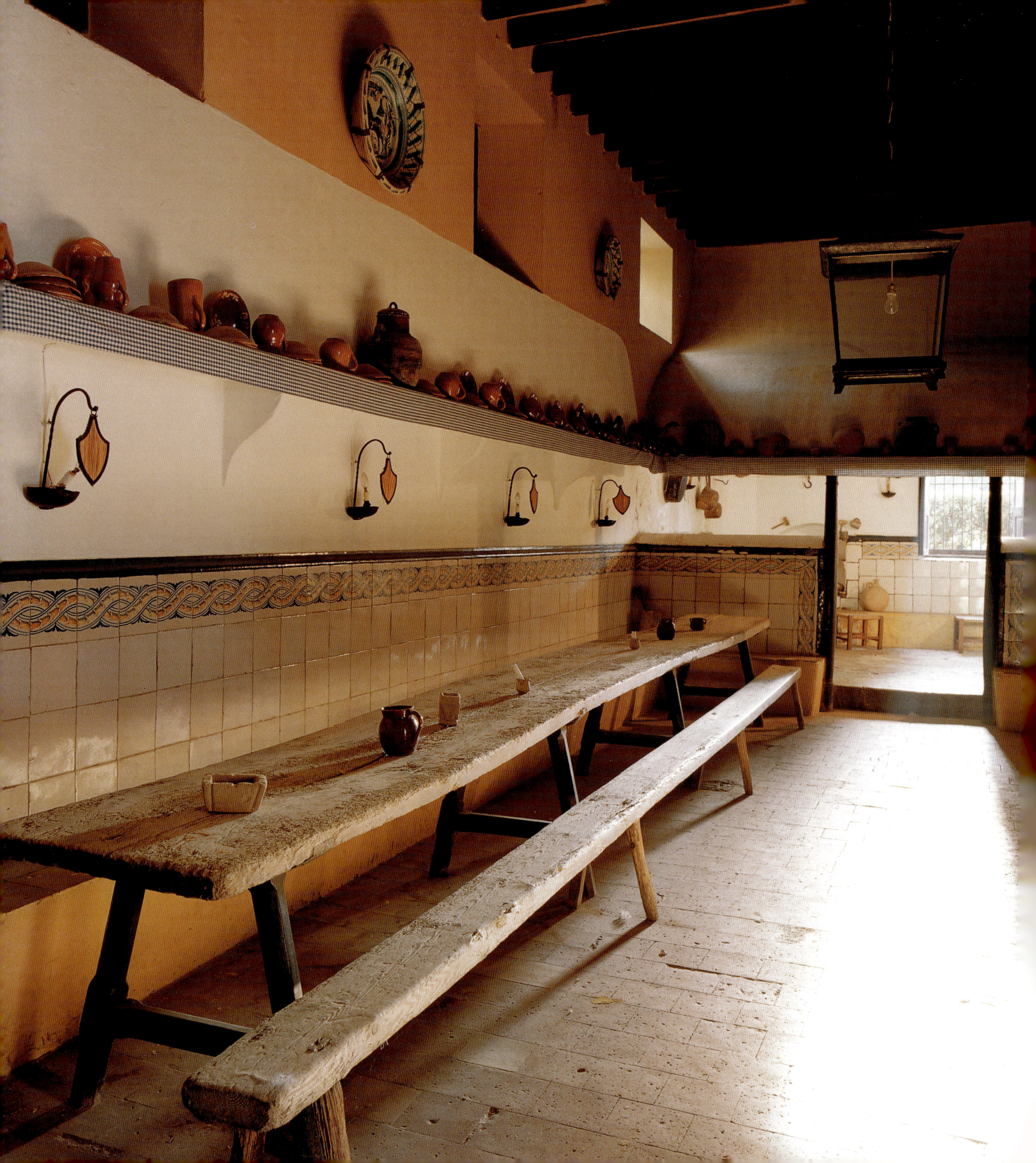

PREVIOUS PAGES Built by Sultan Abdülâziz and designed by the palace architect Nigoğayos Balyan, the Çirağan Palace overlooking the Bosphorus was completed in 1872. The marble walls and floors of the Sultan's Wing were restored, and today what remains of the original palace forms part of a luxury hotel.

OPPOSITE Long scrubbed tables and benches line the ceramic-tiled walls of the great kitchens at Castillo de Bendinat, an 1830s Gothic Revival castle on the island of Majorca.

ABOVE The Old Kitchen in the vaulted basement of Drumlanrig Castle in Scotland is furnished with a Regency pine table and an Arts & Crafts oak ladder-back armchair.

ABOVE Designer John Stefanidis removed the original ceiling of the kitchen-dining room in his former country house; the addition of a window high in the apex of the roof bathes the scrubbed wooden table in natural light.

ABOVE Vaulted ceilings feature regularly in basements to enhance the sense of space, reflected here in this arched kitchen.

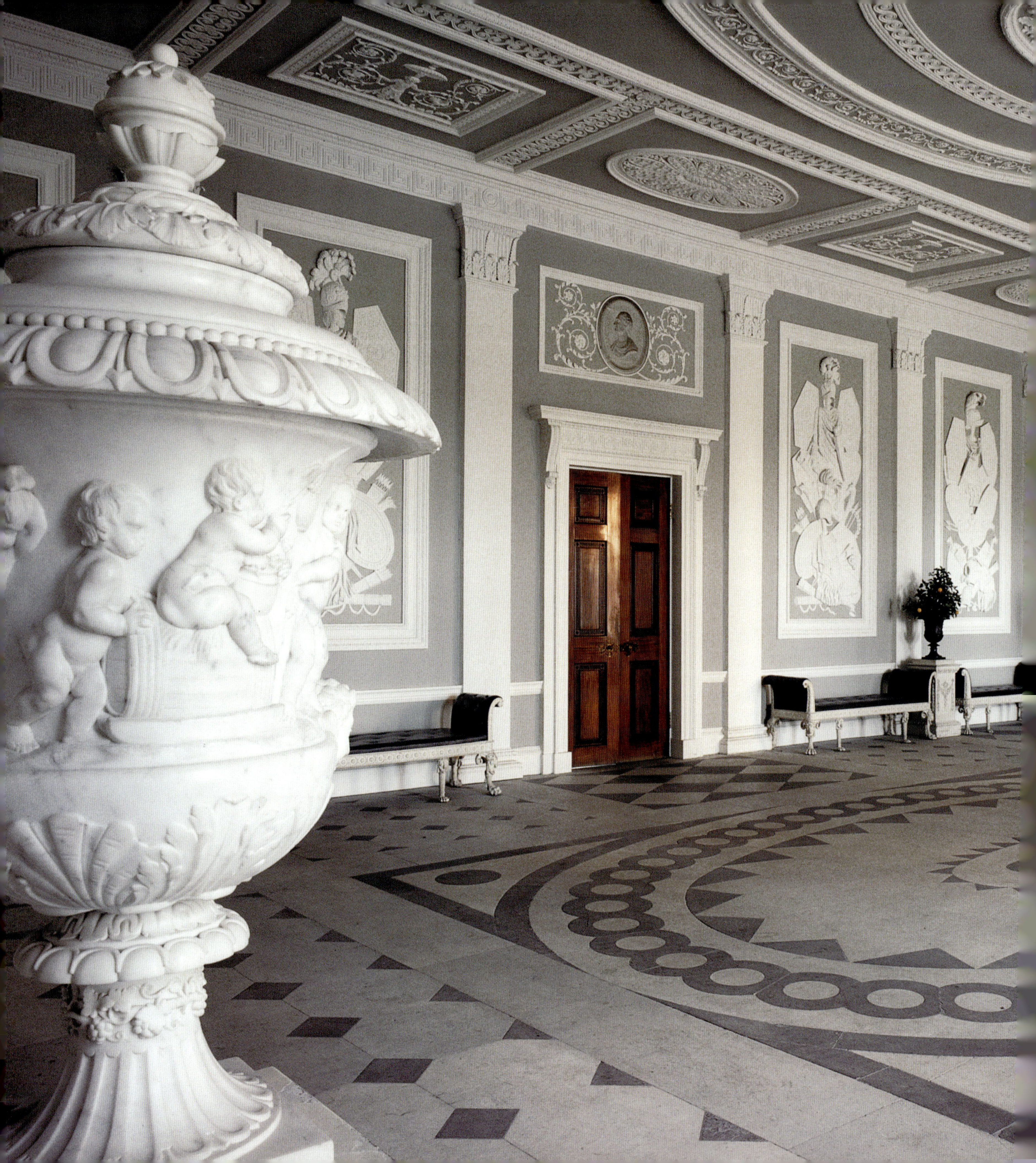

LEFT Created in the late 18th century by architect and designer Robert Adam, Osterley House in London boasts a spectacular Neoclassical entrance hall decorated in ornate plasterwork, with semi-circular alcoves at each end.

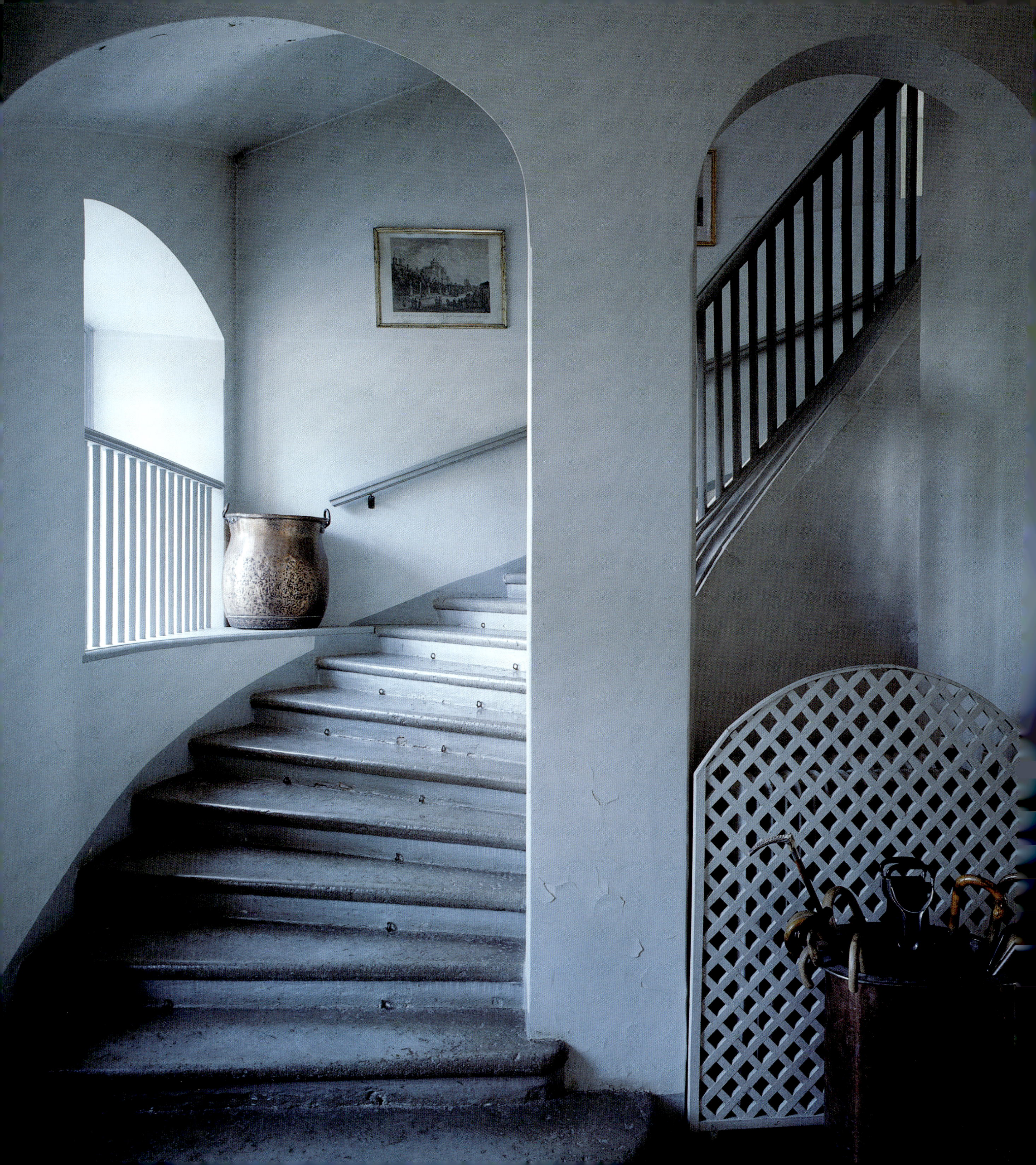

OPPOSITE Framed by a series of narrow archways, the space around this curving Neoclassical staircase is enclosed.

ABOVE Space for a contemporary kitchen has been created under the eaves of the roof, the architectural shape of the room reflecting the semi-circular shape of the window.

'Love architecture, be it ancient or modern. Love it for its fantastic, adventurous and solemn creations; for its inventions; for the abstract, allusive and figurative forms that enchant our spirit and enrapture our thoughts. Love architecture, the stage and support of our lives.'

GIO PONTI, ARCHITECT (1891–1979)

RIGHT The 'world's grandest chalet' was built in Istanbul by Sultan Abdülhamid II in 1889 for the visit of Kaiser Wilhelm II of Germany. The hammam, or bathhouse, is located in the earliest part of the building, where the internal windows allowed lanterns to cast light into the caldarium.

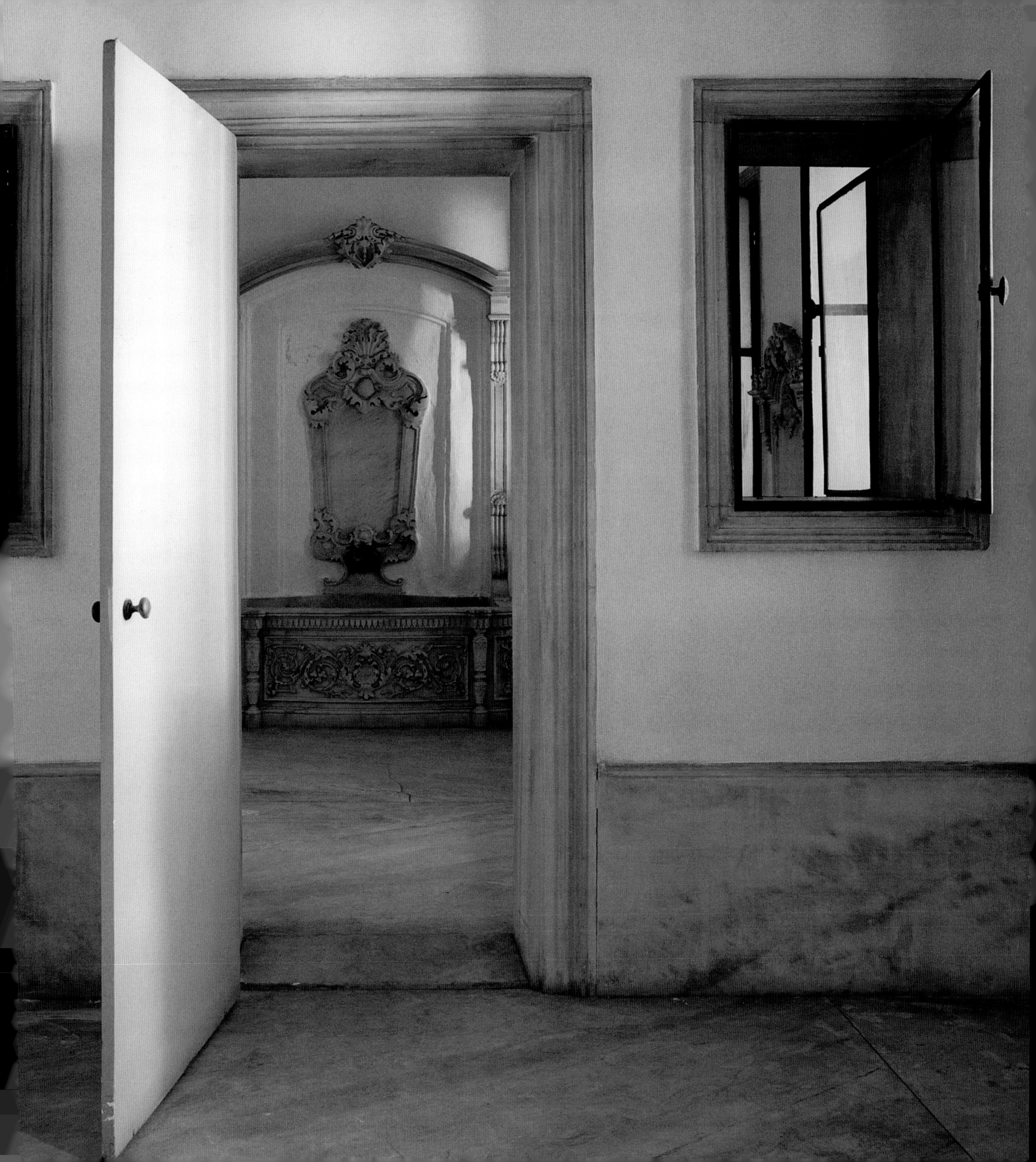

ABOVE The use of marble in architecture and interior design introduced grandeur to a space and was popular in the design of bathrooms, such as this splendidly columned version to be found at Manderston in Scotland (LEFT) and this Art Deco interpretation in a Paris apartment (RIGHT).

OPPOSITE Built by the architect John Kinross in 1900, the Marble Dairy at Manderston is constructed of marble and alabaster, and its shape emulates that of a church cloister. Lit by a single window, the vaulted room, punctuated by dark marble columns, shows how directional light enhances space.

SPACE

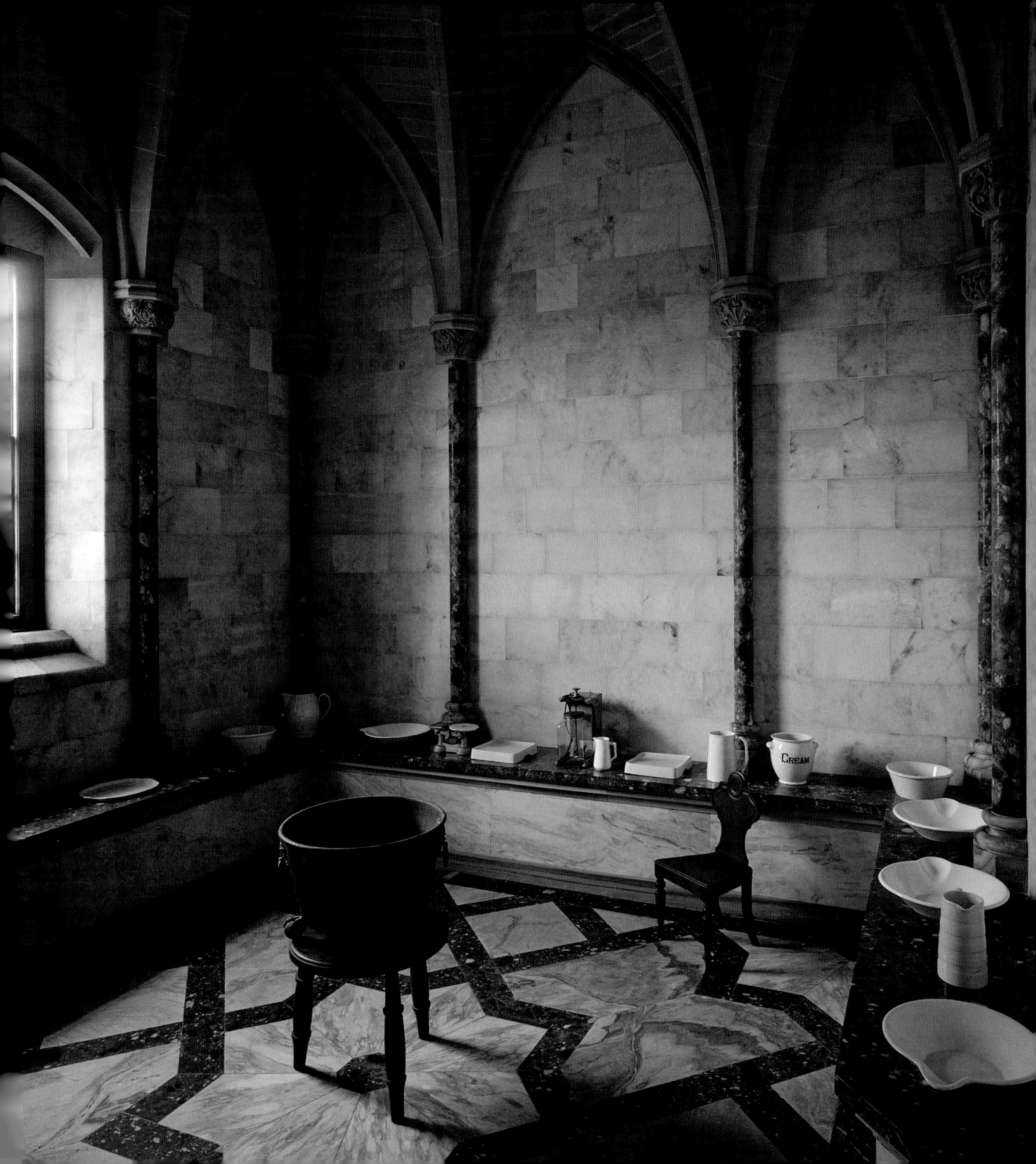
CREAM

ABOVE AND OPPOSITE This double-height entrance hall was created by John Stefanidis. The stone floor is inlaid with mosaic in curves and squares, and there is further mosaic inlay on the pillars of the terrace elevation, which echoes the 19th-century fireplace and clock, re-assembled to fit the hall. The marble balls made to top the over-mantel appear small, but actually measure approximately three feet in diameter. The walls are pigment on plaster, and the red felt curtains are decorated with an armorial motif in white appliqué. The sculpture of Diana the Huntress with an ivory bow is 19th century.

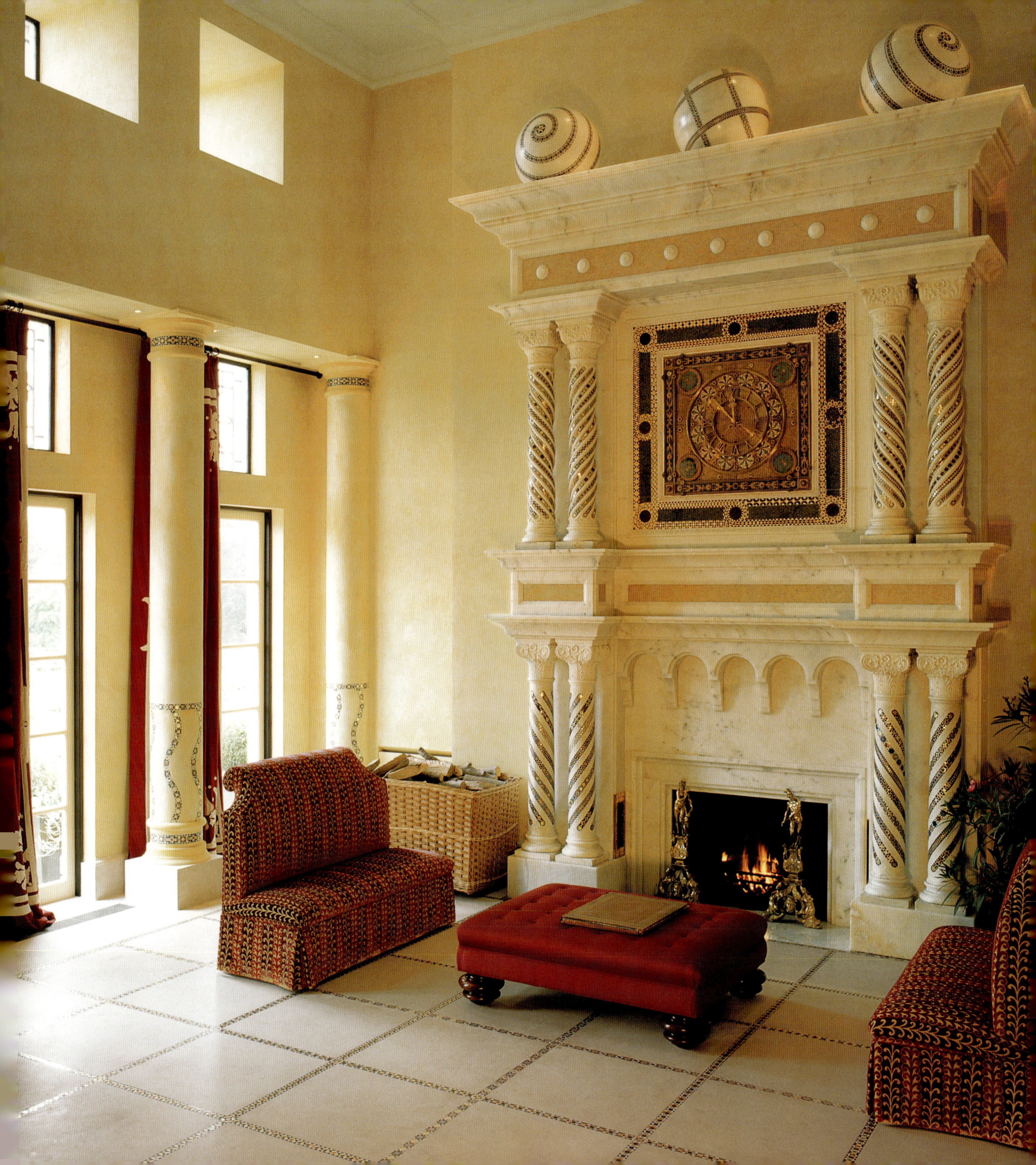

'Space has always been the spiritual dimension of architecture. It is not the physical statement of the structure so much as what it contains that moves us.'

ARTHUR CHARLES ERICKSON, ARCHITECT (1924–2009)

OPPOSITE An ornate 18th-century baldachin towers over a retro workspace in a backroom of the St Petersburg Academy.

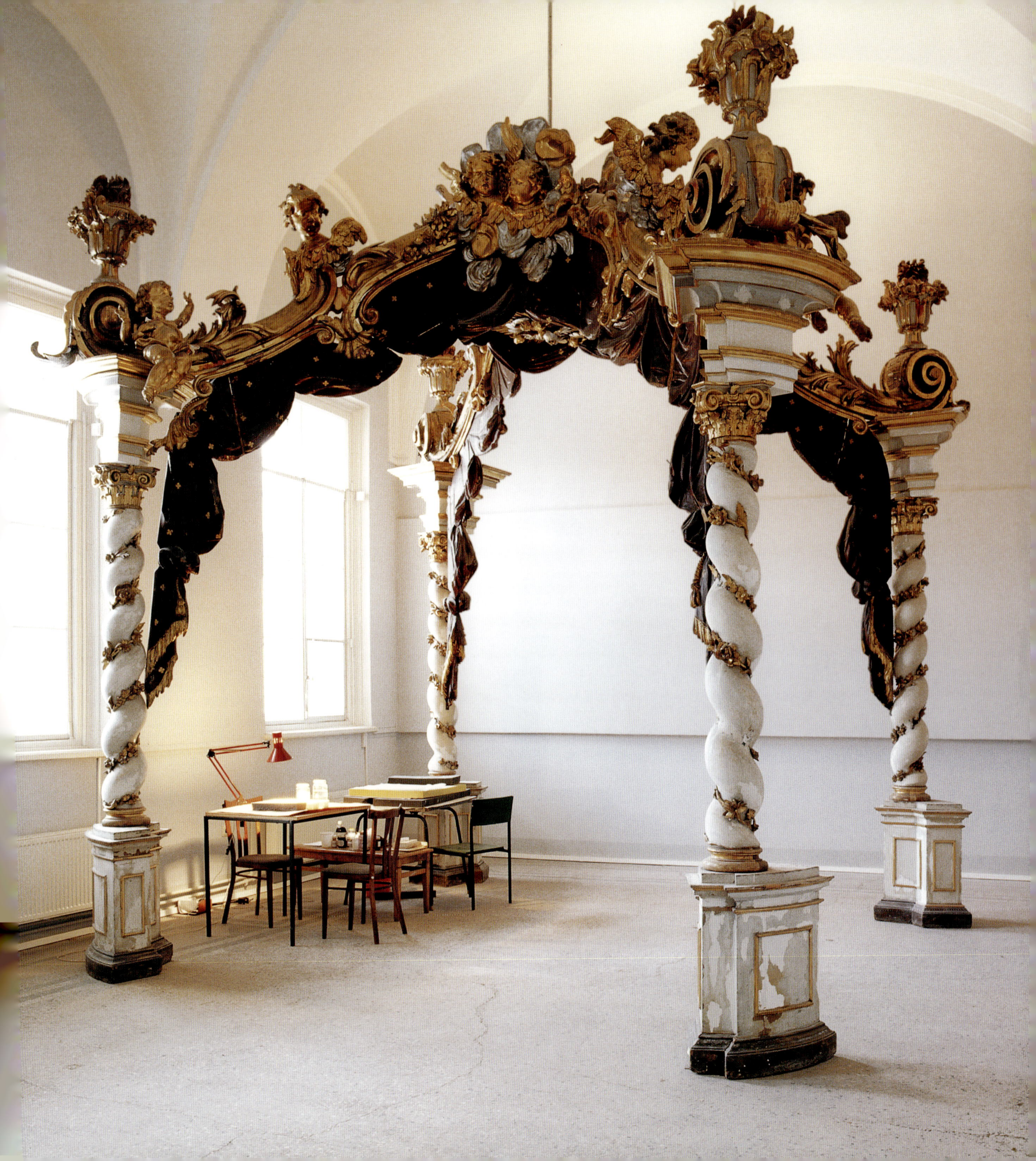

IN CONVERSATION WITH ANNABELLE SELLDORF

'Architecture must first and foremost serve its function. It is not about grand gestures, but rather finding a precise solution to a specific programme, context and client, resulting in space that balances the tension between form and function.

———

I am equally comfortable working in historic buildings and creating new structures. Each has its own set of constraints, but the goal is always the same: to create space where all of the elements, from broad concept to delicate detail, come together in a comprehensive whole.

———

An architect must be in tune with the integral rhythm of an existing building and understand how this can change from room to room. I pick up quickly on the resonance of a place and temper my architectural interpretation according to its specific geometry. It is about combining materials of the period, which give a building its sense of place and historical reference, with contemporary detailing, which brings the property up to date. Yet, at the same time, I like to introduce something mysterious to the mix, whether this is achieved by altering the light source or by using materials with an exaggerated texture, or just creating drama with an unexpected use of colour.

———

It is a related yet different discipline if I am asked to build a new structure. The references have to relate to the context; to the new location, its environment and the purpose of the building. For me to develop an understanding of what is required and to have the confidence to develop new ideas, it is especially important that the client is able to share my passion, my vision and my love of natural materials.

———

When I design a new building, there are two very distinct stages. The first is coming up with the concept; playing with space, volume, light and materials. The second is the discipline and rigour involved in ensuring that the idea actually materializes and carries through. The ultimate test for me is when the end result accurately interprets what my client needs, and the space I have created results in a comfortable environment in which they can live.

———

I grew up in Cologne and moved to the US in 1981 to study architecture, a career path that in many ways felt inevitable for me as my father is an architect and my mother was a designer. I was exposed to all of the elements of architecture at a young age, and in particular my parents instilled in me an appreciation for quality and craftsmanship. I now also have a furniture company called Vica. We design and fabricate sofas, chairs, tables, etc., along with lighting and hardware, still made in small workshops using traditional craft techniques. The company is named after an interior design company that my grandmother founded in the 1950s. You could say that I am continuing a family tradition, but also I think taking it to a new place and scale.

———

I prefer to have the opportunity to complete a building all the way through to the finished interiors. At a point when the structure and floor plan are established, one of my greatest pleasures is to introduce the materials, furniture and textiles I considered in the planning stage.

———

Materials should not just look good together, but should also inject a building with texture and pattern. While I tend to use white extensively, this is because

I prefer to introduce colour into an interior in the shape of furniture and the soft furnishings.

———

I do a lot of looking: at art, at buildings, at the way in which people live. Over the years I believe I have developed a discerning and critical eye. I am quite passionate about art and have had the good fortune to work on a number of architectural projects creating a variety of spaces in which art can be showcased – not just public galleries and museums, but also private homes for collectors and artists.

———

In this context it is important to create the best conditions for the placement of a painting or sculpture. The architecture must complement the artwork without challenging its impact on the viewer or its immediate environment.

———

I have a wonderful client with whom I have worked on several projects. This couple has a vivid imagination and a sense of boldness, which resulted in the creation of the Pika House, in the centre of a beautiful rural site alongside an old mining town in Colorado. This was a dream project, one in which I needed to work closely with the surrounding landscape of mountains and spruce forests.

———

We decided that the footprint of the new property should occupy exactly the same compact amount of space as a traditional log cabin, so as not to be overwhelming. My greatest challenge was then to create sufficient living space for the family. The idea of a wood-clad glass tower evolved. I like to think that the combination of untreated cedar with waxed steel not only gives the building a Neoclassical modernity, but also the necessary harmony with its immediate surroundings. In the summer it reflects the tranquillity of the tall trees that rise on all sides, and in the winter the snow reflecting off the glass façade causes it to sparkle. The house rises over five storeys, with floor-to-ceiling windows on each level that frame views of the surrounding mountains from different vantage points. It is both magical and functional, and I used Mies van der Rohe's Seagram Building as my inspiration.

———

In addition to the building's harmony with nature, the interior possesses a Zen-like quality. While there is a stillness created simply by the humbling views from every window, I also had to come up with a way of controlling the volume of light that floods every floor, a device that could also be functional and protective when the house was not being used. I devised a louvred metal shutter system, somewhat inspired by a trip to Paris, where I noticed that all the 19th-century buildings had protective shutters with slits cut into them. I had never done anything like them before, but we worked with a local fabricator and they came out extremely well. Not only do they function as they need to, they also add a quality of depth to the house which is compelling.

———

I am often referred to as a Modernist, yet I believe that the precision and restraint visible in my work could also be considered Neoclassical. In addition to Mies van der Rohe, Schinkel has had influence on my work. Ultimately, I see myself as a sensualist. I like to work with imagination, traditional craftsmanship, modern tectonics, tactile materials, and above all authenticity. Architecture is not just a statement: it must respond to and enhance its immediate environment as much as it improves the lives of the people who use it.'

ABOVE The master bedroom on the fourth floor of a five-storey wood and glass tower designed by architect Annabelle Selldorf in Colorado. The floor-to-ceiling windows, with views in three directions, are sealed with aluminium shutters, giving texture as well as protection. The headboard of the Vica bed incorporates a desk, a night table and compact storage.

ABOVE Designer William Sofield combines contrasting materials to maximum effect in this New York living room. The walls are of velvet with a bronze trim, the sofa is mahogany and leather, and the chandelier is gilt metal.

RIGHT The panelling in the drawing room at Swangrove on the Badminton estate in Gloucestershire is painted two shades of grey as a foil for the collection of sepia mezzotints, which are from Claude Lorrain's *Liber Veritatis*. The interior of this former hunting lodge, built in 1703 by the Bath architect William Killigrew, was transformed by Robert Kime in his characteristic comfortable and eclectic style.

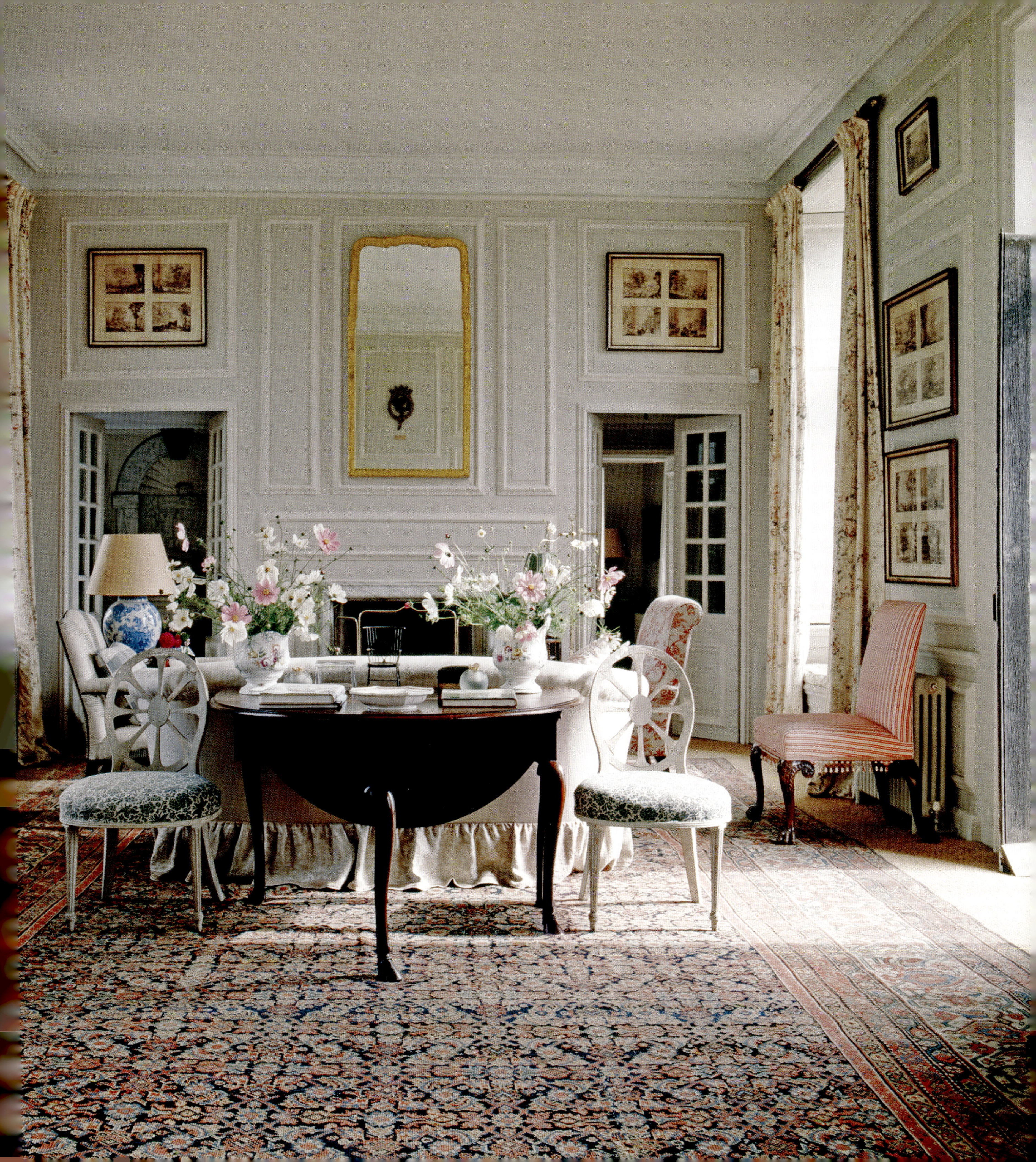

ABOVE Designer Mimmi O'Connell's all-white decoration of this farmhouse bedroom on the island of Majorca enhances the size of the room and its sense of space.

OPPOSITE Designed by Anouska Hempel, the towering four-poster bed at Blake's Hotel in London influences the visual perception of the size of this bedroom.

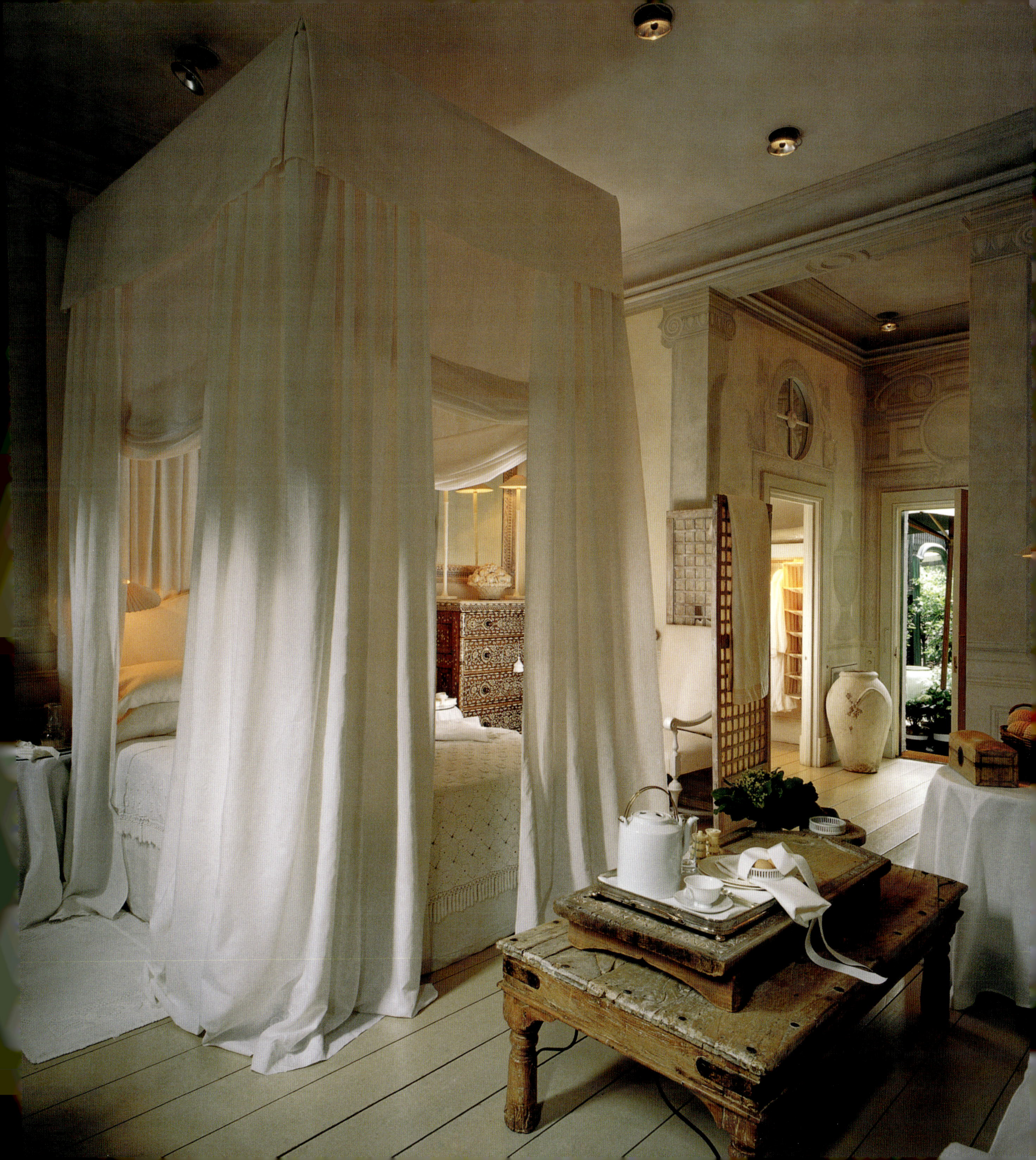

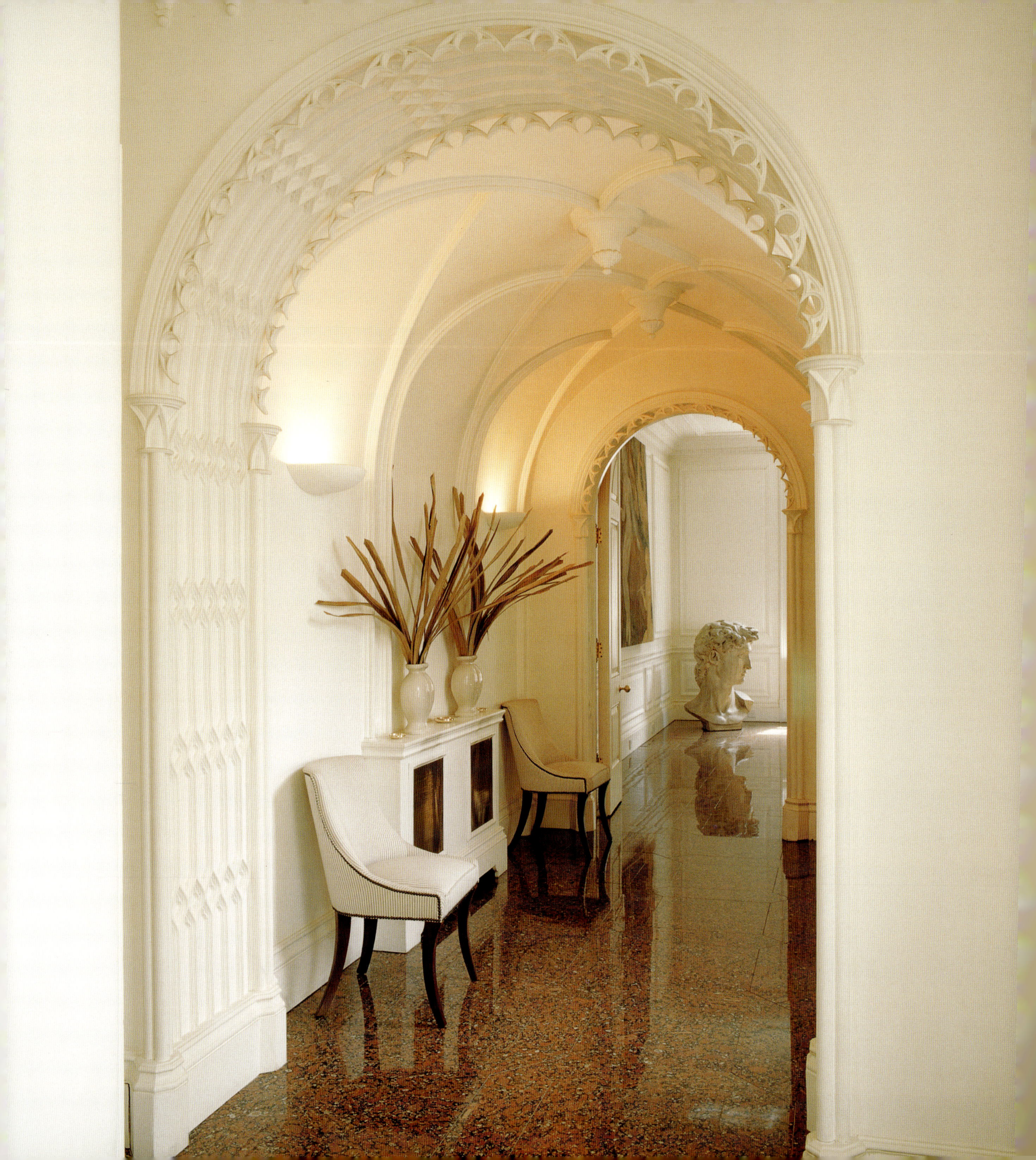

OPPOSITE A Neo-Gothic vaulted ceiling is reflected in the highly polished marble floor of an Italianate villa in central London.

ABOVE Through an archway in the impluvium in Karl Friedrich Schinkel's Roman baths in the Sanssouci Park outside Potsdam, blue-painted niches house Neoclassical sculptures.

RIGHT The octagonal State Dining Room at Sturehof is decorated with carvings and hand-painted murals. Originally the room would have been sparsely furnished, as was the custom in Sweden up to the beginning of the 19th century.

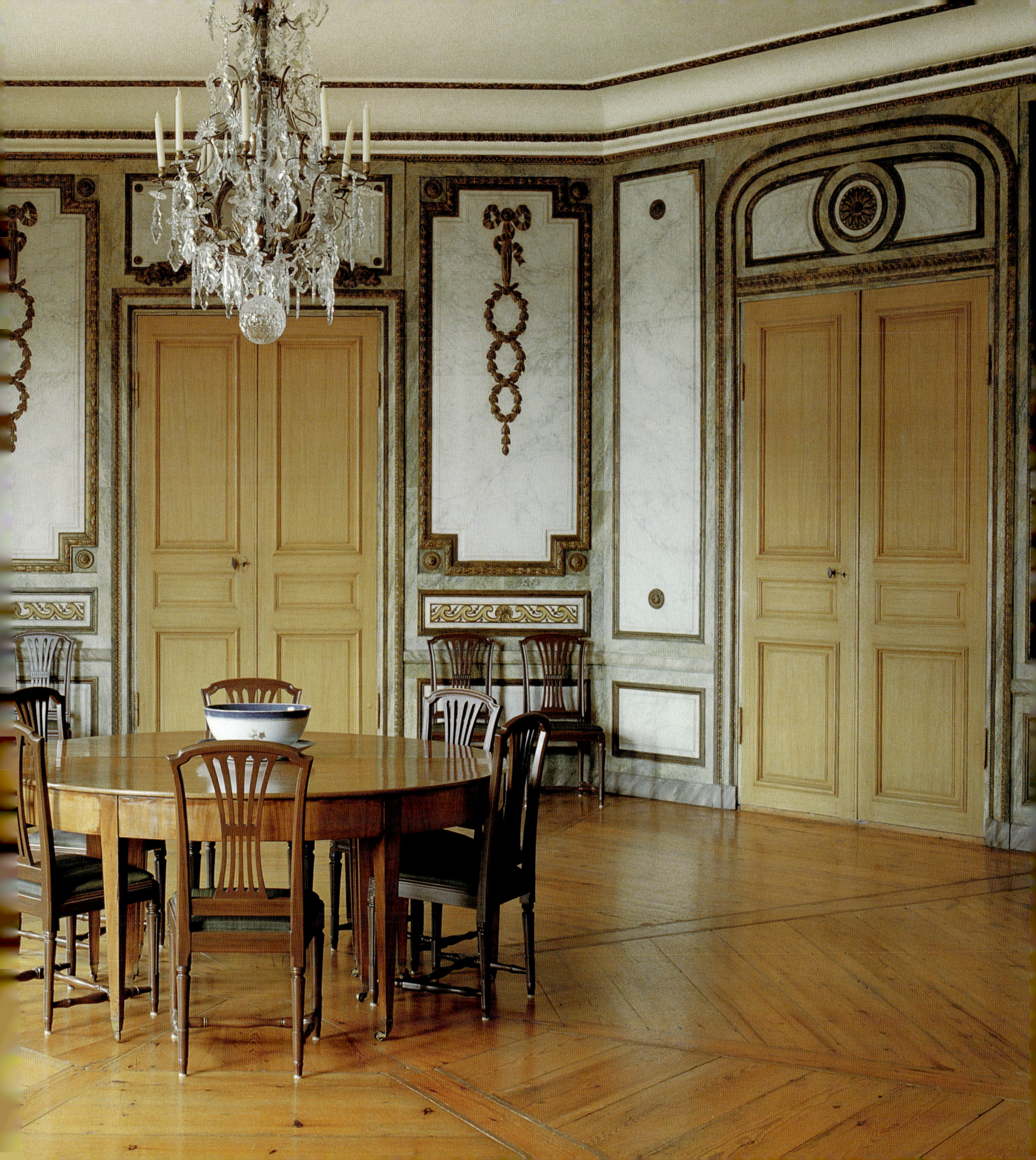

The so-called Escher Room in Kanaal (ABOVE), prepared for one of the art-event dinner parties regularly hosted by antiquarian Axel Vervoordt and his son Boris. In couturier Jasper Conran's London apartment (OPPOSITE), a Minimalist kitchen with a thick stainless-steel work surface contrasts with original plaster mouldings and a crystal chandelier.

OVERLEAF The black and white marble-floored Wootton Hall at Althorp is named after the 18th-century equestrian painter John Wootton, whose oil paintings encircle the room.

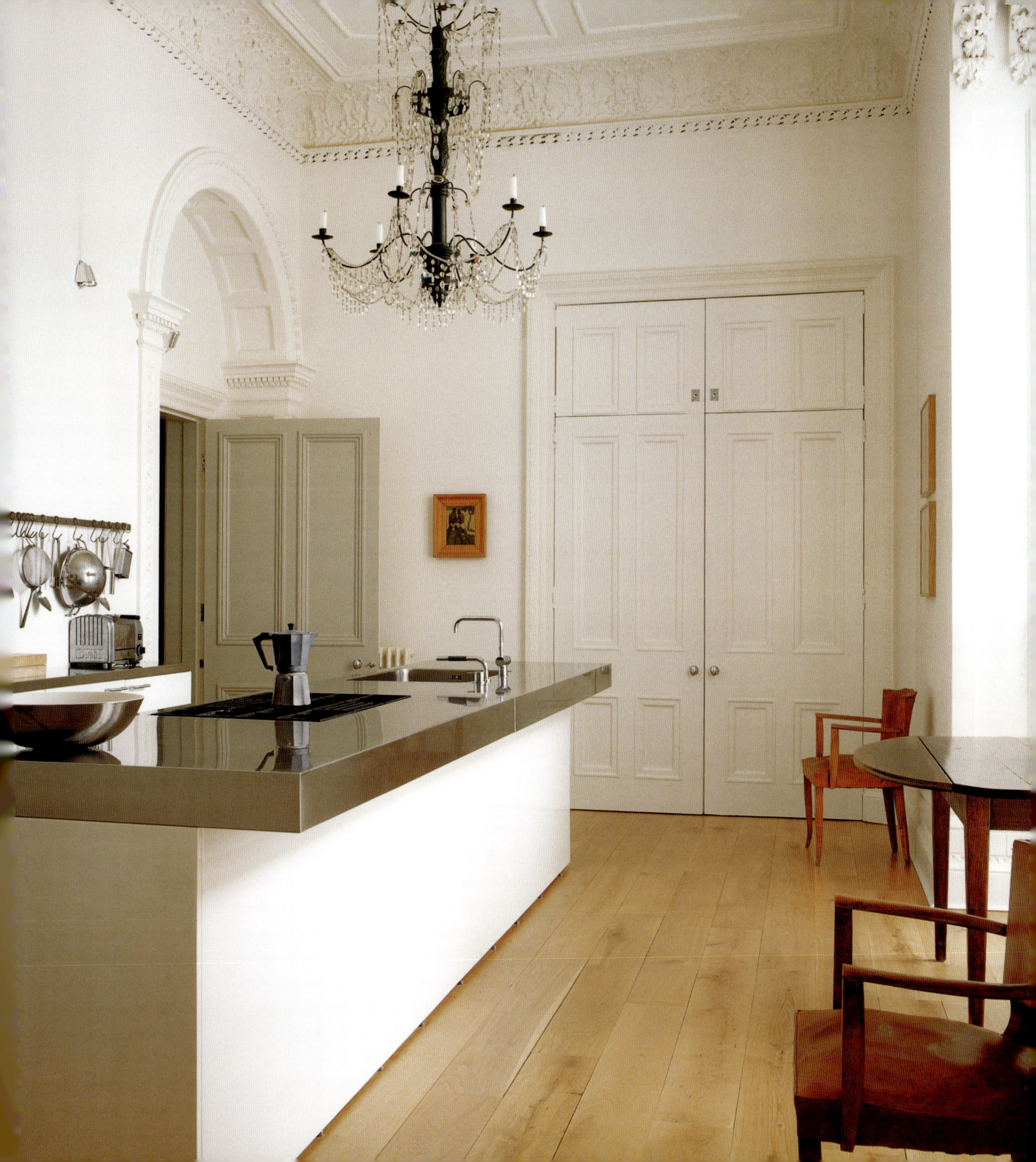

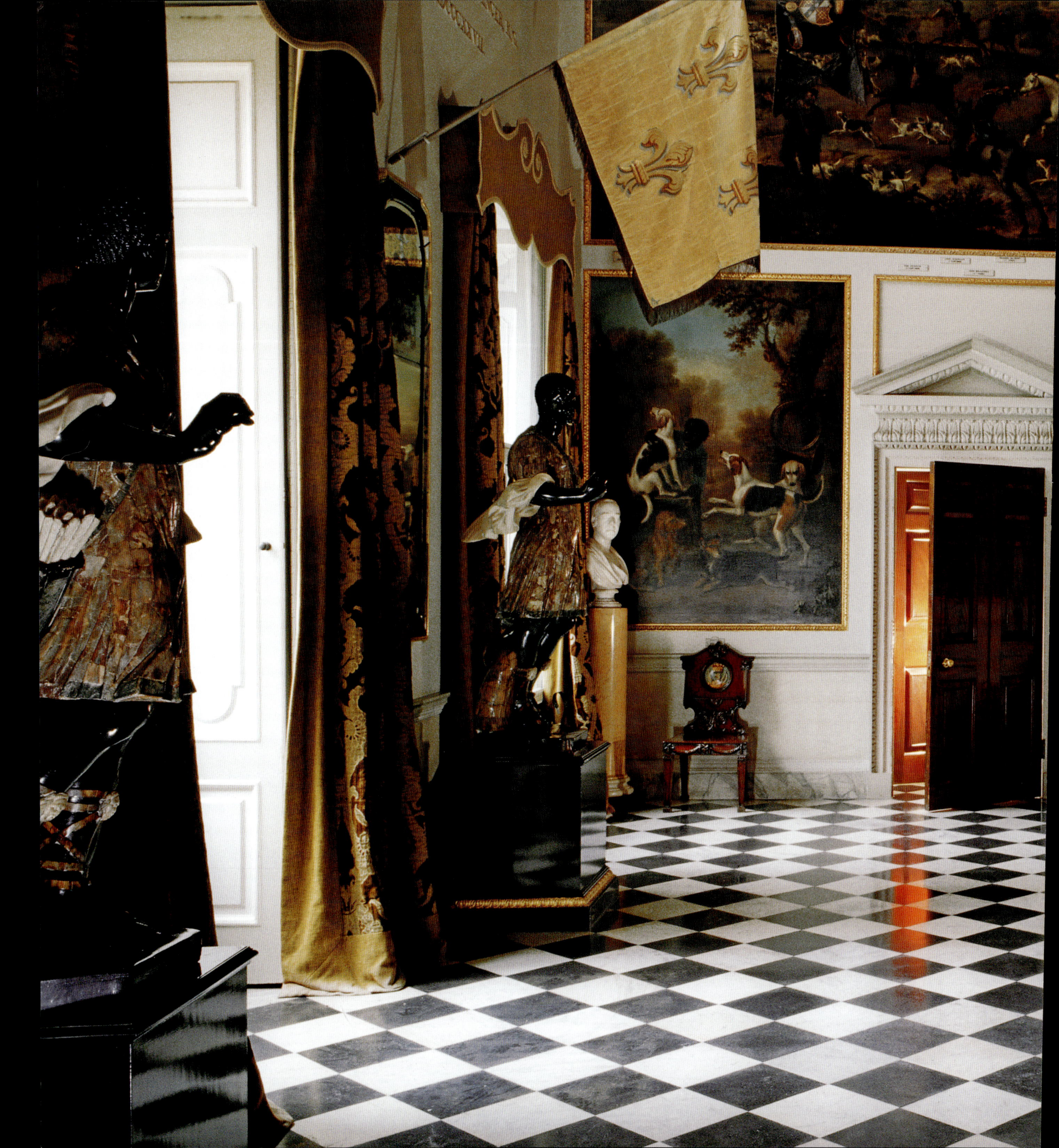

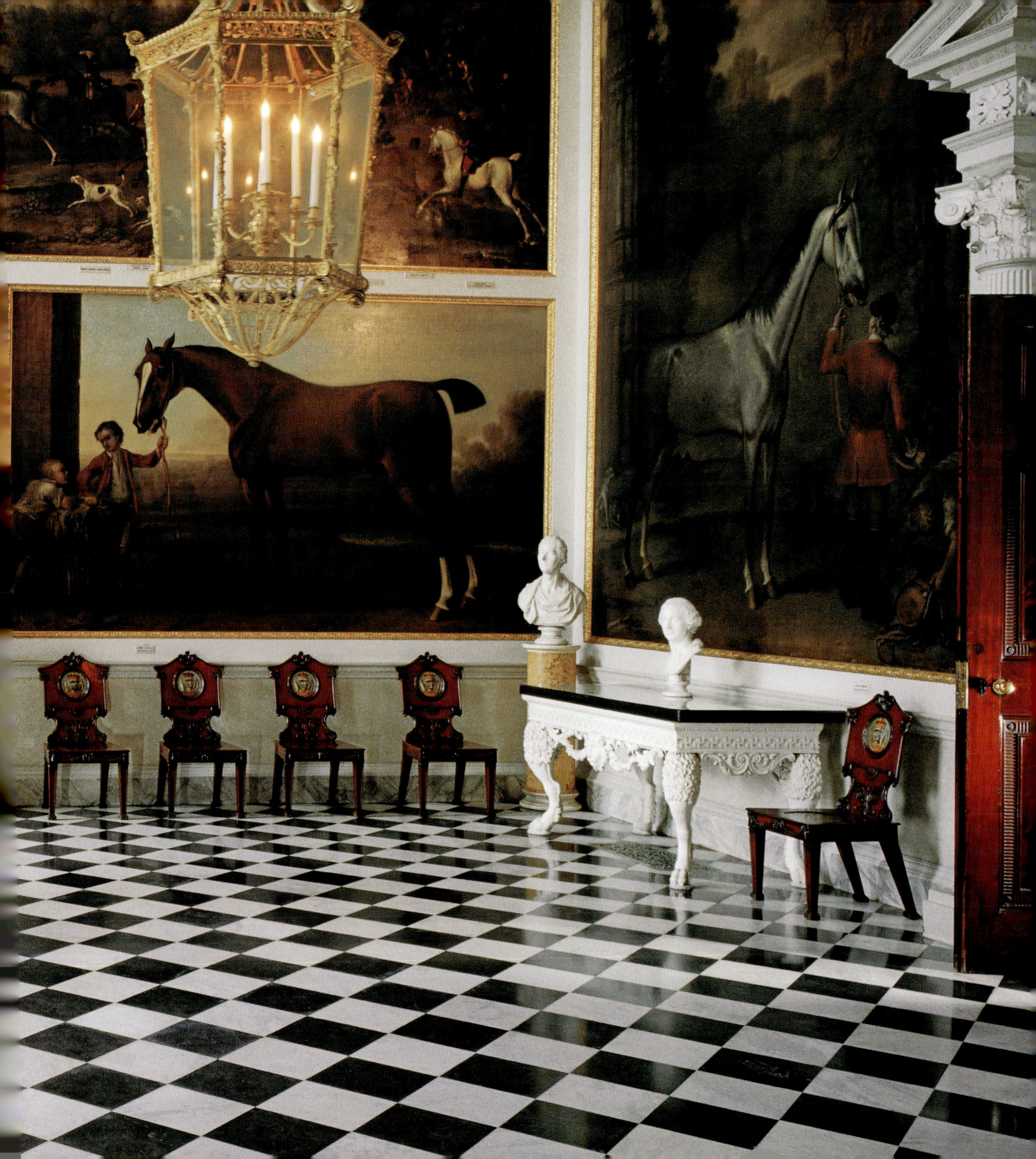

This swimming pool, created in the basement of a London mews house, was designed to resemble a Roman bath (ABOVE). Chiswick House, a Palladian-style villa commissioned by Lord Burlington in the early 18th century (OPPOSITE), boasts an interior of sparse Neoclassical splendour.

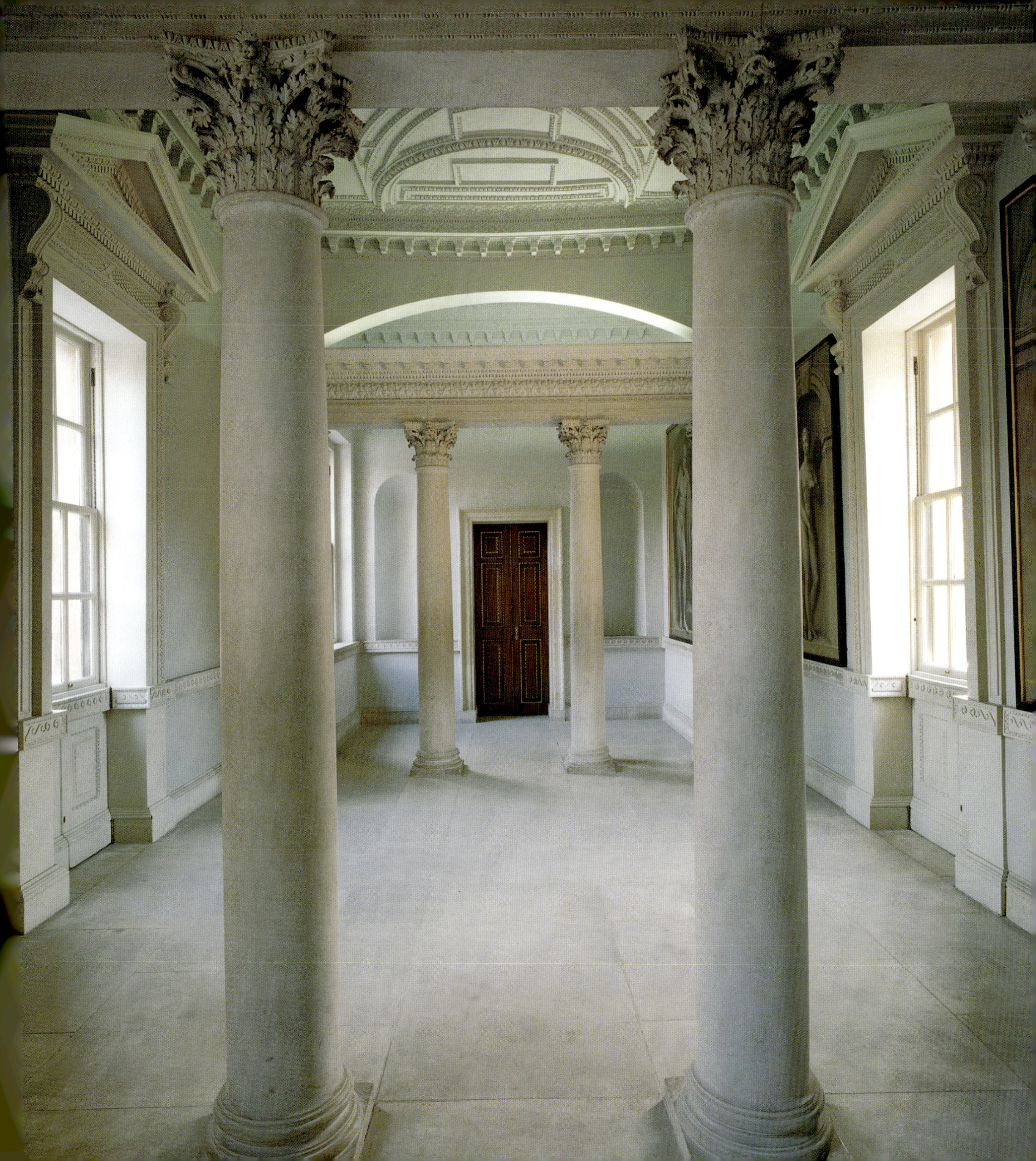

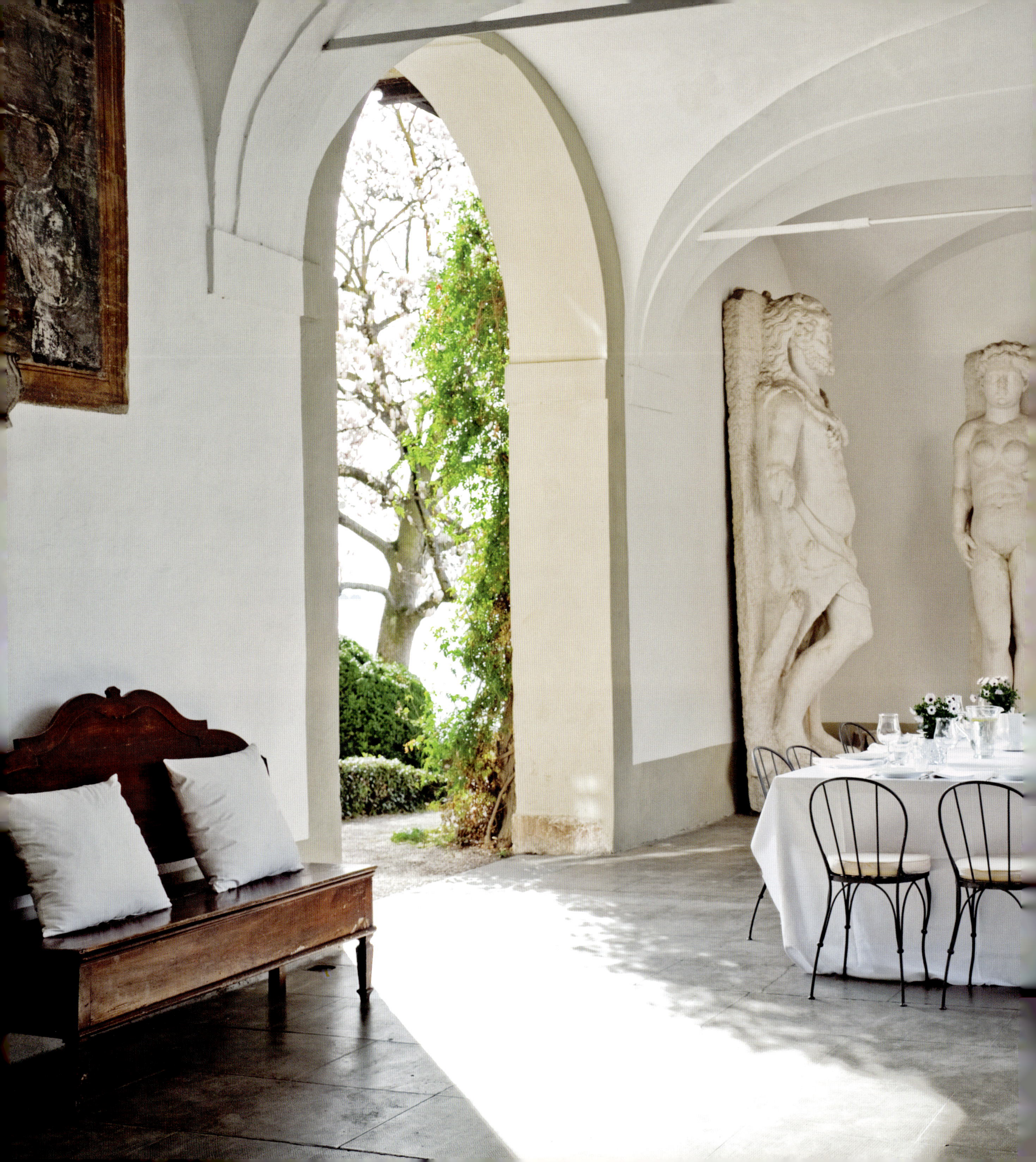

LEFT Guarded by a trio of monumental Classical figures, a table is laid for a formal lunch in the loggia of the Palazzo Terzi Martinengo overlooking Lake Garda.

SPACE

TEXTURE

Everything that has a surface has texture, which means that, as a description, texture can be applied to both rough and smooth surfaces. Texture, in the context of architecture and interior design, plays an important role in the decoration of a property, as the materials chosen for flooring, walls and furniture are integral to the design.

Considered to be one of the more subtle elements in design, texture introduces a suggestion of rhythm, often through repetition of a motif or a shape, which in turn creates pattern. Pattern comprises repetition and the more repeats there are, the stronger the pattern becomes. The simpler the pattern, the bolder and more striking is the overall effect. As William Morris said: 'No pattern should be without some sort of meaning.'

In historic interiors, textural variety was often present on walls and ceilings in plasterwork and mouldings, in the shape of swags, medallions, flowers and shields, cornices and ceiling roses. Parquet flooring introduced wonderful geometric patterns, a mosaic of different woods and veneers, which often incorporated contrasting colour and grain. Floor pattern was also constructed using marble, flagstones and tiles, while carpets and rugs introduced a three-dimensional surface. Walls were enhanced with elaborate wallpapers and fabrics, such as flock, damask and moiré, which relied on light to reveal their subtle texture, while an illusion of texture was created through paint effects such as trompe-l'oeil and faux marble.

Contemporary designers continue to use texture to create contrast and to stimulate the senses. Nicholas Haslam is fond of materials that have depth, with which he can create a sense of drama. He uses veined or even black marble, which he overlays with verre églomisé, and, in a contemporary twist on the period marble-flagged entrance hall, he has designed a floor of bold, fat stripes of contrasting lengths of black and white marble. William Sofield recreates plaster reliefs as focal points for chimneybreasts and, like Jean-Michel Frank, incorporates

OPPOSITE Most of the beautiful walls at Kanaal, where antiquarian Axel Vervoordt displays much of his furniture, were left in their original condition, like a contemporary fresco – old, damaged, and in places simply repaired. The building dates from 1860 and patches of colour have been added over the ensuing 150 years.

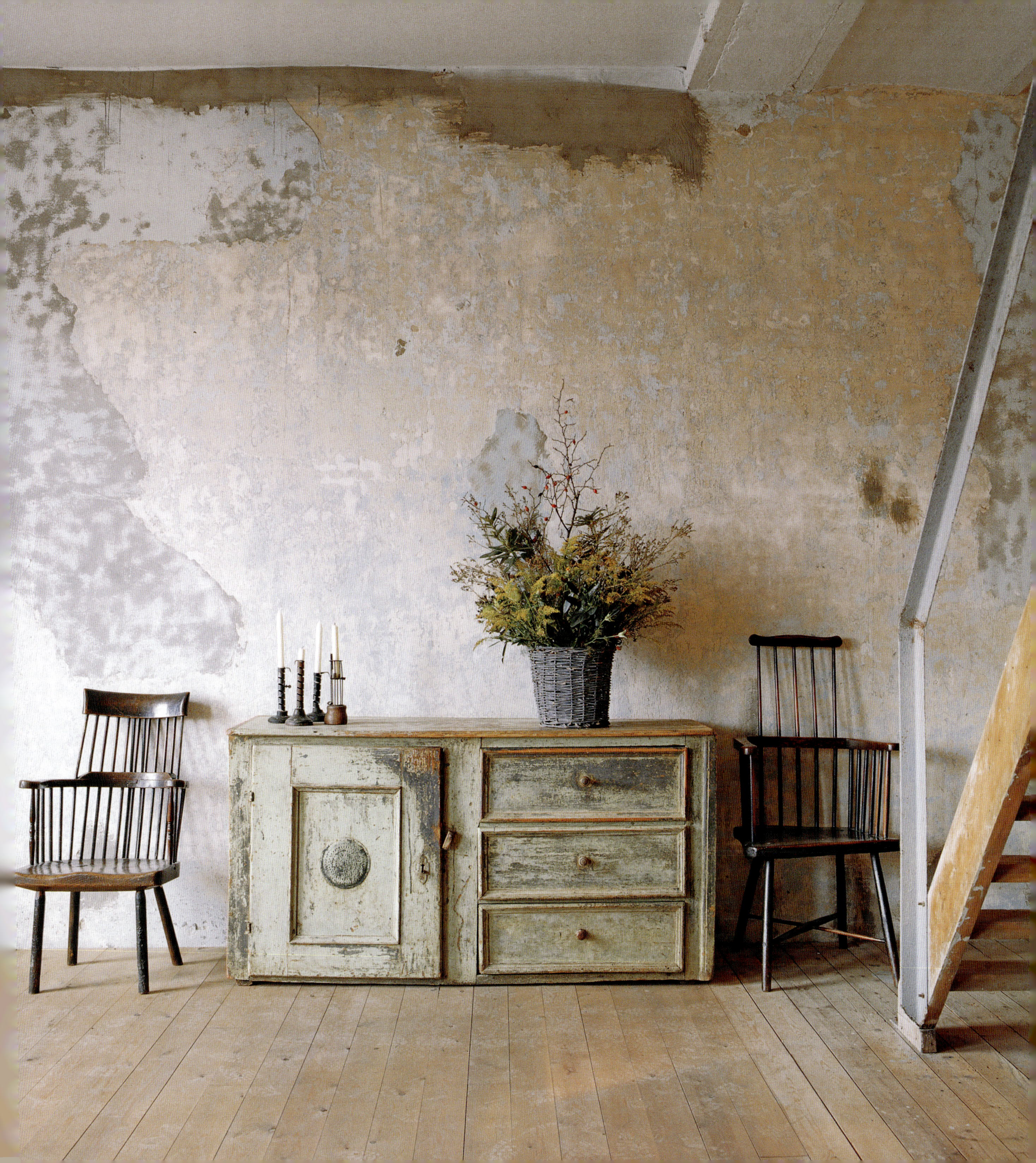

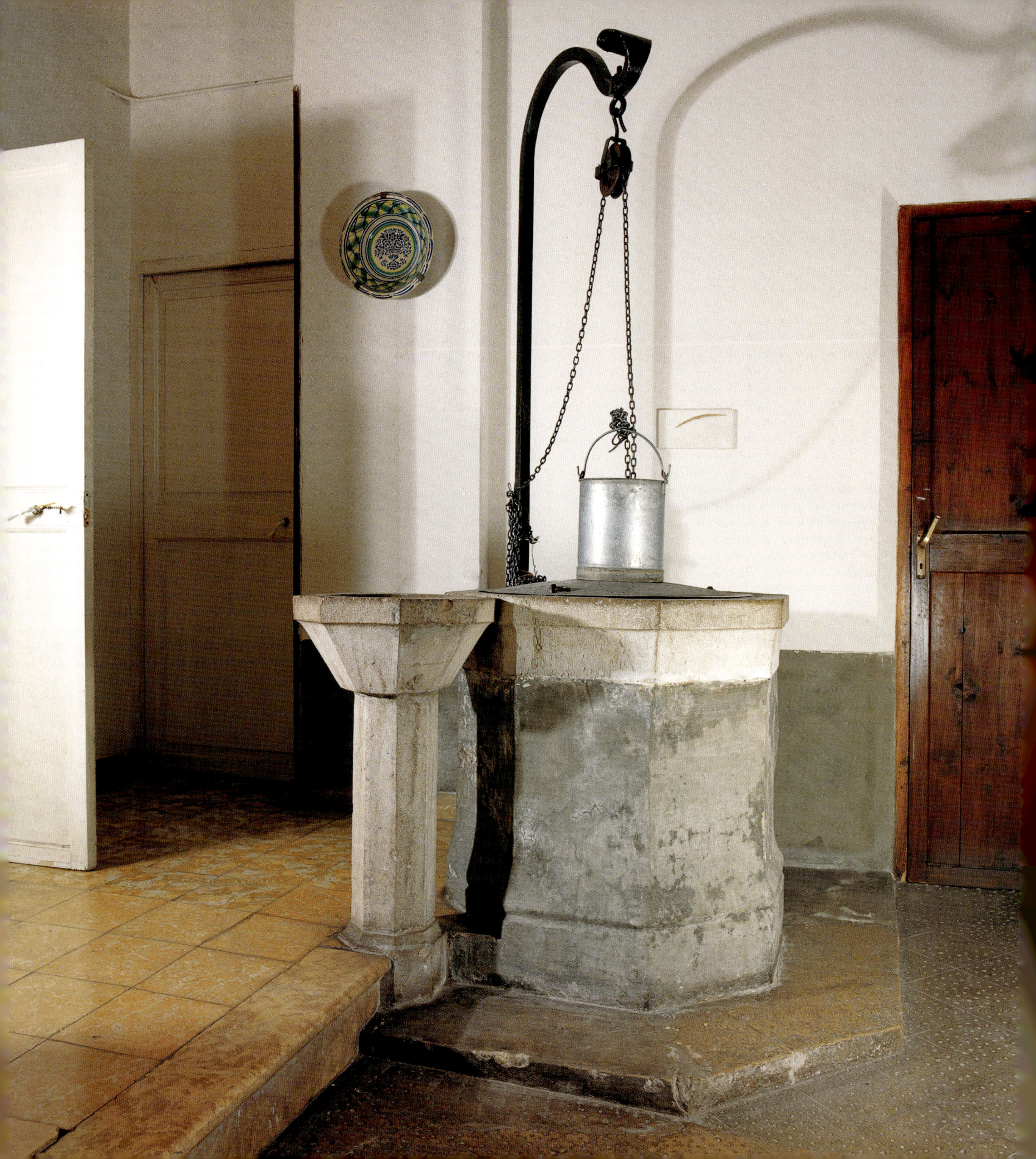

materials including parchment, vellum and bronze into his furniture designs.

Textiles introduce colour, pattern and texture and, in addition, an attunement to the sense of touch. According to Robert Kime, antique textiles that are a little worn and threadbare, unrestored and perhaps even bearing the occasional hole, introduce an important textural balance to a Minimal interior, similar to a distressed paint treatment on a wall or a piece of furniture. By the same token, Kime believes that soft furnishings do not need to be made from perfect lengths of fabric. Curtains can be more interesting if put together from 'bits and strips' and bring a visual texture to a room.

In designing an interior, fabric is first considered for its texture, while its colour, if not a natural hue, is almost an afterthought prompted by the scheme of a design. Designer John Minshaw is fond of layering his fabrics and combining their textures to create added theatre. He puts together sumptuous velvets with plain linens, exaggerating their contrasts.

In the words of William Morris, 'If there is a reason for keeping the wall very quiet, choose a pattern that works all over without pronounced lines. Put very succinctly, architectural effect depends upon a nice balance of horizontal, vertical and oblique. No rules can say how much of each; so nothing can really take the place of feeling and good judgement.'

OPPOSITE This original stone well, in the pantry of the Castillo de Bendinat on the island of Majorca, has an appealingly rough texture.

ABOVE The polished surface of a porphyry urn (LEFT) contrasts with the patina of an old Chinese bottle (RIGHT).

TEXTURE 211

ABOVE Artist Joni Waite's former home in Lamu Town has textured adobe walls, which have been whitewashed.

OPPOSITE In this Swedish burgher's house dating from the second half of the 18th century, paint has been spattered directly onto the wooden wall panelling that lines the simple staircase.

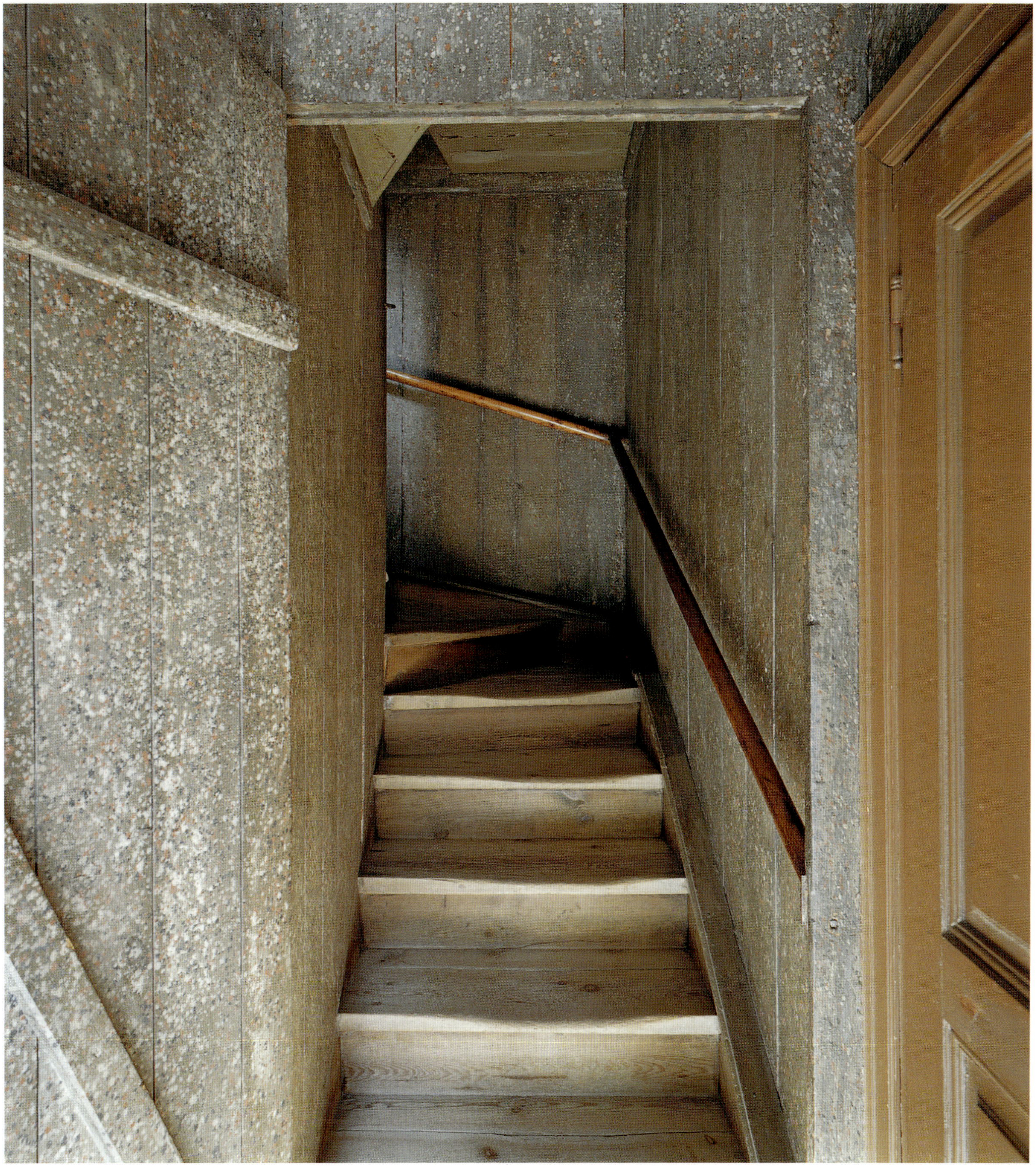

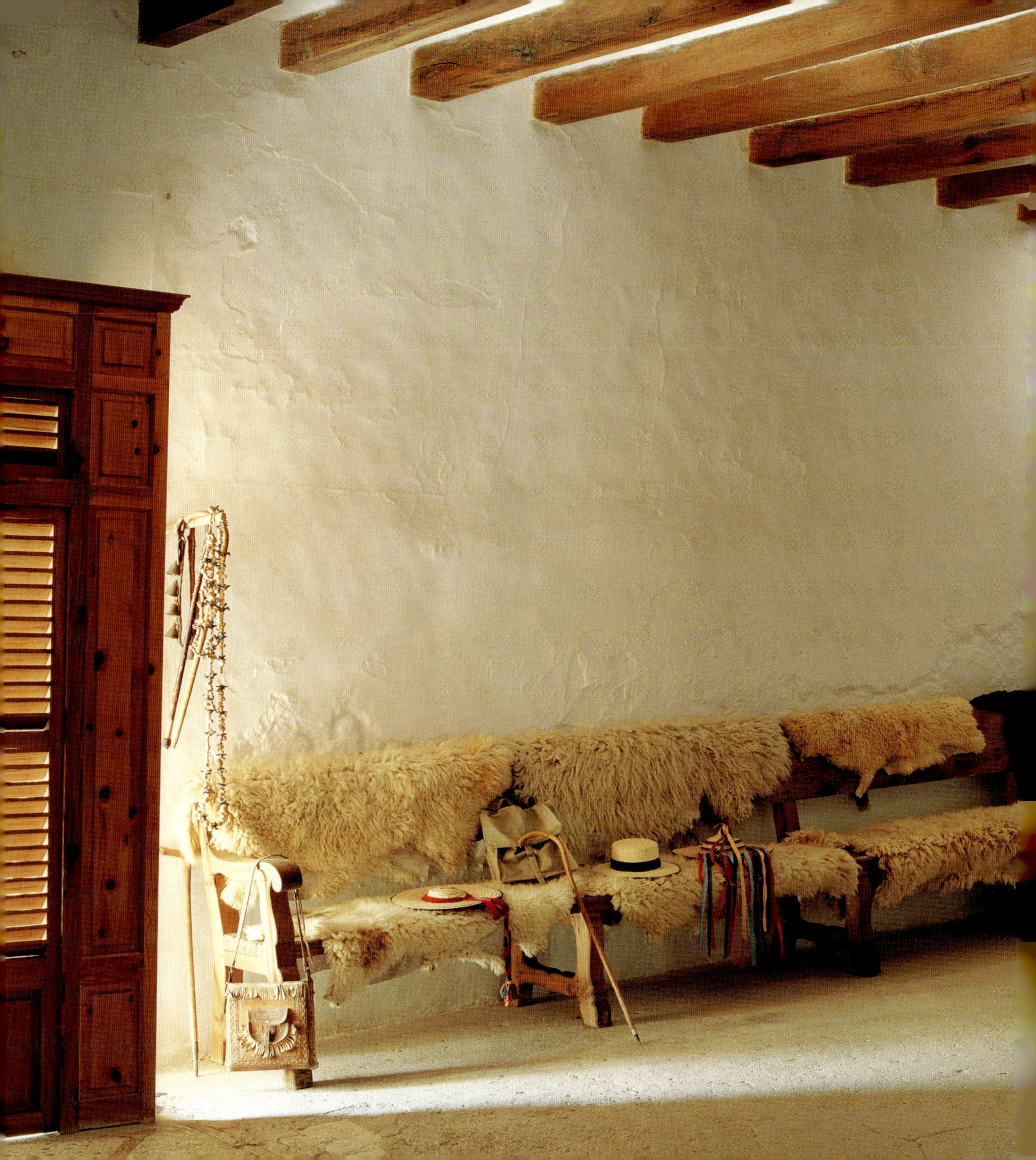

LEFT An ancient wood and leather bench draped in old sheepskins lines the whitewashed wall of this large hall in a Majorcean finca, a room in which the weary farm labourers would originally have slept.

TEXTURE

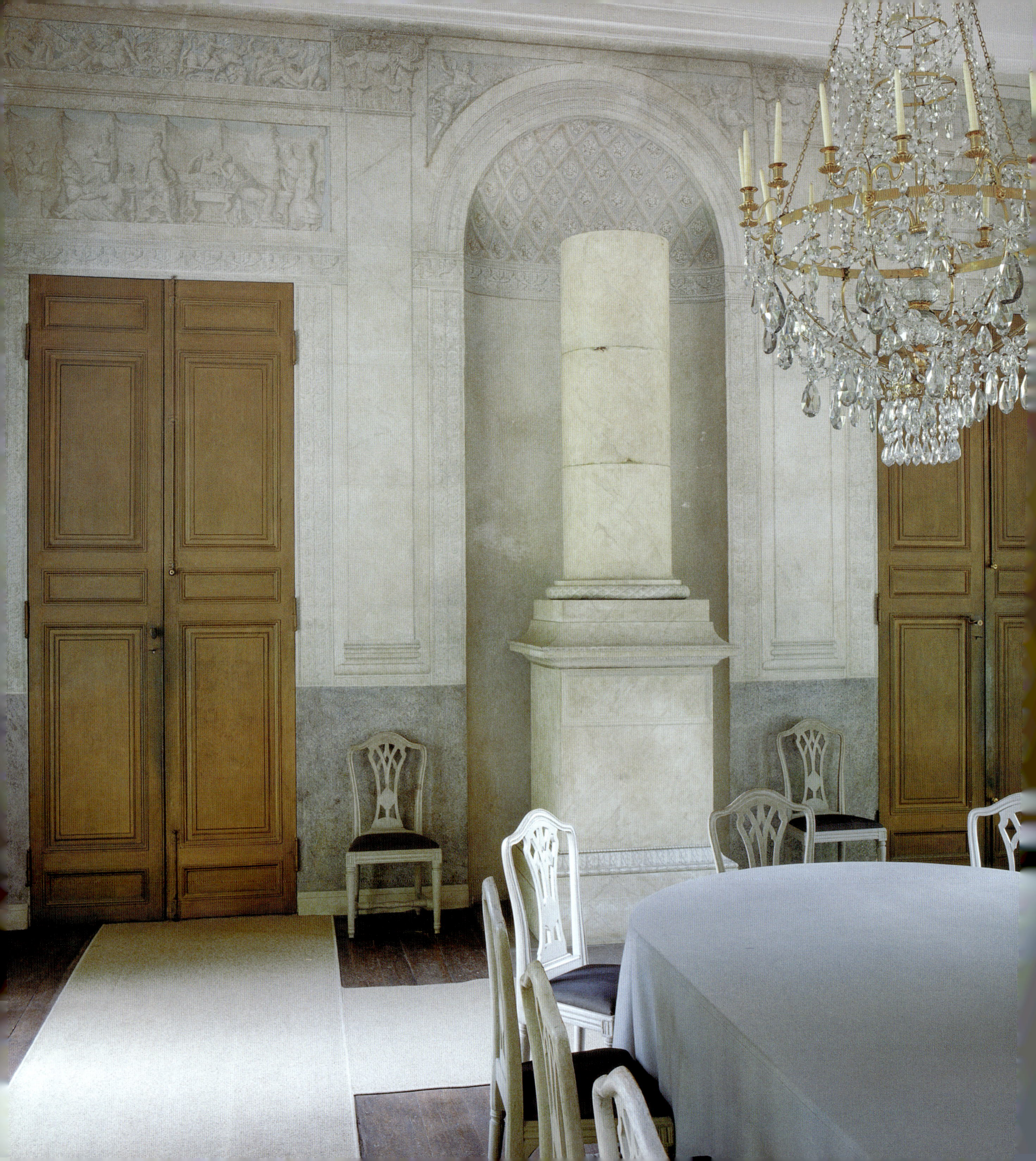

OPPOSITE The dining room at Haga, Gustaf III of Sweden's Trianon, was designed by the painter Louis Masreliez to resemble a Roman interior. The columnar stove is clad in copper and painted to look like marble, while the wall frescoes show scenes from Greek mythology and the doors are trompe-l'oeil bronze.

ABOVE Catherine Painvin has furnished this dining room in a 19th-century former pilgrim's hospice in France with a triangular wooden panel from a Mongolian barn and a distressed wooden bench and table.

ABOVE AND OPPOSITE Four styles of chair have been decorated with different textures. The seat of an 18th-century carved and painted chair has been upholstered in a contemporary patterned fabric; a cane-backed, white-painted chair enhances trompe-l'oeil painted panelling; a Gustavian giltwood chair has been upholstered in a light floral silk; and a simple hand-painted wooden chair contrasts with the marble-clad walls of a bathroom at Manderston in Scotland.

TEXTURE 219

RIGHT The texture of the red-brick floor of the Gallery at designer John Stefanidis's former country home is reinforced by the walls of bookshelves, which divide the space into distinct areas.

OVERLEAF This living room in Axel Vervoordt's castle home in Antwerp is furnished with Italian Neoclassical panelling and a French 18th-century table.

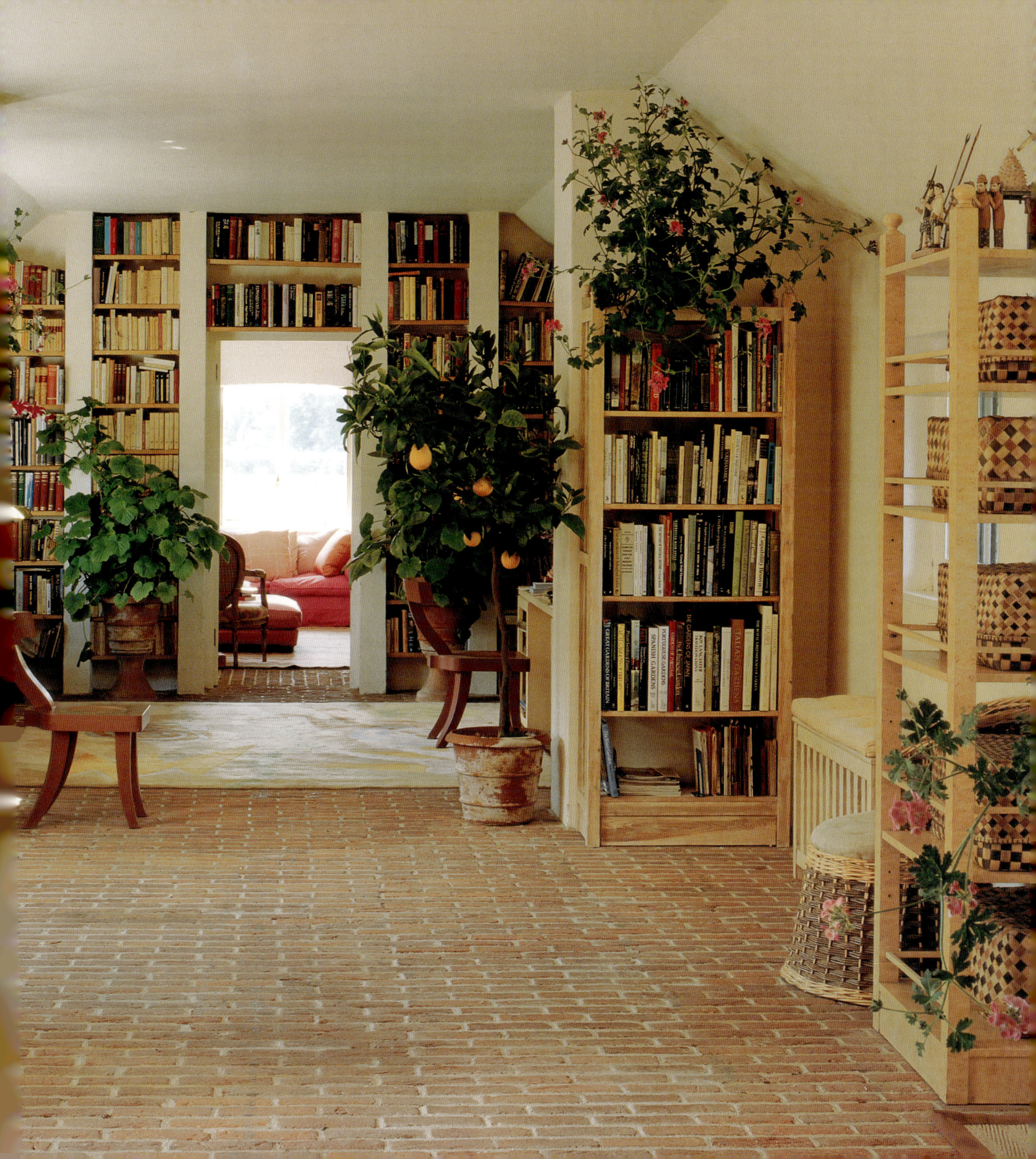

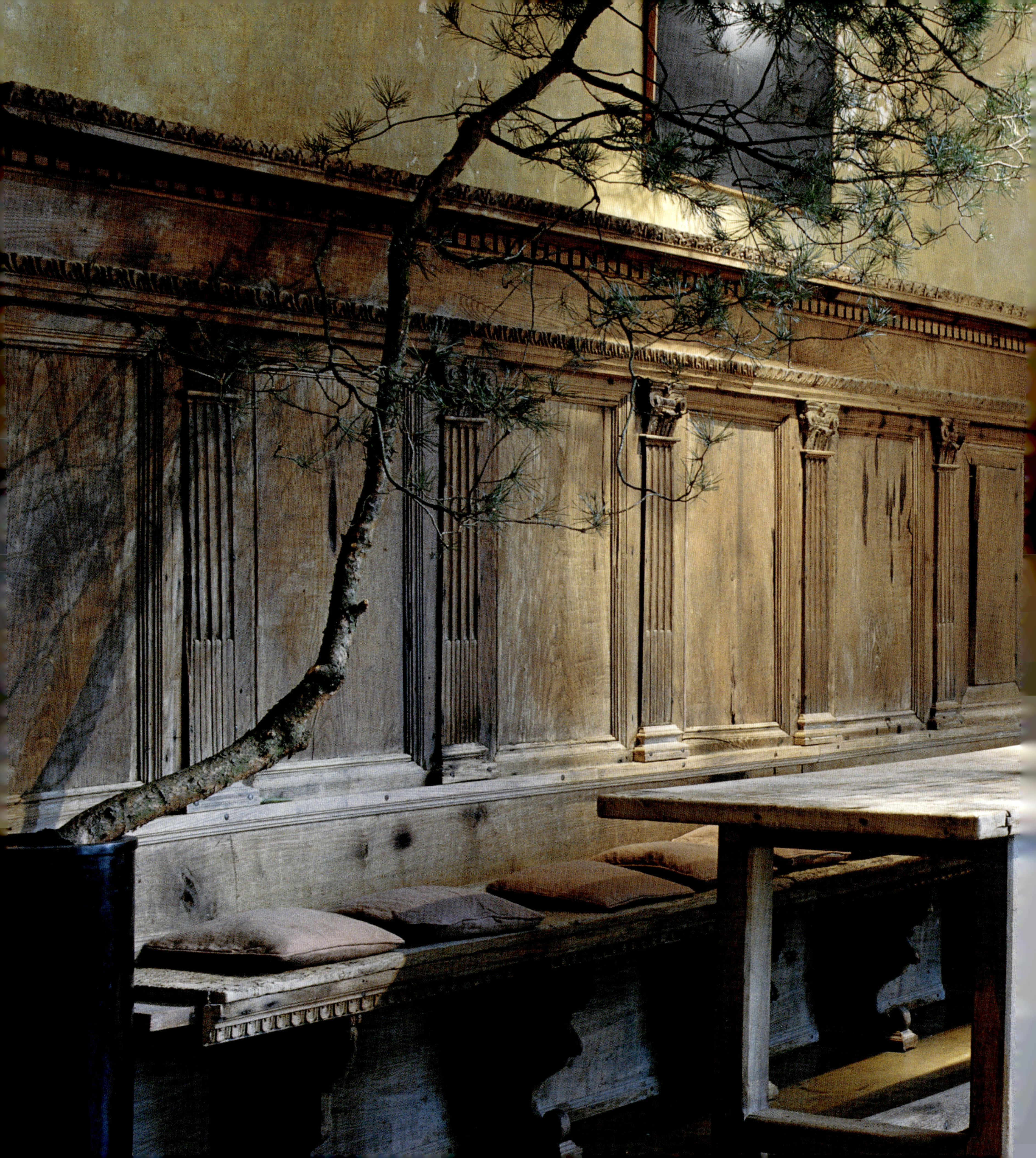

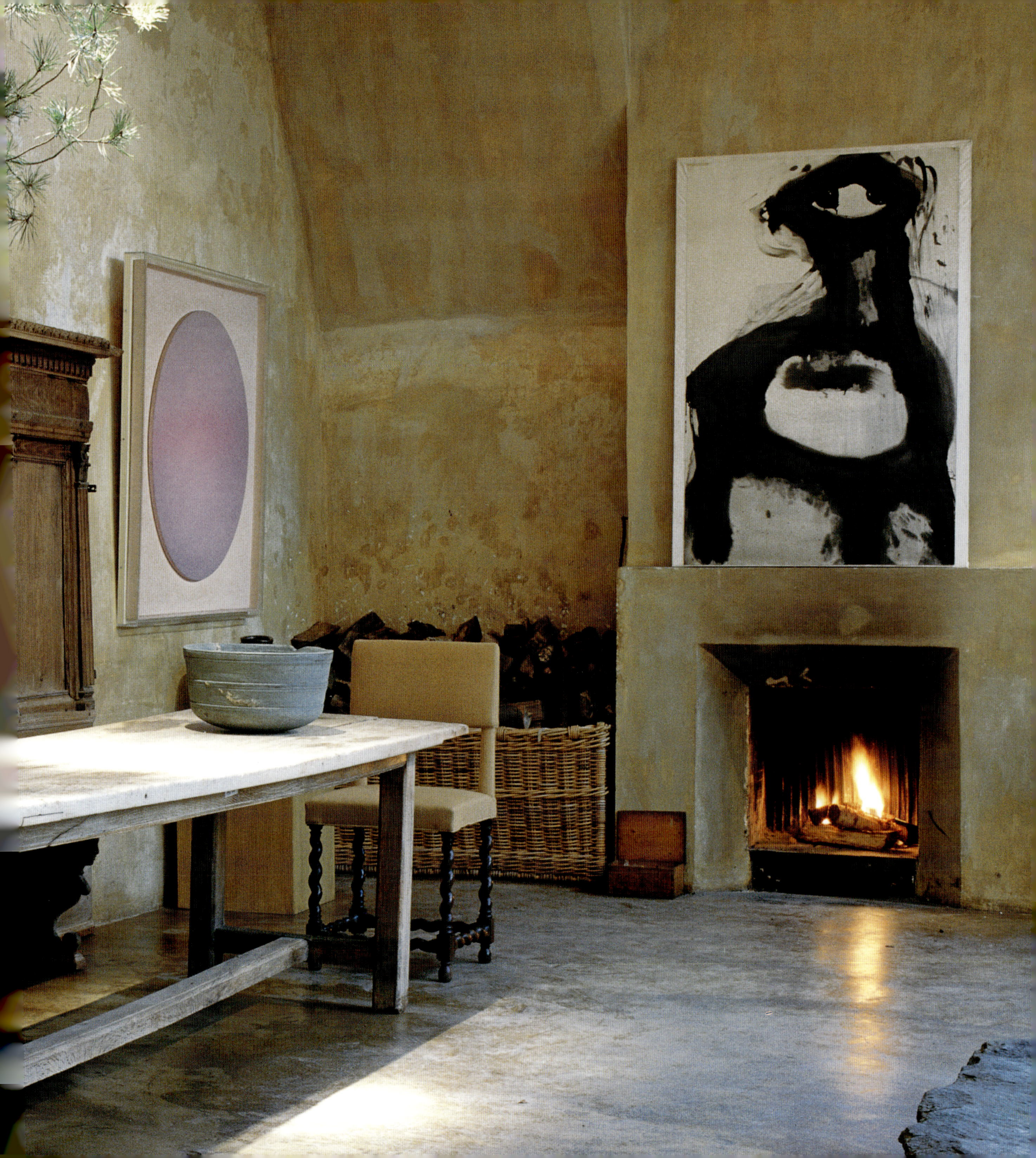

ABOVE The texture of different woods, from the simple oak staircase to the deep mahogany of the pair of 18th-century English hall chairs, contrasts strongly in this eclectic composition by Axel Vervoordt.

OPPOSITE A rustic staircase made of roughly hewn logs provides a contrasting texture to the pale Swedish-style panelling in the living room of this country house in Vermont designed by Jed Johnson.

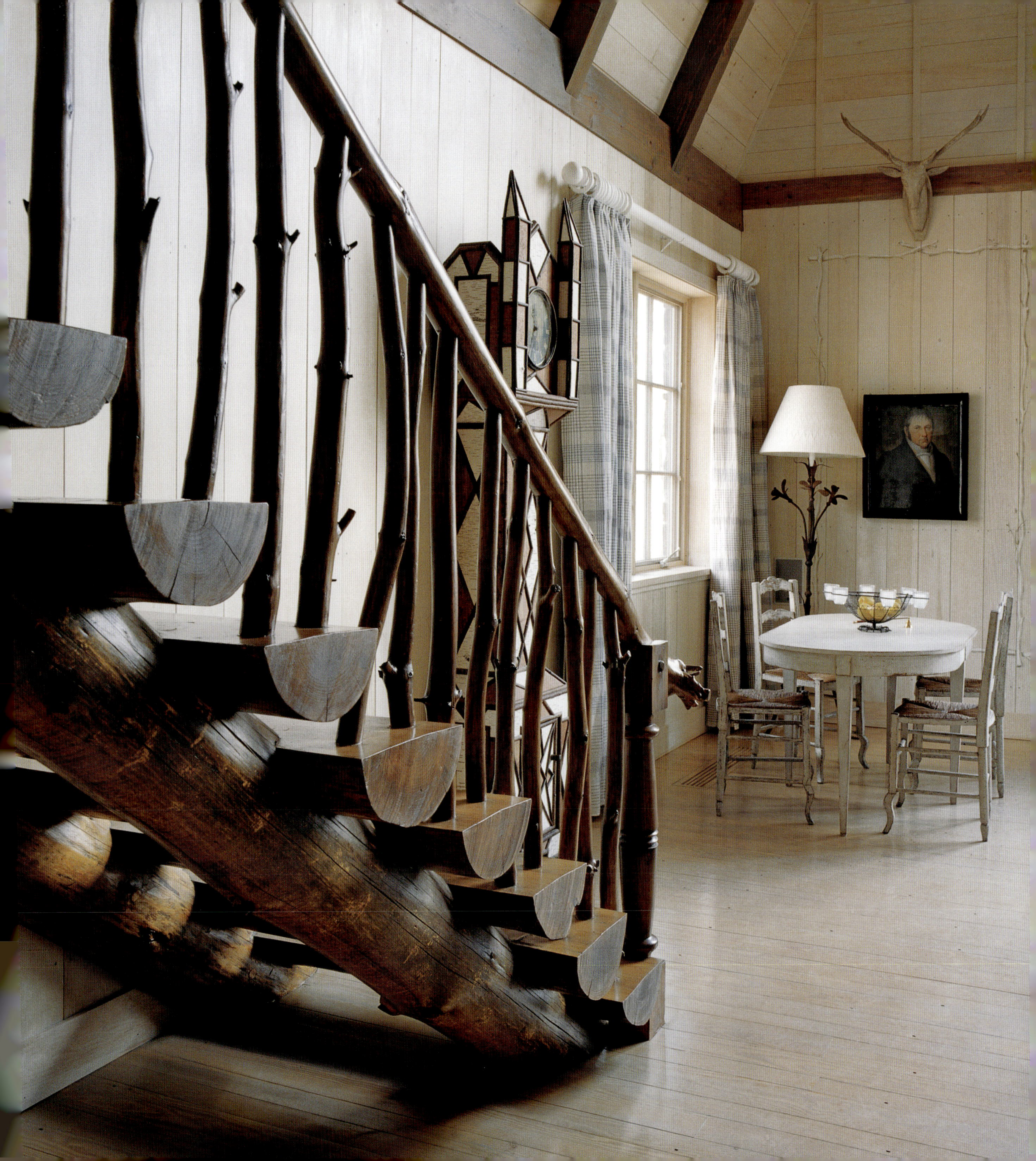

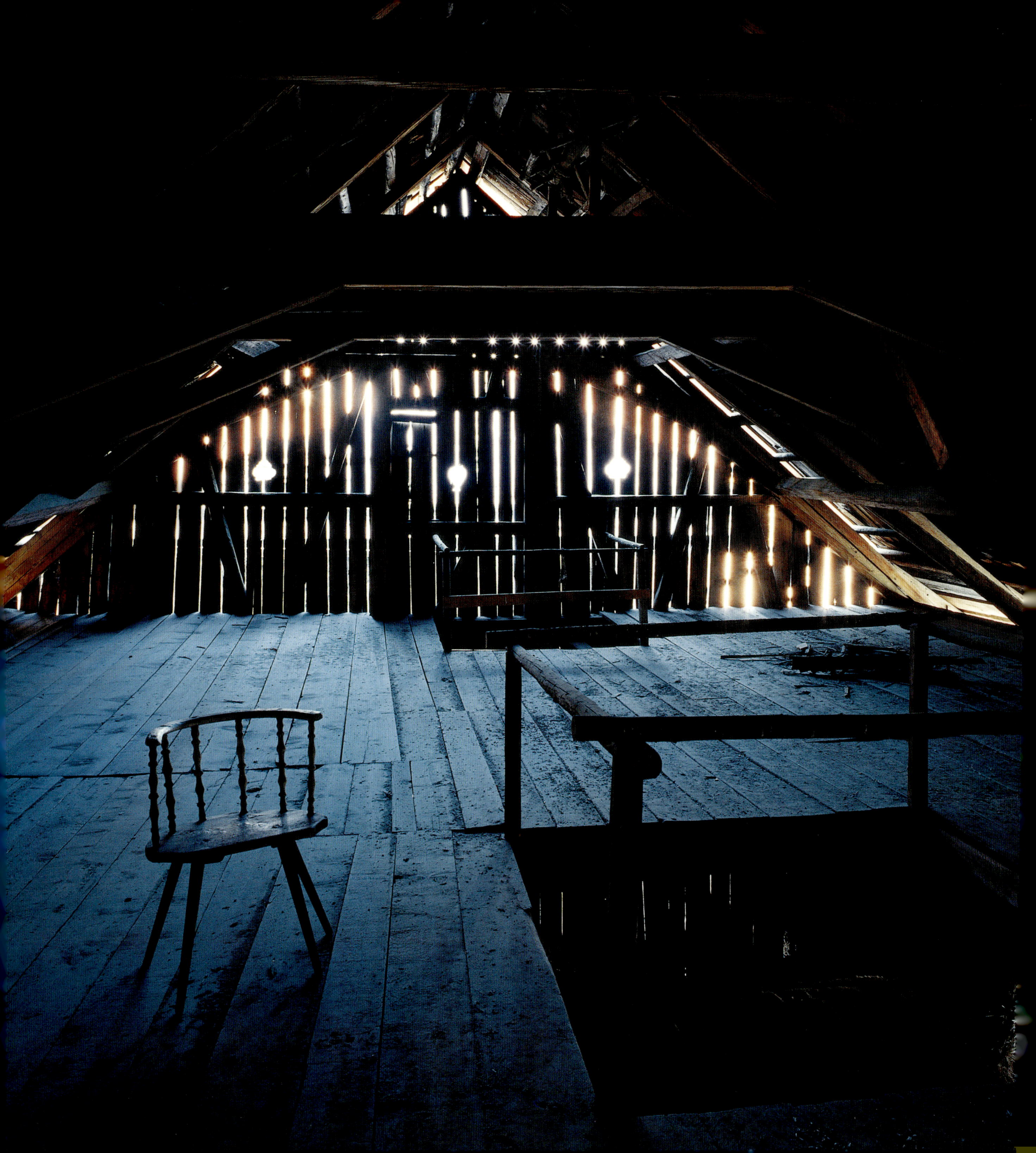

OPPOSITE The light filtering through the wooden planking of this 17th-century hayloft in the Engadin, Switzerland, illuminates the interior structure.

ABOVE The texture of a local-made wooden daybed contrasts with the softness of a mosquito net hanging from the ceiling of artist Joni Waite's former bedroom in Lamu Town.

TEXTURE

IN CONVERSATION WITH WILLIAM SOFIELD

'Texture, whether lacquer or Lucite, is at the root of my design. I have a great respect for the traditions of craftsmanship, and the materials I like to work with include woods chosen for their colour and patina, such as maple and American walnut. I might then embellish these with accents of brushed metal, painted leather and parchment.

———

I love to combine industrial elements, such as cast iron and concrete, with something surprising and unexpected, for example the staircase I created out of glass bottles at the SoHo Grand Hotel in New York.

I guess I am best known for a fusion of modern and traditional design. While there is a part of me that likes to be considered a Modernist, and I have carried out a number of projects that fit the category, I also have sensitivity to a client's needs and to historical context, which will often guide my design aesthetic in other directions. The ongoing challenge is in the initial design and the resulting details.

———

The chance to work with Brice Marden, America's greatest living artist, and his wife Helen on their house overlooking the Hudson, was a privilege as well as a great learning experience. We reworked the house in every sense, building up layers of texture by using a variety of different materials, from stone flags and stone set in concrete to a mezzanine of floating glass blocks in a steel frame for the flooring; fireplaces in limestone and marble, and bathtubs in copper and resin. Everywhere there is contrast. The sitting room we created has walls lined with velvet, while there are areas of the basement where the walls have been left just as they were found: untreated, half-painted or with the plaster falling off, like abandoned collages. The rooms are sparely furnished, albeit with iconic pieces, including a charred chair from a hotel fire, and Helen Marden's collection of colourful and textured textiles works a great counterbalance to the volume of each room.

———

I am an enthusiast of Art Moderne and the styles and designs of the 1920s and 1930s, and, in complete contrast to the Marden home, I have referenced many of the nuances of this period in a private project that I completed recently. On reflection, it is probably the most appropriate of my designs to the title 'Minimalism in the Grand Style': although not strictly Minimal, it certainly has a Grand Style, in addition to a strong visual sense of drama and mystery. The property is a historic five-floor townhouse in New York's West Village, dating from the 1860s, with one of the smallest footprints I have ever been asked to renovate and redesign.

———

I grew up in a house that would have been called Minimalist if the term had existed at the time, and I knew from a very young age that I wanted to be an architect.

———

My life and my career were turned around when I had the good fortune to meet Ignacio, an Italian woodworker who was a master craftsman at a collective on the Upper East Side. Appreciating his skill, his innate knowledge of his craft and above all his great love of wood, I recognized that for years I had been missing the essence of what design is really about. I ended up working with Ignacio as an apprentice for three years and relearned my trade from a craft perspective, a knowledge that I have since been able to translate into the furniture line that I have been designing for Baker for some years now.

I have always been a believer that design should live as well as it looks, so my approach is essentially practical.

I don't have too many preconceptions at the start of a new project, but I have been fortunate in the inspired clients that have sought me out. The commercial projects, particularly working with Tom Ford, Bottega Veneta, Gucci and Ralph Lauren, allowed me the luxury of working with a rich and continuously varied palette of materials under the ever-spinning umbrella of fashion. I revelled in the dramatic possibilities we were able to achieve, in the combination of colour and texture, as well as great lighting effects. Somehow there needs to be a sense of cinema about the interiors I create.

The work of Sir John Soane has been a strong influence in my approach to certain elements of design in both a conscious and a subliminal way. His use of colour has been an example to every aspiring designer, particularly when combined with the subtle lighting techniques that he employed all those years ago, and I also learned through his work the way to display objects and furniture to their best advantage.

More recently, I revisited an old favourite of mine, beautifully bound and quite forgotten on an upper shelf. It is an essay by a Japanese novelist called Jun'ichirō Tanizaki, under the English title 'In Praise of Shadows'. Essentially a book on Japanese aesthetics, Tanizaki's text, among other things, reflects on architecture and the use of space in buildings. The parallels he draws with Soane are uncanny. While heavily symbolic, his essay compares light with darkness and the appreciation of shadows. He discusses the layered tones of the different kinds of shadow and their power to reflect even the dullest of materials, and distinguishes between the values of light, both direct and indirect.

Tanizaki's writing greatly influenced my approach to the design, and in particular the colour scheme and paint treatment, that we applied to the house in the West Village. I used a palette of ivory, smoke blue, slate, persimmon, chocolate, mahogany and antique bronze, and combined the subtlety of these shades with such materials as mica, parchment, macassar and shagreen, while the walls are lacquer-painted or plaster hand-rubbed with wax. Reflective surfaces, mirrors and lacquered walls are all ways in which the space of a small property can be increased in a visual sense. The work in this house is exquisitely detailed, full of texture, mood and shadow, subtle lighting and some beautiful period pieces in the shape of sculptural chandeliers and wall sconces. I guess, rather than Modernist, it would be more accurate to call it Modern Glamour!

I would like to think that a few of my designs will outlive me and that the work I do does not necessarily have my stamp as a designer on it. I don't like to impose my taste on others, yet I feel proud to think that there might be a sense of inheritance associated with some of the furniture I have designed.'

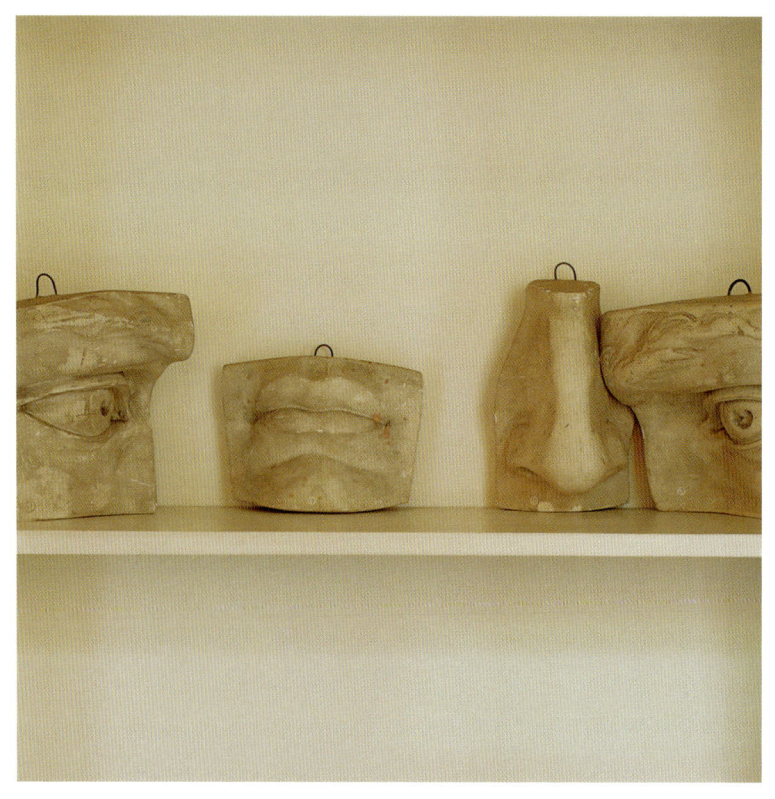

A collection of marble dust copies of the facial elements of Michelangelo's David (ABOVE RIGHT), available from London-based antiques dealer Anthony Redmile, is displayed on a simple shelf, while his foot (TOP LEFT) is used more practically as a doorstop.

An antique Khmer torso in bronze (TOP RIGHT) is displayed on a contemporary side table, sold through Jim Thompson, against the textured background of a pair of closed, louvred shutters in Jim Thompson designer Gerald Pearce's home in Bangkok. A Neoclassical marble bust of a young girl (ABOVE LEFT) placed on a pedestal in a corner of the room is simple and eye-catching.

ABOVE This plaster relief, based on a design by Armand-Albert Rateau, gives texture to the contemporary fireplace in a New York bathroom designed by William Sofield.

TEXTURE 231

'Perfection is achieved, not when there is nothing more to add, but when there is nothing left to take away.'

ANTOINE DE SAINT-EXUPÉRY, WRITER (1900–1944)

OPPOSITE The benign expression on the face of this Asian head reflects the sense of tranquillity that antiquarian Axel Vervoordt creates in all of his compositions.

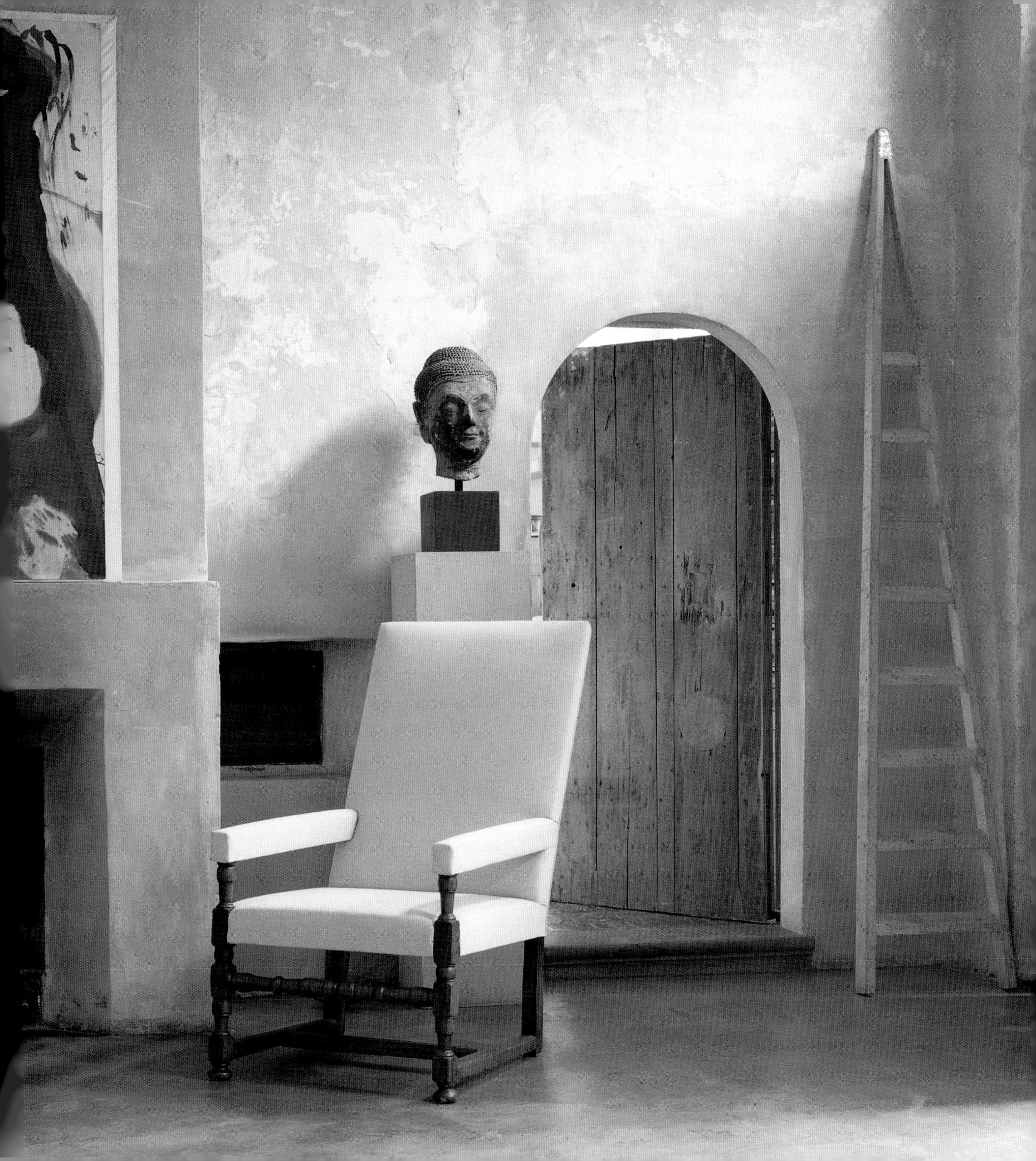

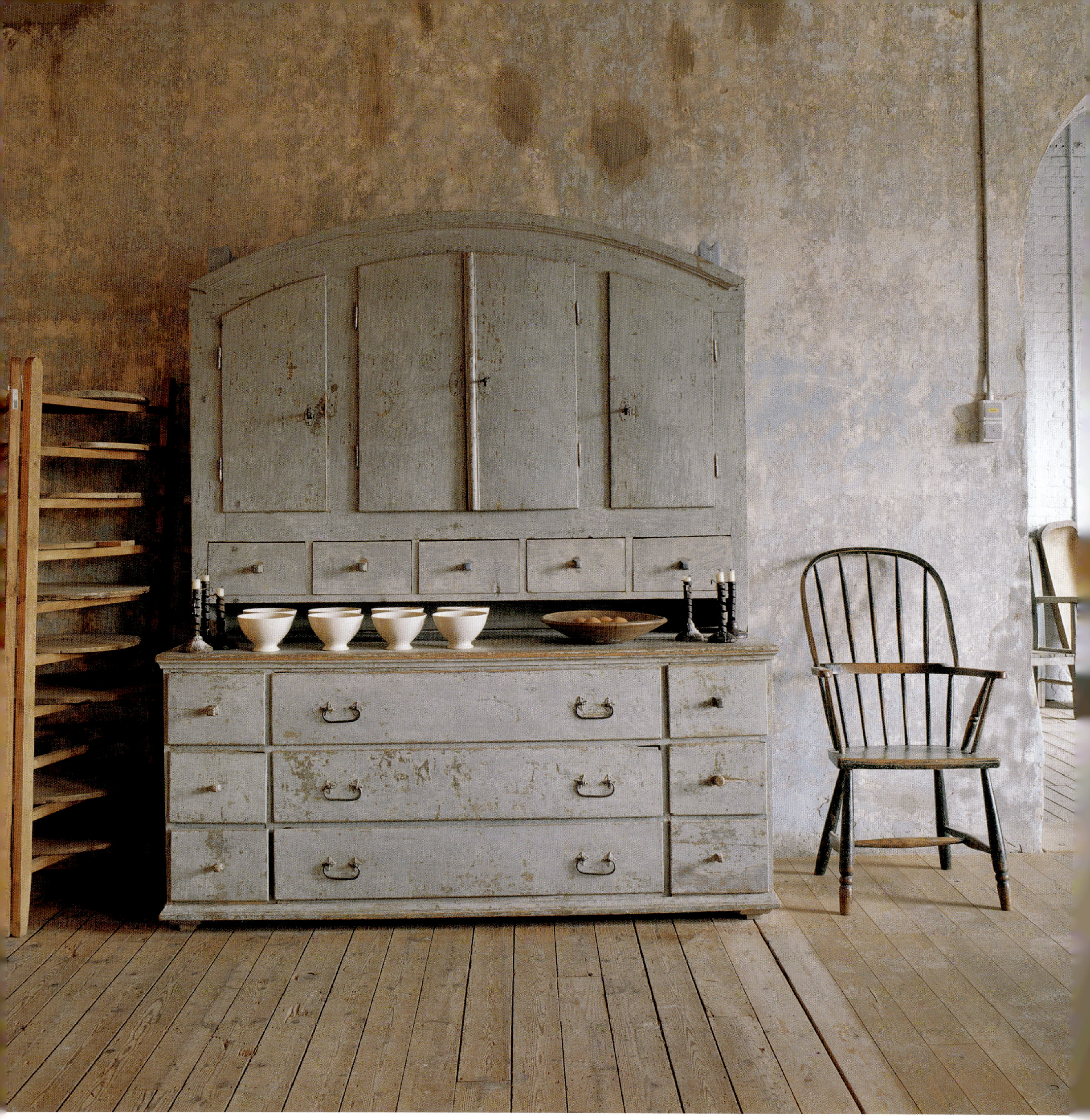

OPPOSITE AND ABOVE Axel Vervoordt allows himself to be inspired by the emptiness around him, as well as by the beauty he finds in imperfection, illustrated by the patina of wood and the authenticity of materials that are the legacy of time and use.

TEXTURE

ABOVE Late 18th-century peasant furniture, made of birch blackened from the smoke of an open fire used to heat this simple dwelling in Karelia, has acquired both texture and patina as a result.

OPPOSITE A collection of old planks that Axel Vervoordt has been amassing all his life are put on trestles to create impromptu tables, just as was done in the Middle Ages.

TEXTURE

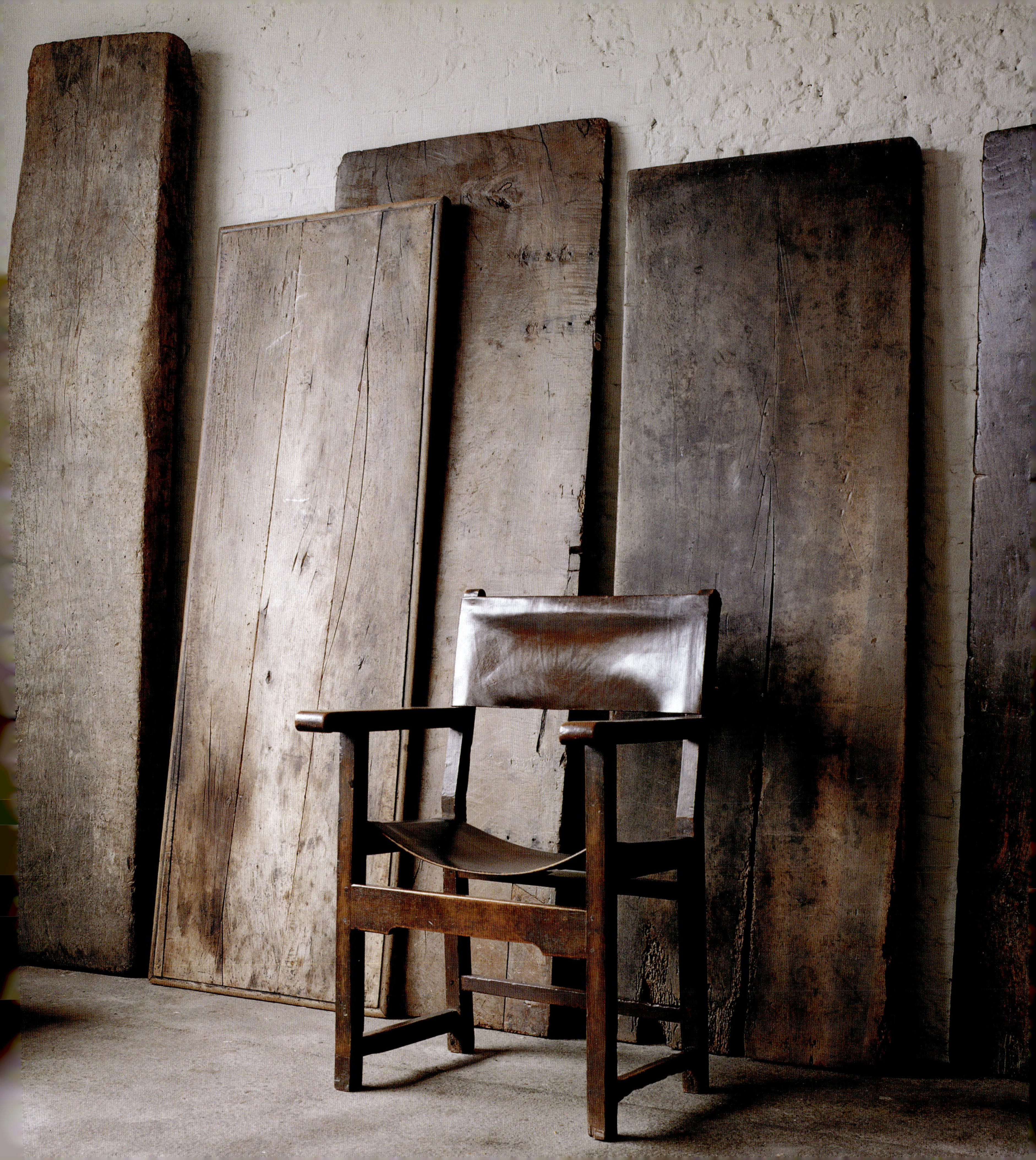

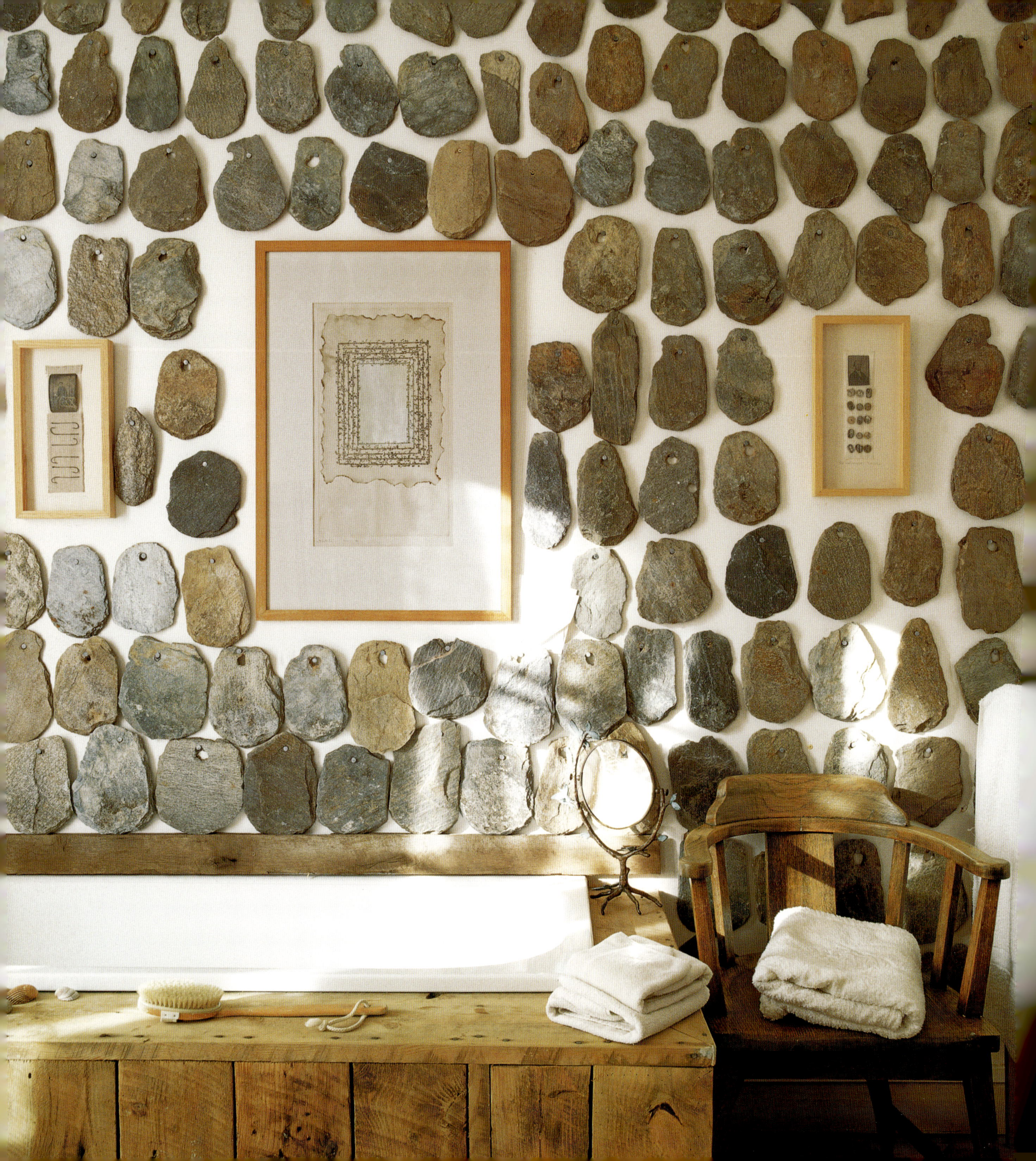

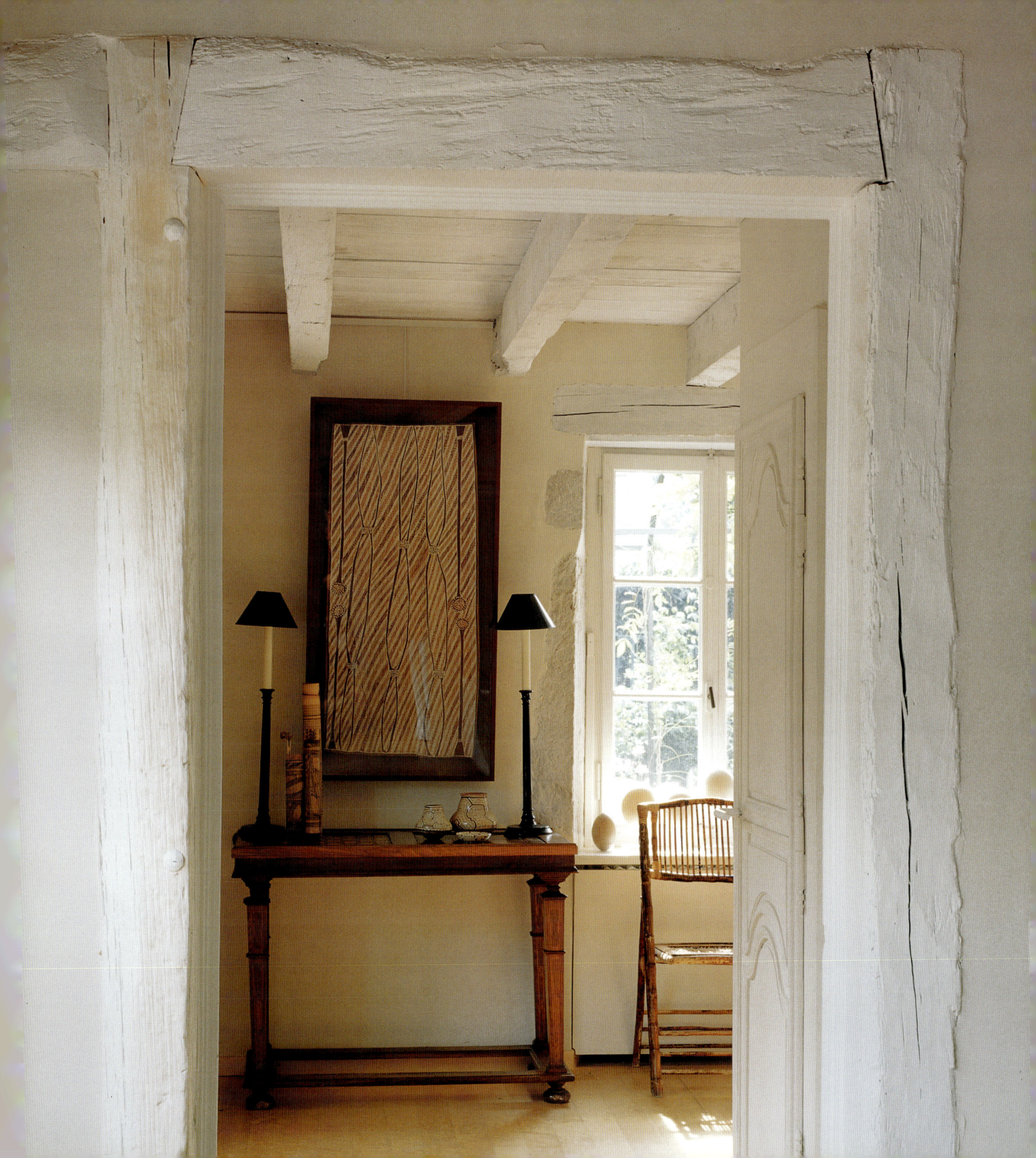

TEXTURE

PREVIOUS PAGES Catherine Painvin has used stone roof tiles to decorate the walls of her bathroom, while the bathtub is encased in simple planks of wood (LEFT). A rough, white-painted wooden doorframe echoes the treatment of the beams in the room beyond (RIGHT).

OPPOSITE The textures of fur and fabric contrast with the subtle Neoclassical-style painted panels on the walls of this Swedish country house.

ABOVE A worn leather, buttoned armchair is placed against an antique map of Rome, which antiques dealer Axel Vervoordt purchased from the sale of Rudolf Nureyev's estate.

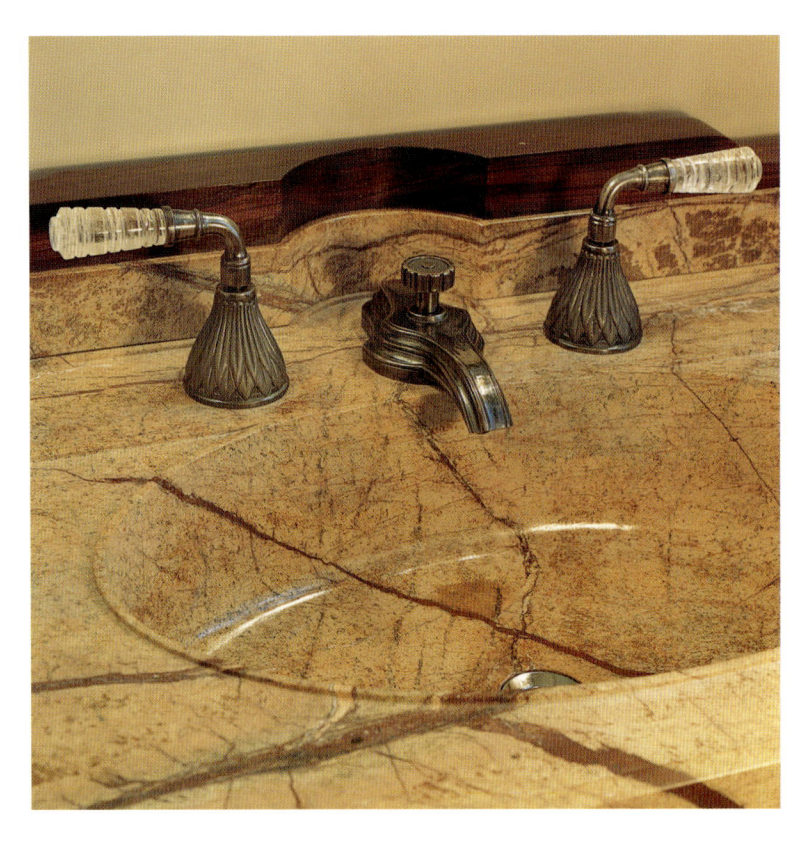

CLOCKWISE FROM TOP LEFT Designer William Sofield considers texture to be an important part of any design scheme, from a marble wash basin with rock crystal handles and a black nickel finish by P. E. Guerin to a 22-arm 1940s Veronese Murano glass chandelier; and from a 1940s French gilt iron sconce to an antique gilded picture frame.

TEXTURE

ABOVE The polished wood of an antique piano contrasts with the rough plaster walls of the sitting room in this Majorcean farmhouse.

TEXTURE

ABOVE The guest bedroom in this Welsh farmhouse retains the rough stone walls of the original stables, while the bed hangings are Irish horse blankets.

OPPOSITE The striped pattern and texture of the linen and hangings for this twin bedroom designed by Mimmi O'Connell contrast with the solid stone doorframe of the Tuscan farmhouse.

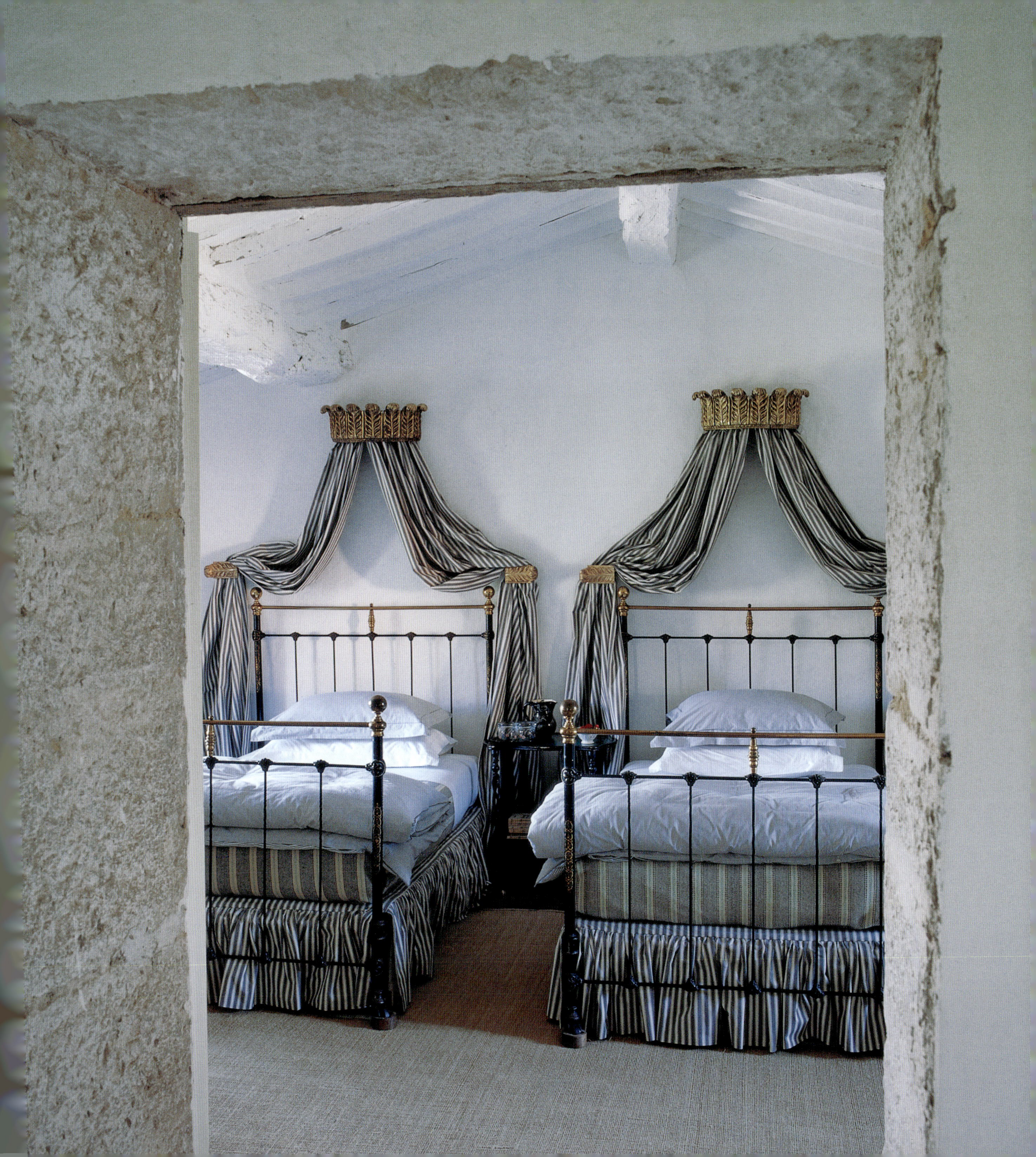

ABOVE A majestic ceramic stove in the octagonal State Dining Room at Sturehof in Sweden (LEFT) is flanked by wall decorations. A grand black and white marble basin, or buffet, set into an alcove in the drawing room at Swangrove on the Badminton estate (RIGHT) was designed by John Harvey. Fed with water by a concealed system of ropes and pulleys, it was used by guests to wash their hands after dining.

OPPOSITE The pale cream painted dining room in the Château de Montmirail in the Loire valley owes its original elegant panelling and decoration to the Princesse de Conti, whose husband, Louis Armand de Bourbon, acquired the property at the end of the 17th century. Situated in an arched recess is an 18th-century tiled ceramic stove used as a *chauffe-plats*, flanked by a pair of hanging shelves on which is displayed a white porcelain dinner service.

TEXTURE

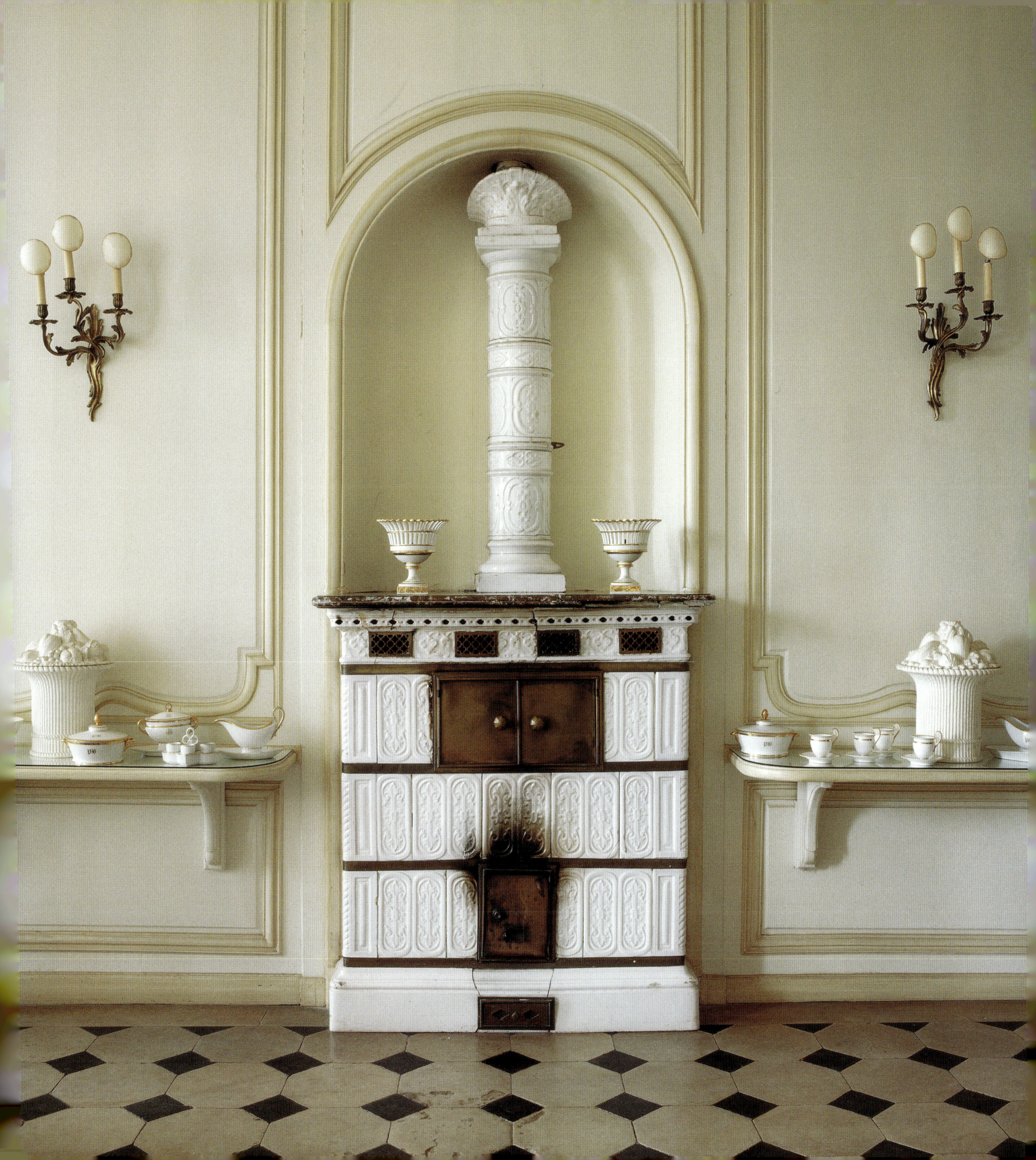

An antique painted sleigh bed made up with antique lace-edged linen (ABOVE) contrasts with the contemporary crispness of designer Mimmi O'Connell's guest bedroom in her home in Tuscany (OPPOSITE).

TEXTURE

250   TEXTURE

OPPOSITE AND ABOVE A collection of wooden chairs illustrates the different textures and patinas that come with age, finish, restoration and use.

TEXTURE 251

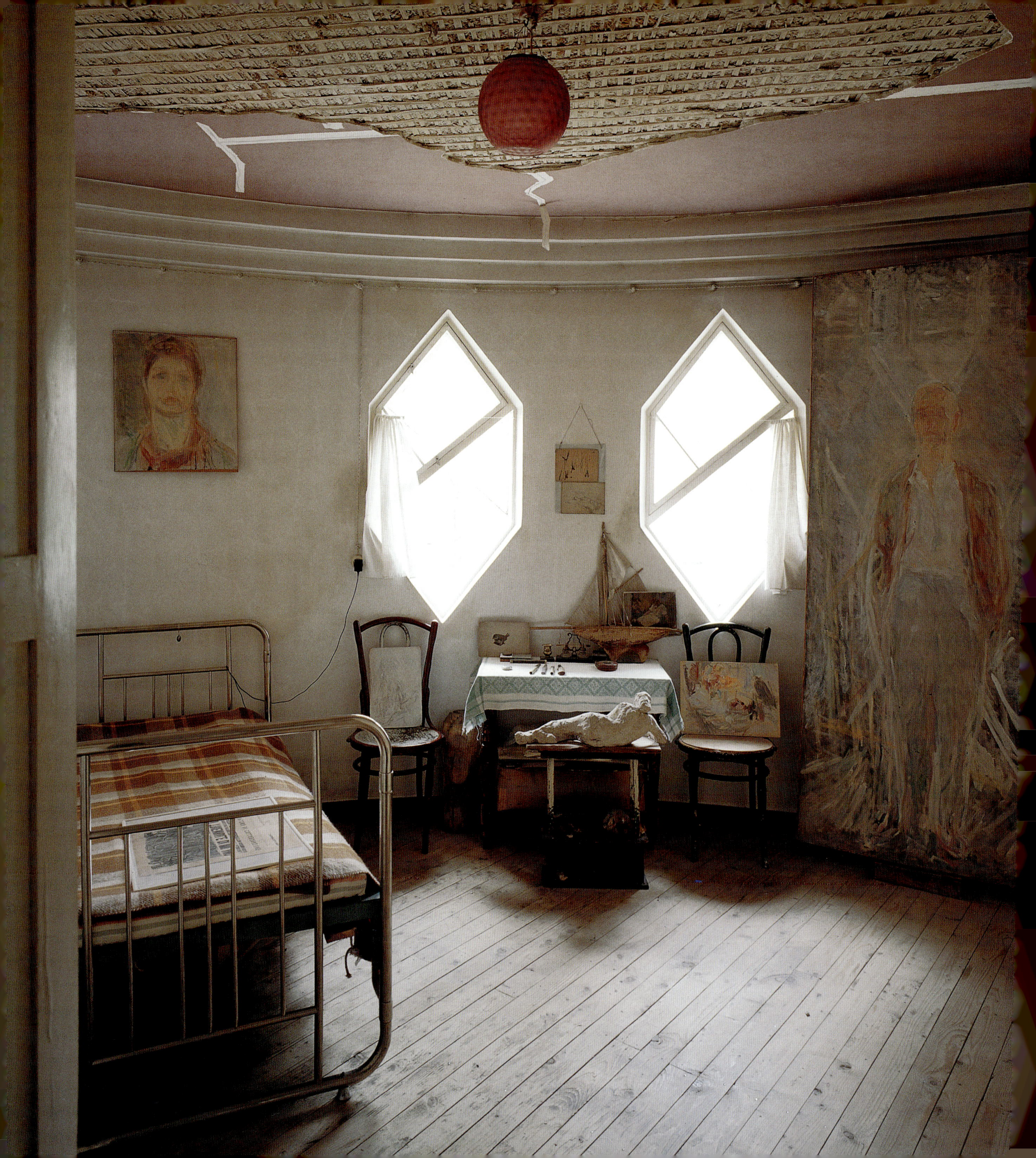

OPPOSITE The intriguing ceiling of architect Konstantin Melnikov's bedroom in his former home in Moscow in fact shows the effect of neglect, resulting from water damage, rather than design.

ABOVE The distressed paintwork on the walls of this bathroom in Afra on the island of Corfu is the result of age and damp conditions.

ABOVE Designer Gail Behr has created an interesting bathroom full of contrasts in her home in Plettenberg Bay, South Africa, with a free-standing zinc bathtub lit with silver candelabra against rough unplastered stone walls.

OPPOSITE Antiques, vintage objects and rustic pieces in Axel Vervoordt's Kanaal warehouse are displayed in a casual way against the neutral background of the building's distressed painted walls.

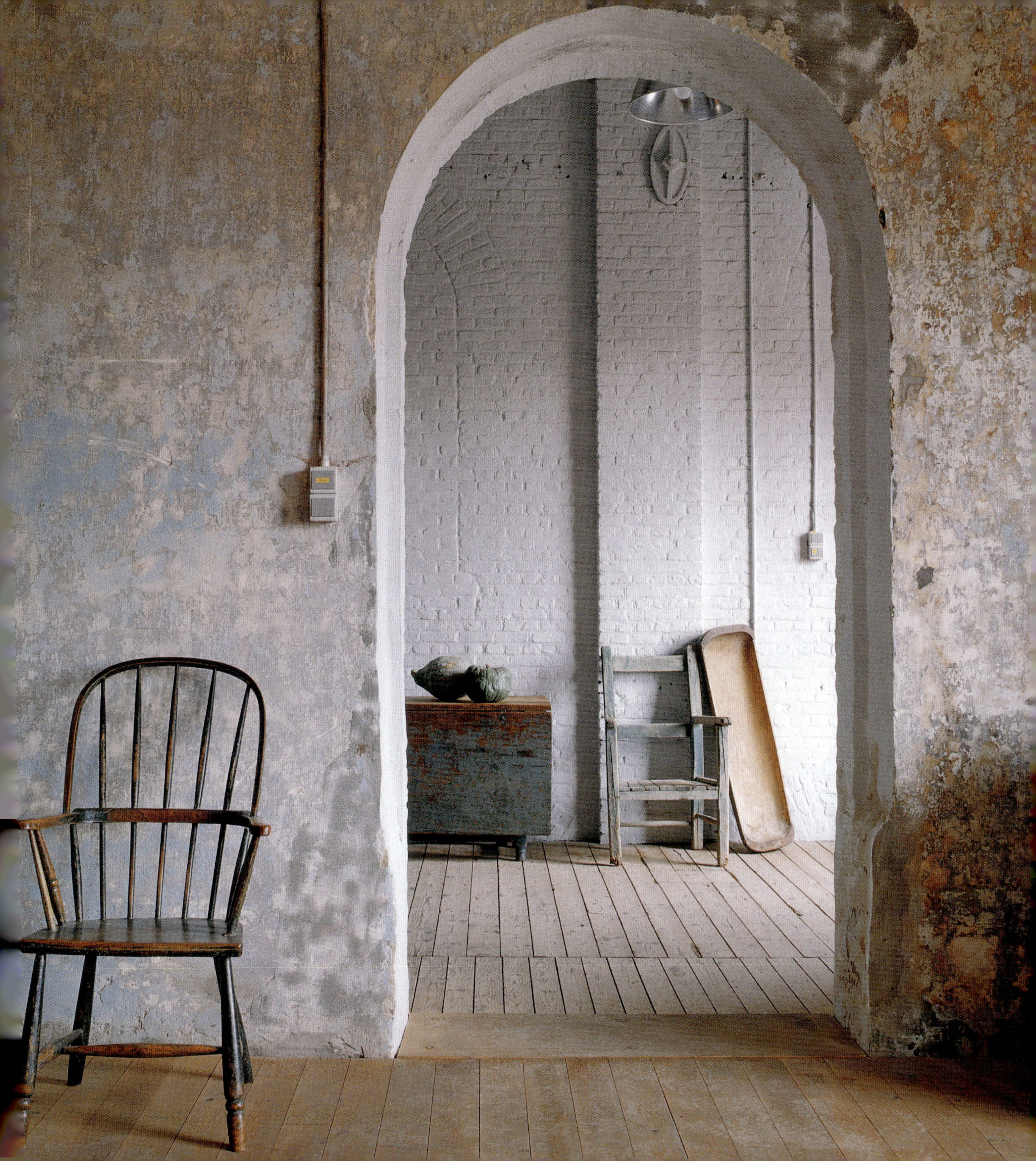

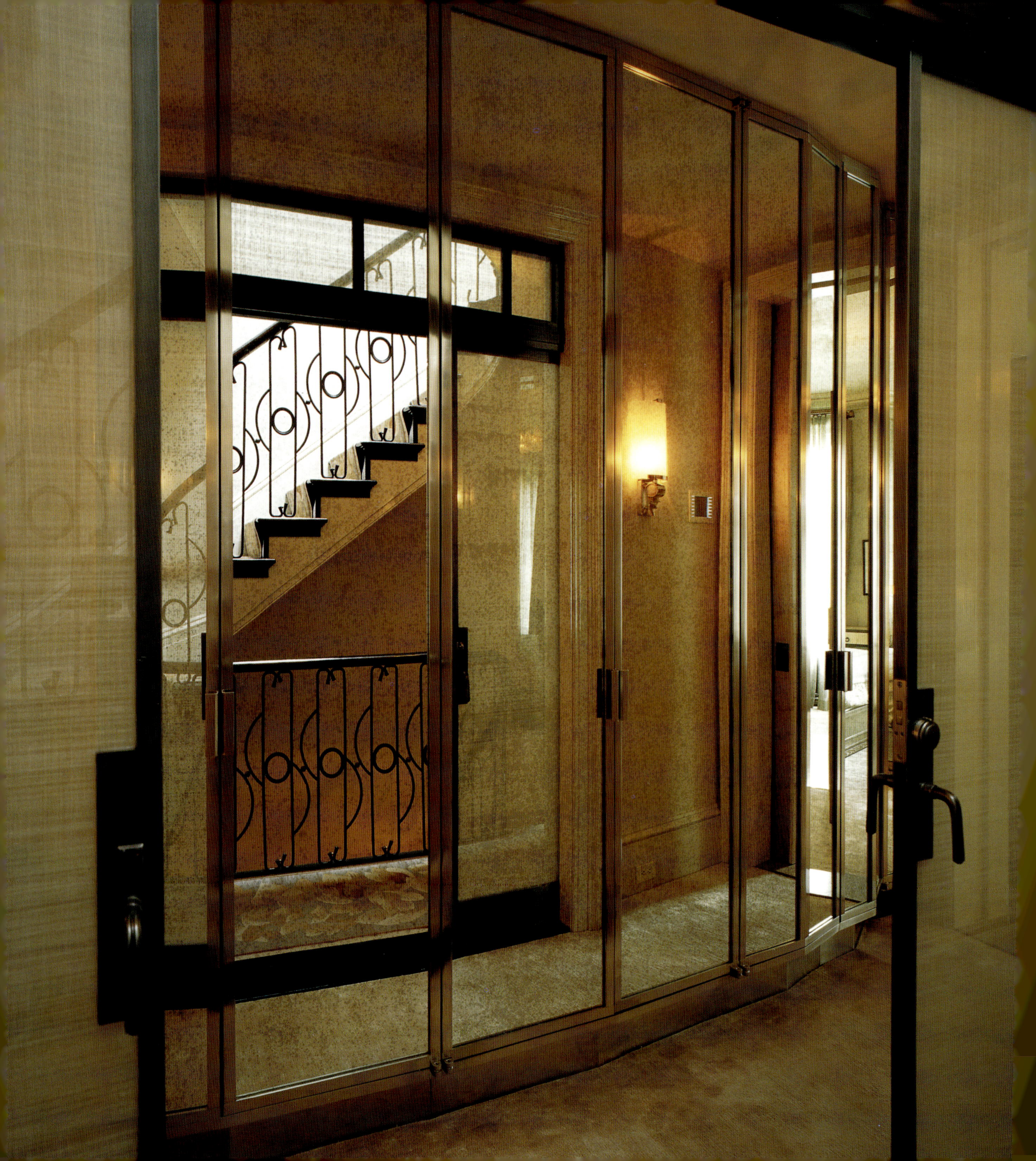

OPPOSITE This narrow New York house required clever storage, so designer William Sofield devised a faceted nickel and antique mirrored wardrobe, which spans the hallway between the master bedroom and bathroom.

ABOVE One of the small, low-ceilinged guest bedrooms at Tullgarn, the summer palace of the Swedish Prince Fredrik Adolf, is simply furnished with scrubbed pine floor and walls decorated with Piranesi prints.

COMPOSITION

Composition is about balance and space. The addition of personal elements can influence the visual interpretation of an interior that has been pared down to Minimalist simplicity. It is the combination of choices of colour and texture, light and rhythm that creates harmony and makes the space work.

According to Jean-Michel Frank, the balance of an object or a piece of furniture depends on its association with the various elements surrounding it. His sense of composition was influenced by the subtle relationship between the length of a sofa and that of the mantelpiece, which, in turn, related to the dimensions of the window, the height of the ceiling and the spacing of the doors. While Frank was able to reduce objects and furniture to their simplest expression, that of function, it is clear that his composition and spare, sometimes isolated placement of furniture in a room was due entirely to his awareness and understanding of space.

Reel forward several decades. Belgian antiquarian Axel Vervoordt has educated many of the world's contemporary interior designers, subliminally as well as consciously, in an understanding of composition. Vervoordt has a talent for composing interiors in a way that suggests they have been there forever, and his creativity in the juxtaposition of furniture and objects, irrespective of their origin and historical period, has changed global perspective on how to create a successful interior.

Vervoordt thinks in terms of spatial context, interrupting the planes of a room by bringing together different, sometimes opposing, objects to inspire contemplation, even meditation. Asked to describe his approach, he compares his arrangement of objects to the choreography of dance and the fluidity and ethereal quality of music. As musical tastes are influenced by mood, so too are compositions, and Vervoordt habitually rearranges his things to suit new contexts.

'I learned from artist and close friend Jef Verheyen about the importance of the way in which we look at things,' Vervoordt explains.

OPPOSITE A minimal loft space in an outer building of Axel Vervoordt's Belgian home is furnished with a Vervoordt-designed 'Zurbarán' table in schist, its dense black colour exaggerated by a charcoal drawing by Renie Spoelstra and balanced by a plaster replica of Michelangelo's *Dying Slave*.

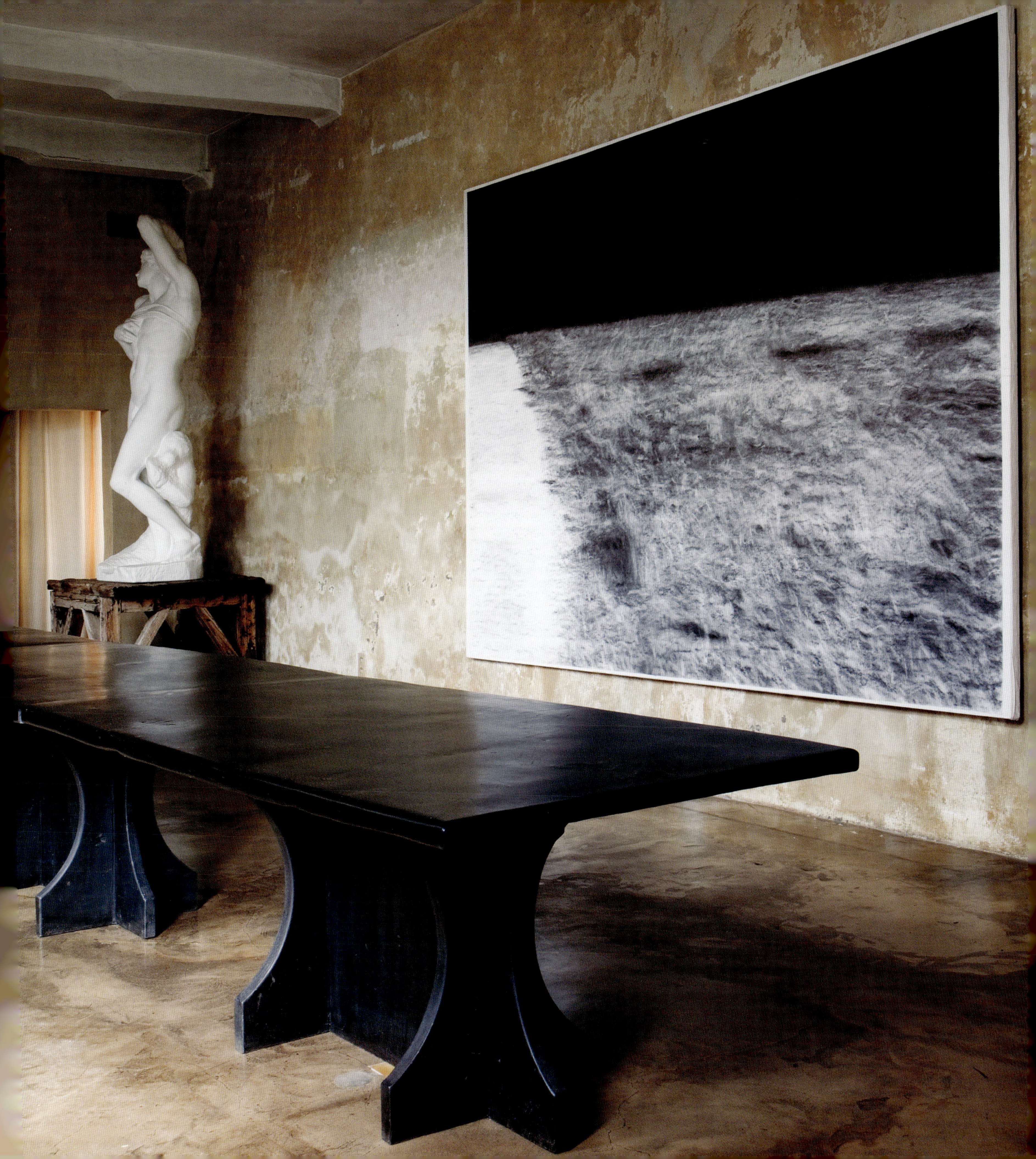

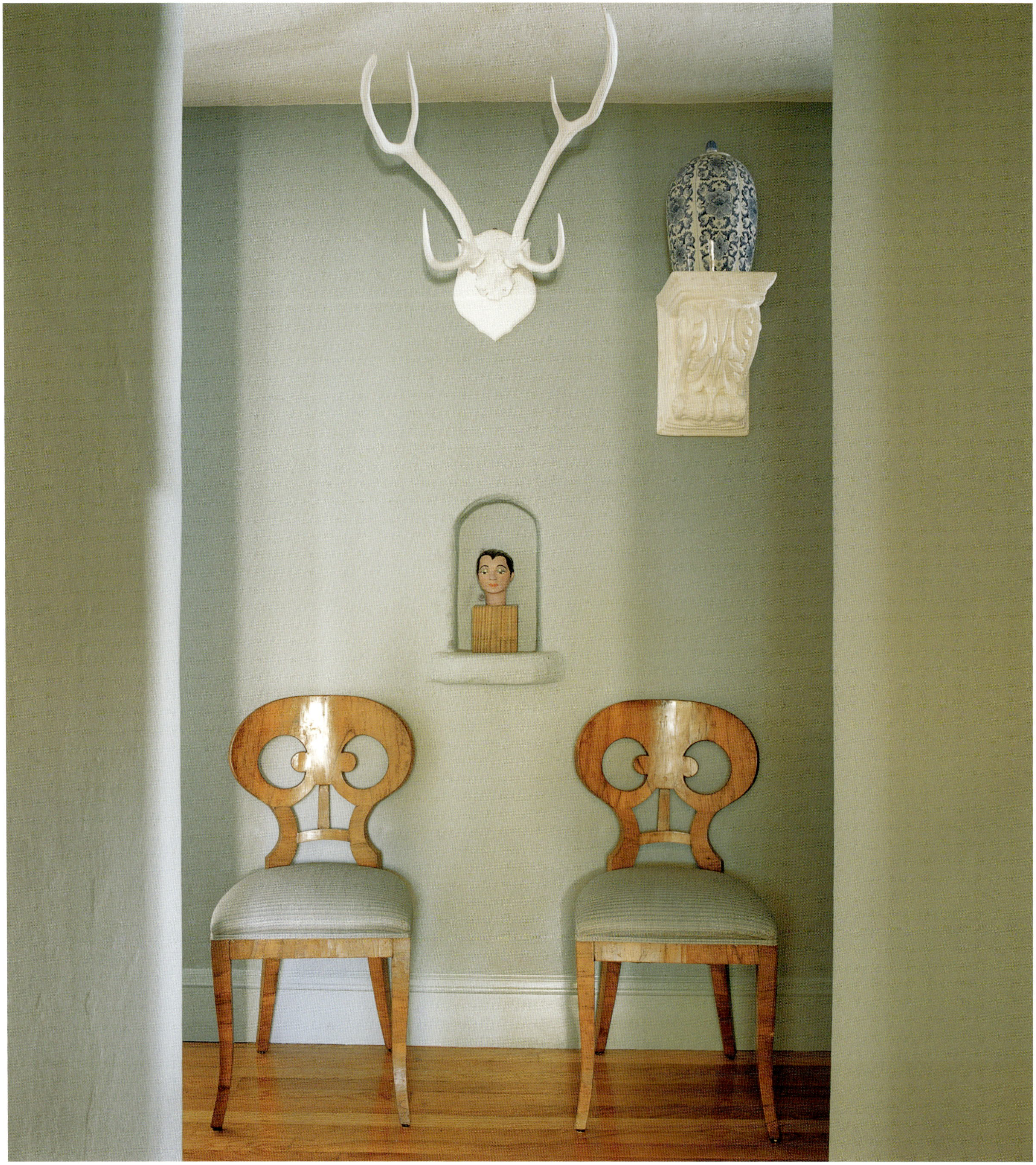

'It has nothing to do with seeing an object, but has everything to do with our appreciation of emptiness, in which the essence reveals itself and in which nothing can also mean everything.'

John Minshaw, a designer who freely acknowledges Vervoordt's influence, regards objects as magical touchstones that reveal what people were thinking about in another time. This sense of history adds to the pleasure he experiences in discovering a different way in which to display someone else's genius.

For Robert Kime, composition is 'all in the mix'. While there needs to be a synergy between objects, such as a similar use of material, ultimately it is the texture that prompts the rhythm, which in turn energizes the composition. A Kime composition and interior might involve a threadbare Bargello textile used to upholster a grand pair of chairs, combined with a cut-up old rug draped over a 17th-century faux-marble-topped table, completed with a personal object discovered in the client's attic.

If Minimalist composition represents simplification – elimination until what is left is completely balanced – then the underlying influence has to be the recognition that the less is included, the stronger a composition becomes. Vervoordt explains this in terms of a void filled with a magnetic field: it requires not only an awareness of space but also a tension between objects for a composition to work perfectly.

OPPOSITE A touch of humour is important in any composition. Here, the objects displayed on the wall offset the formality of a pair of antique Biedermeier chairs.

ABOVE The success of any composition is in the mix and placement of objects. German artist Karl-Heinz Scherer's country house (LEFT) is a homage to Biedermeier, each piece of furniture placed like a sculpture. The stone sink in this Directoire entrance hall (RIGHT) has been filled with a collection of Bohemian glass baubles.

COMPOSITION 261

ABOVE The luminous beauty of a Classical head is displayed on a simple plinth in the gardens of Oranienbaum, an 18th-century Chinese palace outside St Petersburg designed by architect Antonio Rinaldi.

OPPOSITE At Gunnebo near Gothenburg, the serving room, which is furnished with a cistern used for rinsing wine glasses during meals, leads off the dining room, which is decorated with carvings by the Italian sculptor Gioacchino Frulli.

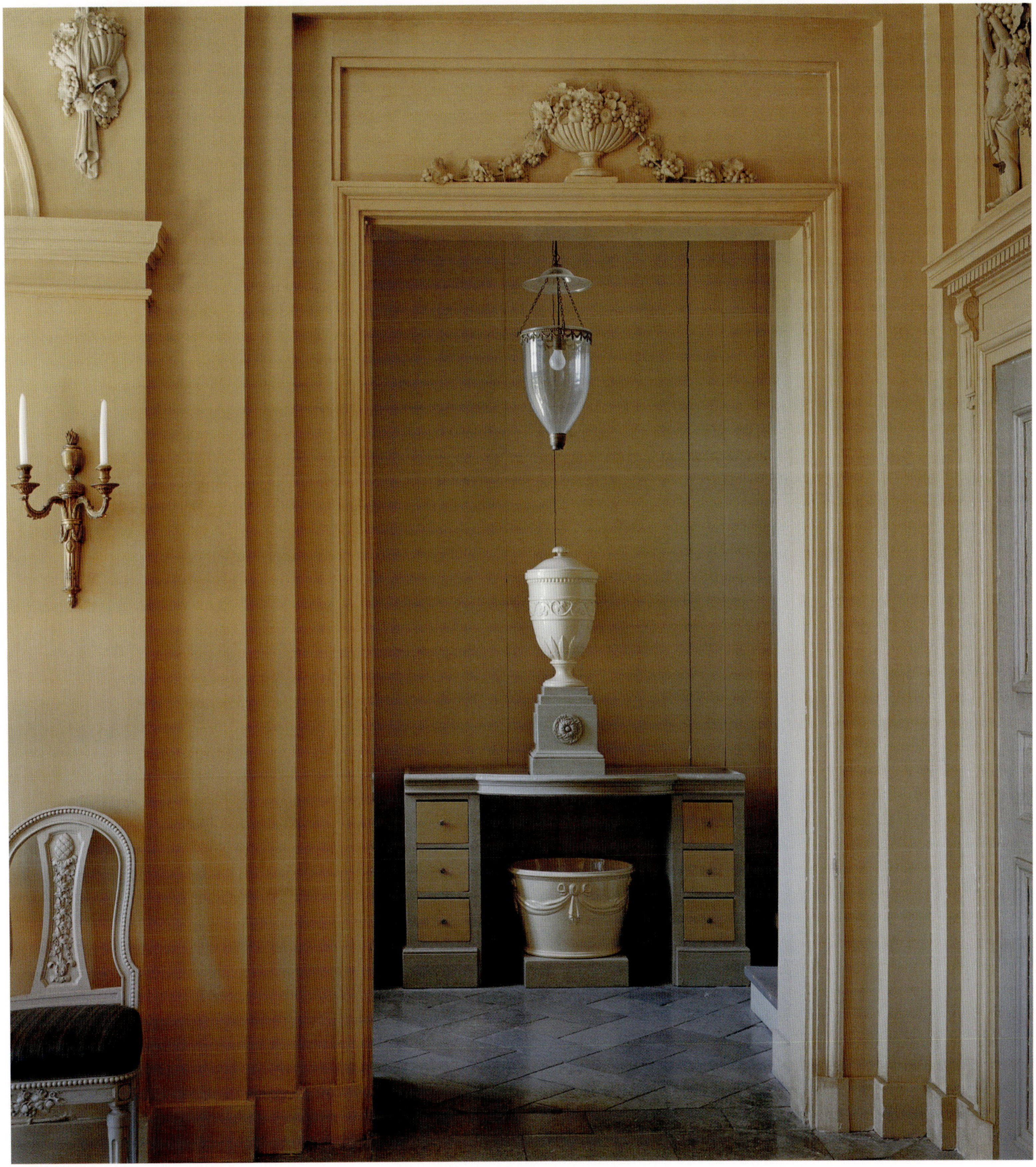

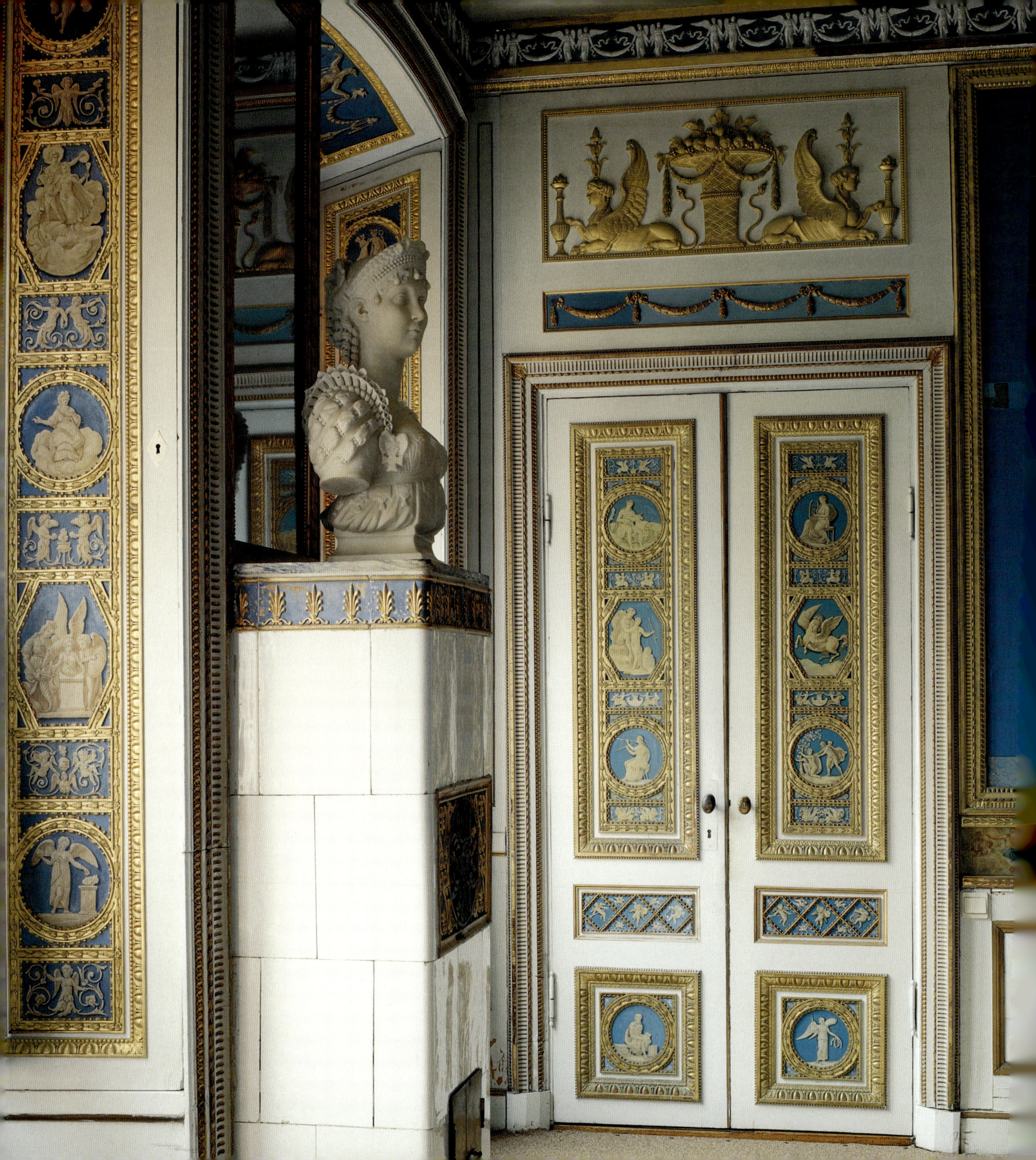

OPPOSITE The writing room at Tullgarn in Sweden has elaborately decorated doors and a narrow frieze depicting scenes from Swedish history by Anders Hultgren. The bust on the ceramic stove is of Napoleon's second wife, Marie Louise.

ABOVE This minimal master bedroom, designed by Collett-Zarzycki, combines a variety of reflective materials. The bed is the clear focus of the room.

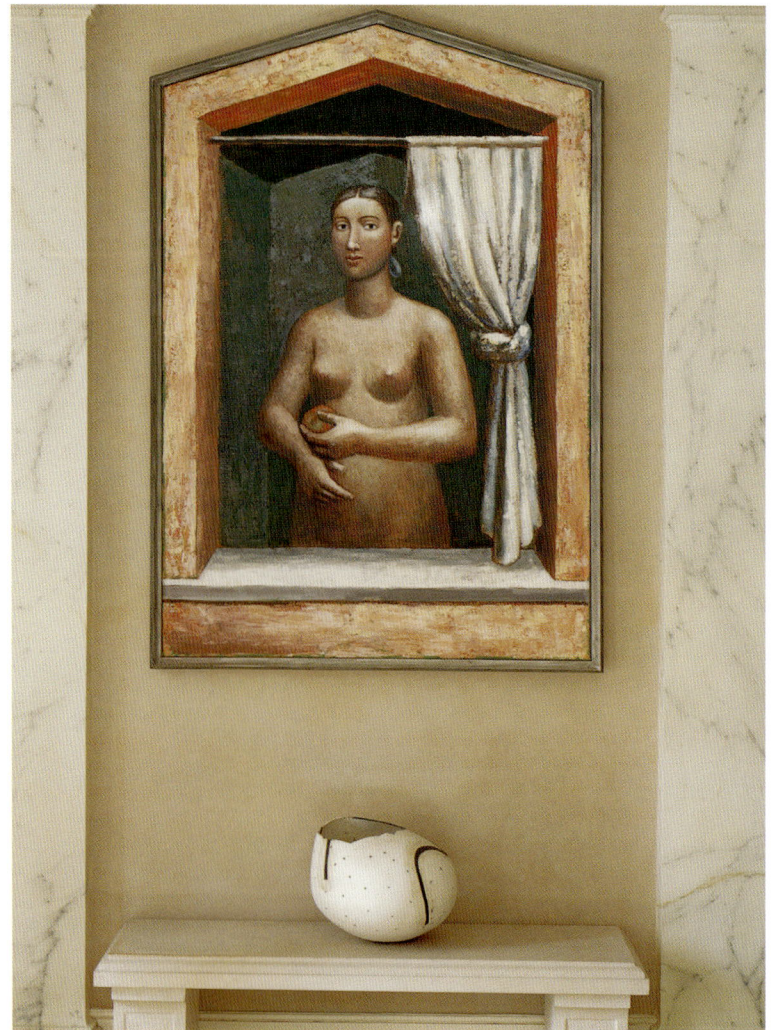

Display is about striking the right balance and achieving a sense of symmetry between artwork, furniture and objects. Rhythm has been achieved in an Austrian castle by mounting a collection of hunting trophies on the walls (ABOVE LEFT AND OPPOSITE), while a single object makes a bold statement beneath an elegant painting in a London hallway (ABOVE RIGHT).

COMPOSITION 267

IN CONVERSATION WITH AXEL AND BORIS VERVOORDT

'The concept of perfect minimalism is something with which I disagree. In my opinion, perfection is unknown and may not even exist, which is why we must appreciate instead the beauty that is to be found in imperfection, and the authenticity that time and use leave behind. As human beings, we are born imperfect, and we struggle for perfection all our lives. It is this quest for the unachievable that I find so exciting and that continues to inspire me to greater understanding. And I have still so much to learn.

———

Looking back over the last forty years, my life has seen a slow progression rather than a revolutionary change. As a child, I had a love of simple things and the sense of purity that these evoked. This early appreciation was influenced further by my friendship with Jef Verheyen, whose introduction to Lucio Fontana and to the influential ZERO movement in the late 1950s resulted in the purchase of my first Fontana work.

———

Over the last decade I have sought increasingly to find harmony and balance in what I do and how I live. I have found answers to many questions in the Japanese philosophy of Wabi, which embraces a simple aesthetic, one in which all inessentials are eliminated. There is also the concept of 'ma', which is the 'framed' emptiness between two objects – in essence, the space. 'Ma' is important in any great architecture since correct proportions create a beautiful emptiness, and it is what surrounds this emptiness that is so important.

———

A brief tour of our home outside Antwerp reveals the road I have travelled since starting my career as a collector at the tender age of fourteen. The period in which each room has been designed is enhanced by the composition of furniture, art and objects, the whole influencing the ultimate use of the space. Composition and juxtaposition affect the mood of a room, rendering my library, for example, which has a very English feel to it, more suitable for conducting business, communicating and entertaining. The tranquil meditation room on an upper floor, which is simply furnished with a couple of low platforms, requires you to bow low as you enter and to remove your shoes at the door as signs of respect. This beautiful space has a different ambience from the library, and the objects it contains are of great personal and often spiritual value. I go there for serious discussion or sometimes to say nothing at all, simply to reflect.

———

I have always bought things that caught my eye, even if in those early years I did not have enough money. I bought things I knew nothing about, purchases prompted by a gut instinct that an object was special, exceptional even. I would never sell an item on until I had discovered all I could about it, often consulting experts and other collectors in my quest for knowledge. It was then, and still is today, a real passion.

———

It is fortunate to be born with an eye for beauty and composition. Personally, I do not consider myself to be a collector in the classic sense. For many collectors it is enough to display their art and objects. I need to live with mine, to touch them and to use them every day. Our home is not a museum; nothing should be valued so highly that you are unable to touch it. I have always wanted clients and friends to understand how they can live with their precious possessions.

———

We all need an interpreter at some stage in our life. At times I have been accused of being merely decorative in my composition and of devaluing art by placing a rare painting above a mundane chest of drawers. A growing awareness that even well-educated people did not understand the energy created by the unexpected juxtaposition of objects prompted me to set up the 'Artempo' exhibition in Venice in 2007, which examined the relationship between nature and our man-made world, obliging each and every one of us to re-evaluate our perceptions of reality. I wanted to show that the essence of all art is about how we live with it; that it should not always be viewed in isolation, but also understood out of context, juxtaposed with other things. Art is inter-reactionary; art is human. The idea behind the exhibition was to start a dialogue, a new learning process. It succeeded, and was followed by 'Academia: Qui es-tu?' and the finale 'In-finitum'.'

'Growing up in a household filled with beautiful things, it was inevitable that I would succumb to my father's passion for collecting and eventually join the family firm. I always enjoyed being a part of it all, watching him in action at auctions and fairs, and the buzz of giving visitors a tour of our home and being able to explain in my own words the reasons behind the purchase of certain furniture and objects.

I share my father's philosophy, his quest for authenticity and love of the genuine article. The first thing I bought was a piece of Khmer pottery, inexpensive yet very precious, and this was followed by other things over the years. The pieces you never want to sell tend to be those whose intrinsic importance you appreciated at the time, yet the world did not. As a family, we have often bought pieces that no one else has understood. These pieces now form the anchors of my father's collection. They were simply too great at the time and are therefore no longer for sale today.

Over the years my father has inspired designers, architects and clients alike, many of whom have become good friends. They understand the philosophy and want to be a part of it, yet, like mine, their interpretation is different, individual. In order to emulate our philosophy, one must try to understand it. If one doesn't, the resultant interpretation will be empty and meaningless.

For me, true colour is expressed in natural pigment, which is enhanced over the years by the patina of time. If colour is contrived, it becomes decorative and lacks soul. I like to play with light and dark and prefer not to live in a space that is lit evenly. I find the contrast of rooms that are filled with light but where dark corners co-exist both energising and vibrant. Flickering candlelight adds rhythm, and rhythm for me is life, the heartbeat of a property, its emotion and its core. Space is all about proportion and balance. The grandness in grand minimalism is in the proportion. In my opinion, Palladio's interpretation is the best: his proportions are in perfect harmony, yet the design of the whole is extraordinarily simple.

My father and I hate the idea of 'decoration', so when it comes to creating a space or a home, we think as architects and not as decorators. Like Palladio, we try to find the harmony between client, home, belongings and, most important of all, surroundings. Ultimately it is about energy.'

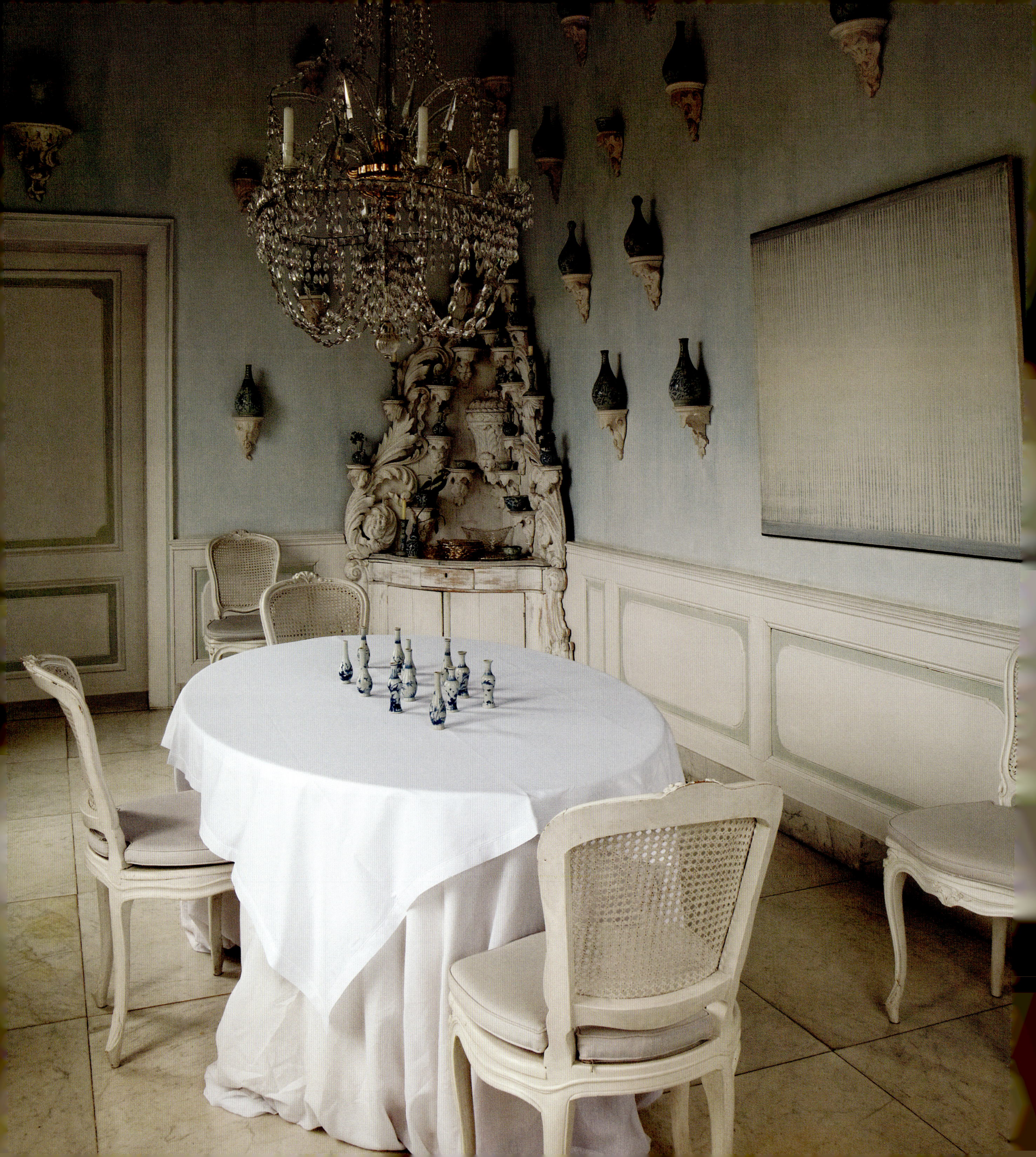

The white dining room in antiquarian Axel Vervoordt's castle home near Antwerp (OPPOSITE) displays the Hatcher collection of Late Ming china on the walls and an 18th-century painted corner cabinet by Daniel Marot, with a ZERO painting by Heinz Mack as a counterpoint to a Bohemian crystal chandelier. A sculpture by Otto Boll in aluminium and steel (ABOVE LEFT) seems to float in the vaulted emptiness of a tower room, while (ABOVE RIGHT) a marble-topped Italian table displays a 2nd-century AD Roman spherical vase in white marble.

COMPOSITION

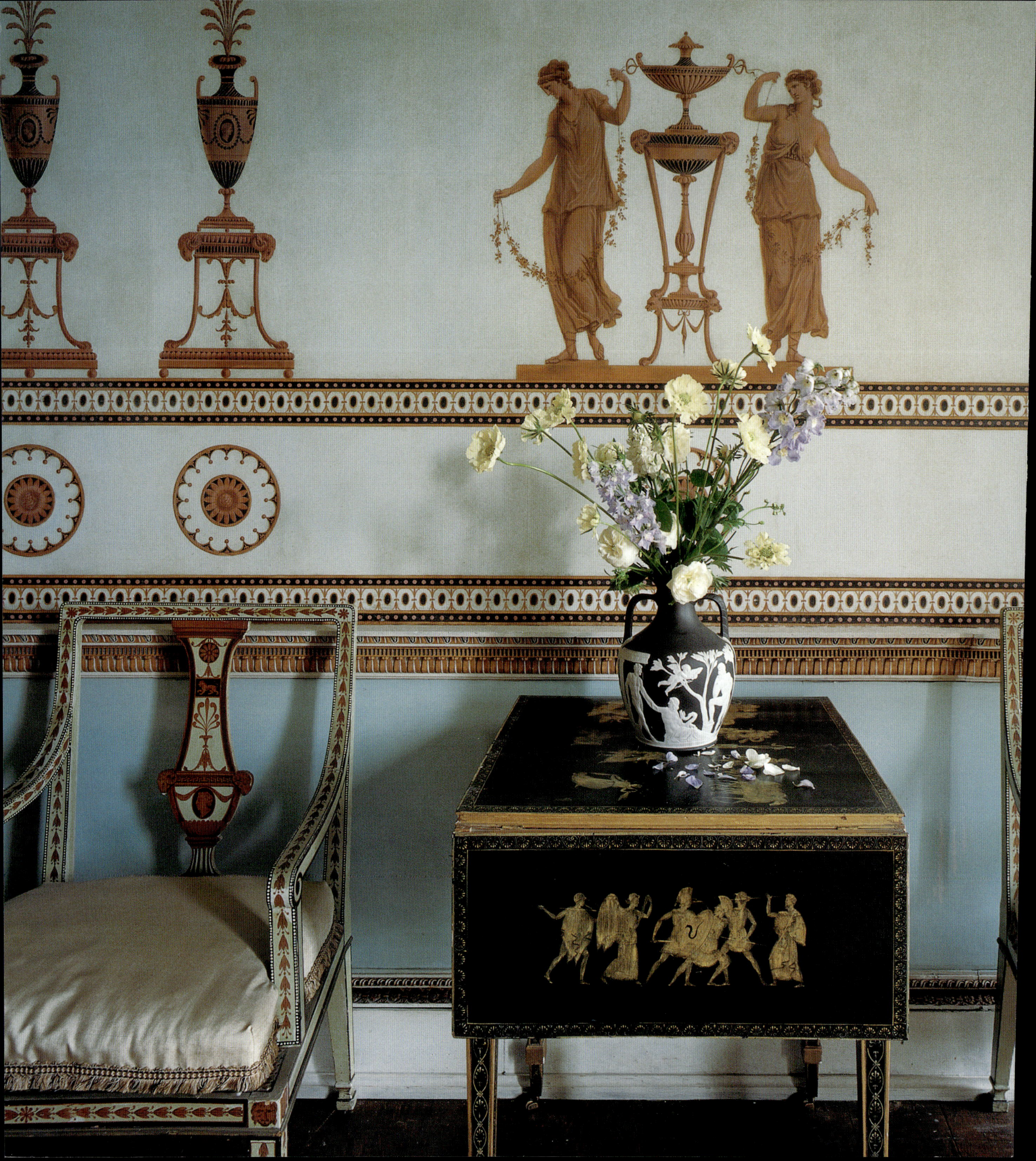

LEFT AND ABOVE The Etruscan Dressing Room at Osterley House was created by Robert Adam, who used the Etruscan vases in renowned antiquarian Sir William Hamilton's collection as inspiration for the decoration.

COMPOSITION 273

Architectural elements such as fireplaces and columns provide the structure and symmetry for good composition and the display of Classical and contemporary artwork and objects, as illustrated in a London entrance hall created by designer John Stefanidis (ABOVE LEFT), a New York apartment (ABOVE RIGHT), and the late Bill Blass's New York home (OPPOSITE).

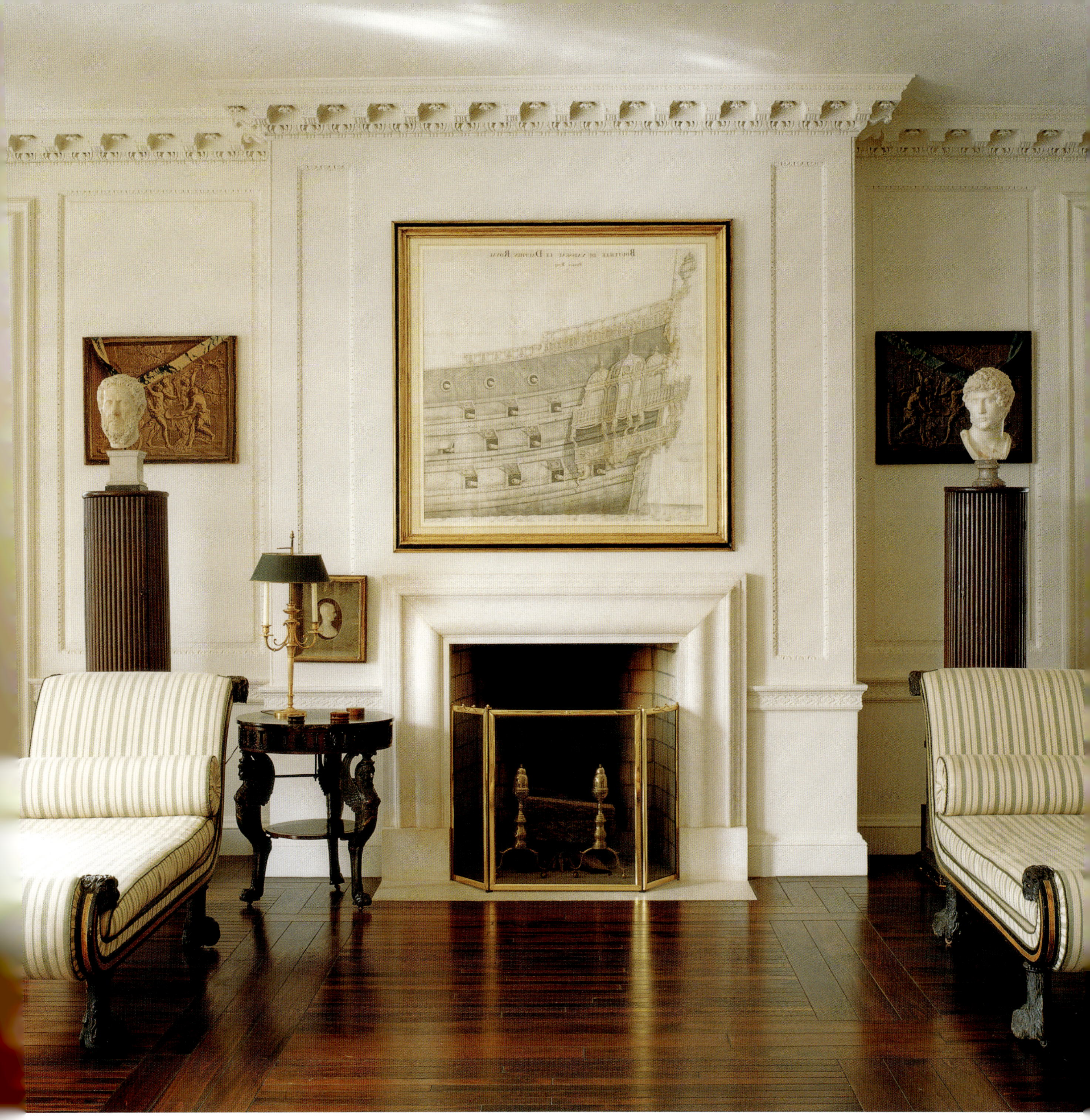

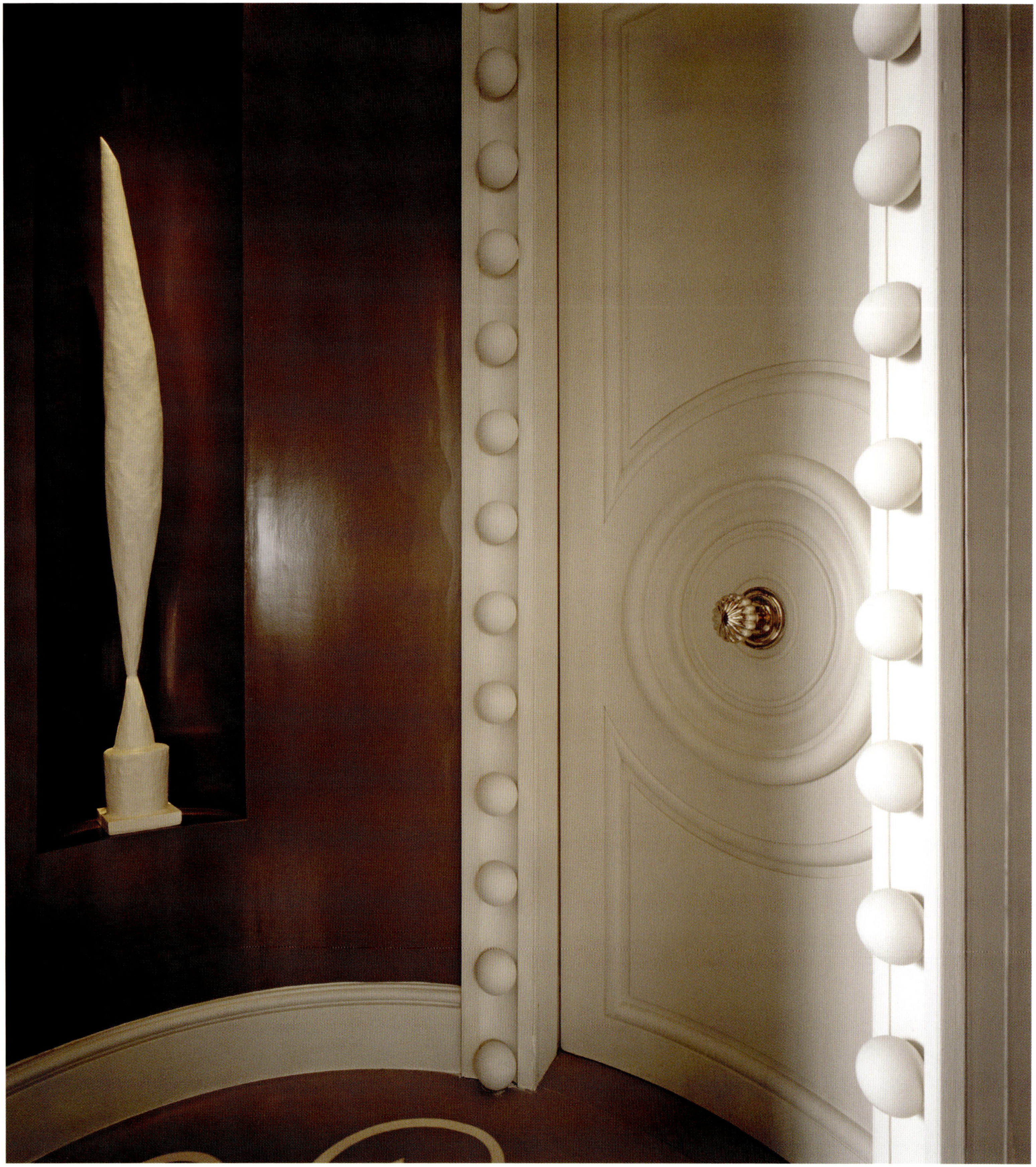

OPPOSITE One of the secrets in Nicholas Haslam's approach to the decoration of this London house was to over-scale. The curved doors to the small connecting hallway are framed with a row of plaster balls. The Brancusi-inspired bird is, naturally, a fake!

ABOVE Another of the imaginative touches that Nicholas Haslam brought to the decoration of this London house was a plaster urn, situated at the head of the stairs and filled with an abstract red and white creation of Haslam's own devising.

ABOVE A late 18th-century Italian Classical bust on a simple pedestal in a corner of a Neoclassical anteroom (LEFT). The Neoclassical Grand Staircase at Gunnebo in Sweden (RIGHT), which was built by the architect Carl Wilhelm Carlberg, is remarkable for its carved balustrade and ornamental urns.

OPPOSITE On the staircase of the Neoclassical house at Hylinge in Sweden, a Gustavian column supports an early 19th-century Italian alabaster urn.

OVERLEAF A vast George III oak table dominates the Serving Room at Drumlanrig Castle in Scotland. The portrait to the left of the open door is of the chef Joseph Florence.

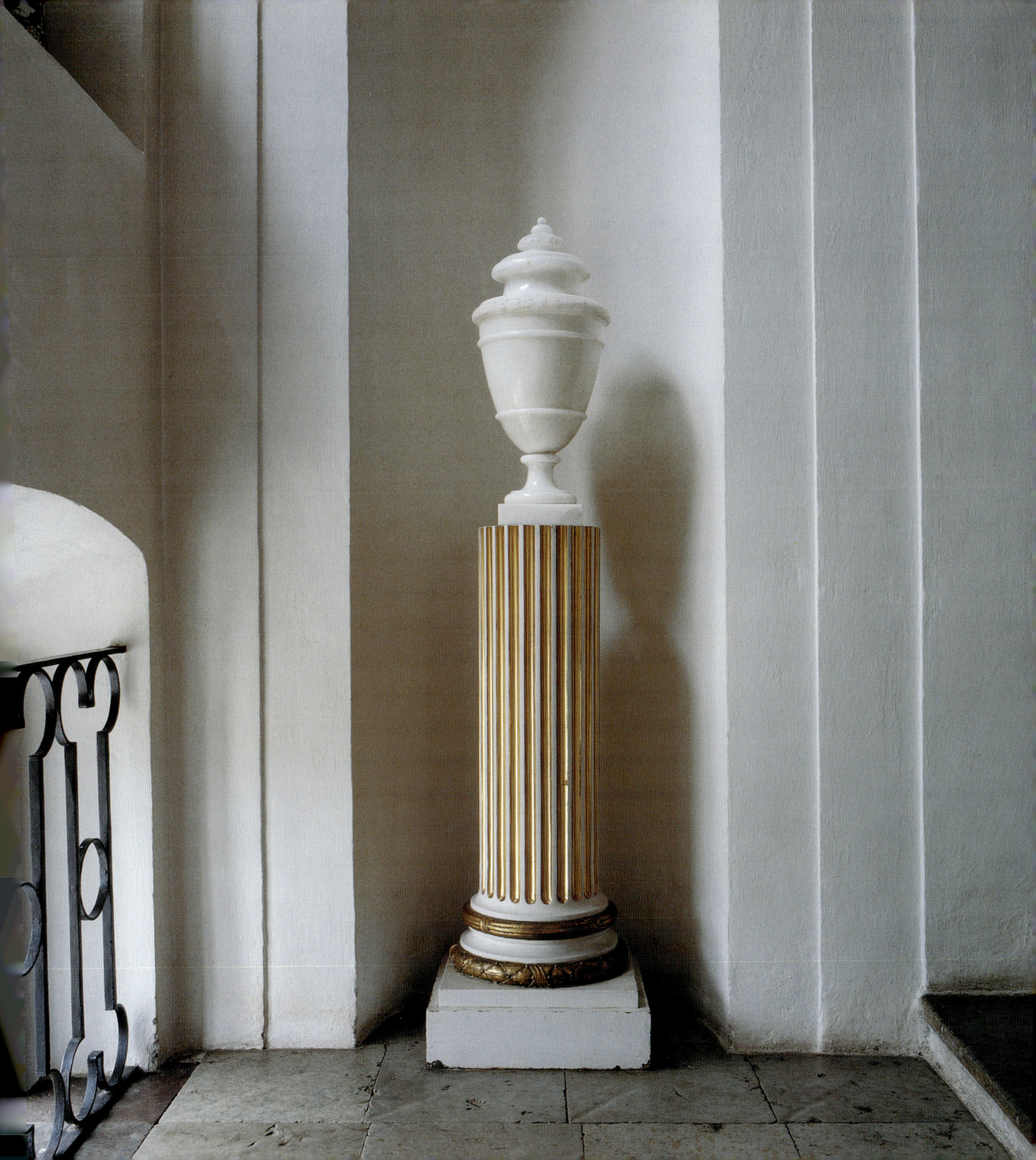

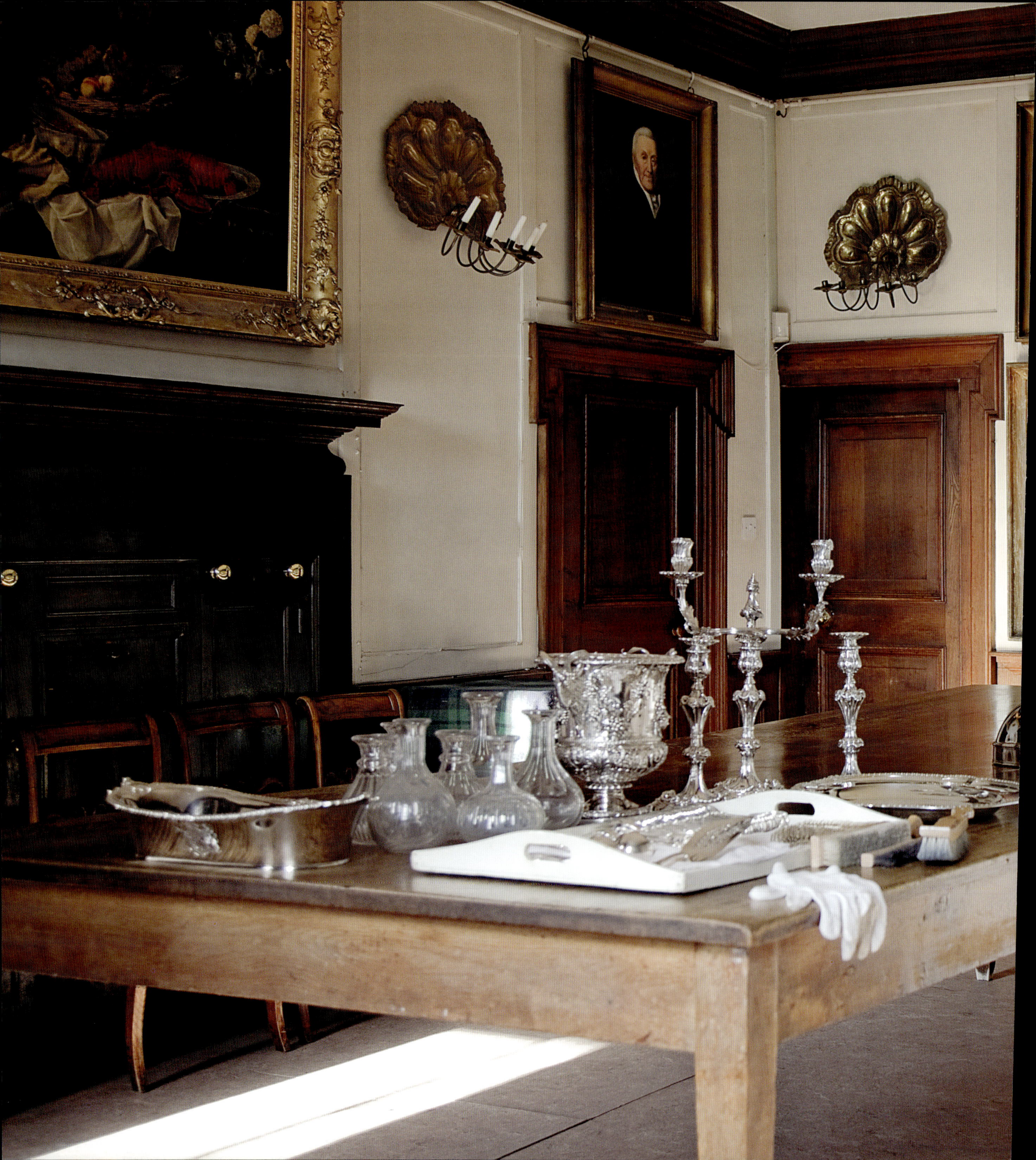

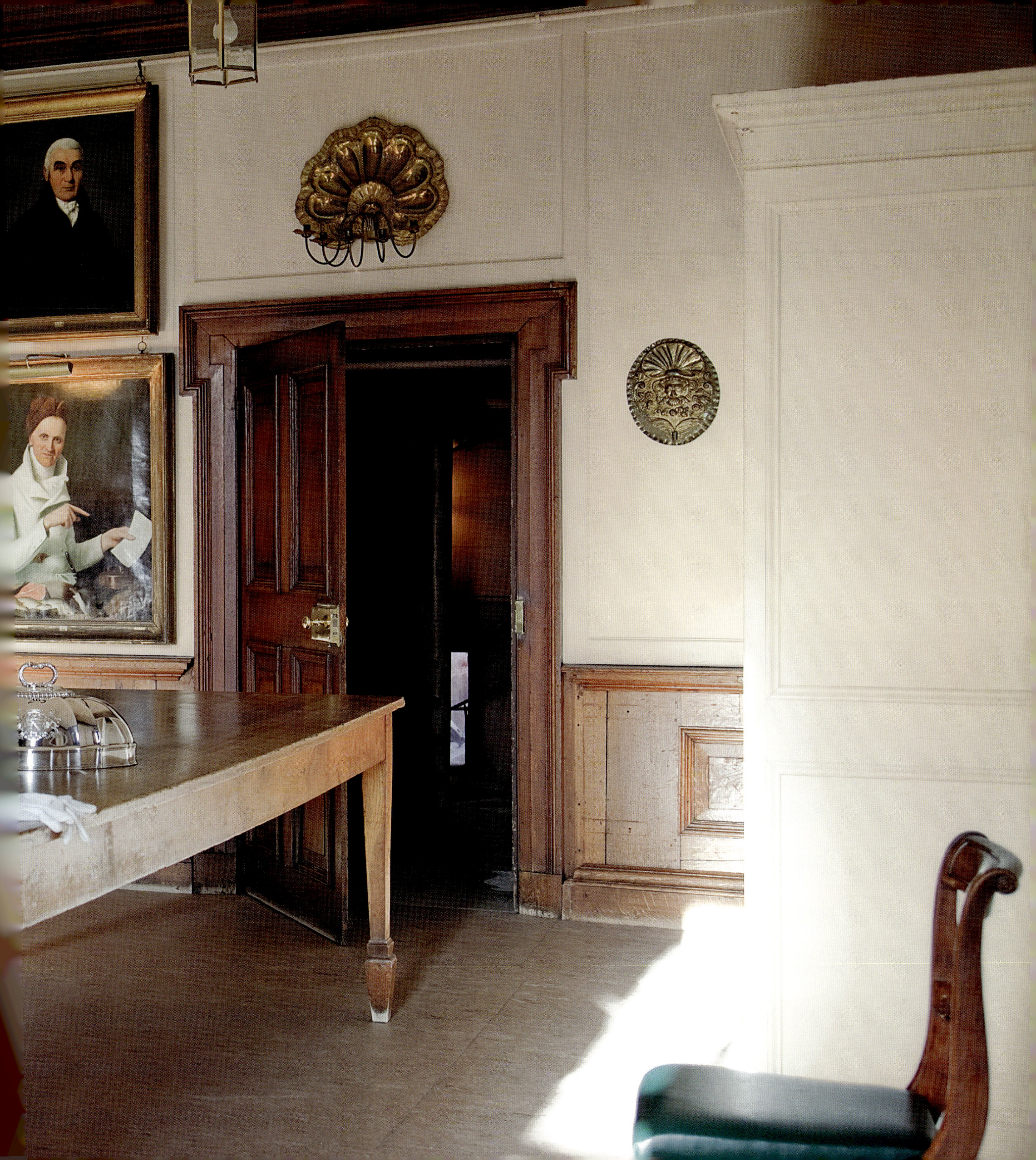

Artwork plays an important part in any composition, whether a discreet contemporary mix (ABOVE) or a wall dedicated to a particular style of art, as illustrated in the central saloon of Sadullah Pasha Yali (OPPOSITE), on the shores of the Bosphorus in Istanbul.

سلام عليكم بما صبرتم فنعم عقبى الدار

ادخلوا الجنة بما كنتم تعملون

كل من خان عليها هالك وزينا كالمحراب

محمد

ABOVE Mantelpieces give composition a platform, their shape, style and texture often contributing to the overall display.

OPPOSITE An English Regency fireplace in designer John Minshaw's London home is contemporized with a modern steel grate and firedogs, and an eclectic collection of framed artwork and sculpture is displayed on the mantelpiece.

284   COMPOSITION

COMPOSITION 285

ABOVE The dining room at Malmaison was decorated in 1800 by Charles Percier and Pierre-François-Léonard Fontaine. The murals of Pompeiian dancers painted on large stucco panels are by Louis Lafitte. The room is equipped with a marble fountain, a new trend for dining rooms of the period.

OPPOSITE The Salon of the Four Seasons in the Hôtel de Beauharnais, Paris, is one of the most sumptuous Empire interiors and has beautifully painted door panels.

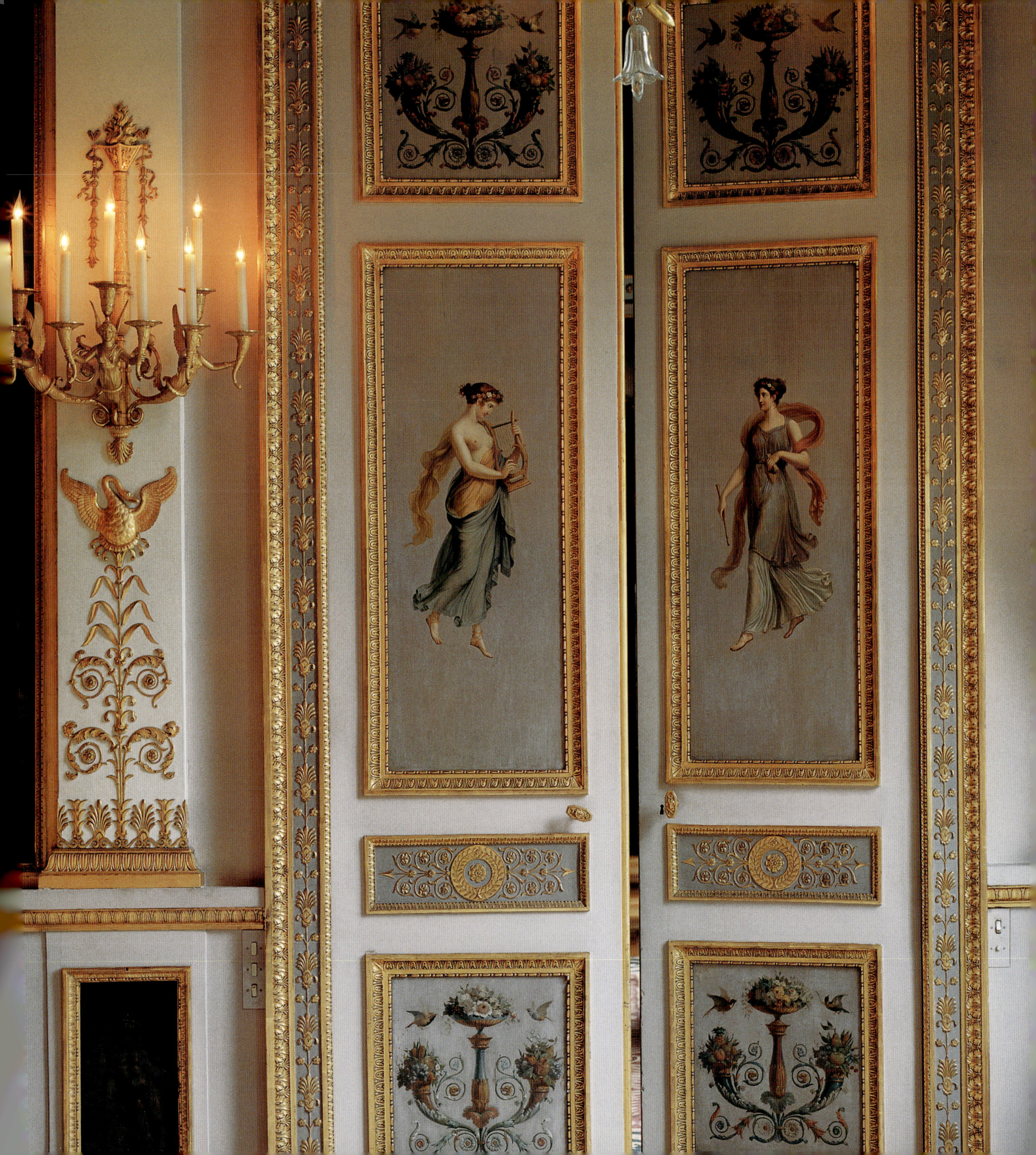

IN CONVERSATION WITH ROBERT KIME

'I didn't really see myself as a decorator at Swangrove, more an arranger.

———·———

Swangrove, a hunting lodge on the Badminton estate, is perhaps the closest I have come to addressing the various paradoxes encapsulated in the title of this book. The design of this house in the forest is the simple result requested of me from a very complicated set of requirements. I would like it to appear effortless and without concentration, but nevertheless this small-scale ducal go-down might be the best example of my interpretation of 'Minimalism in the Grand Style'. In essence, this is what I am about: this is the bit of decorating that I can relate to, where it is all about composition, collection and elimination.

———·———

The living room at Swangrove has windows on opposite sides, with three on each long side. Therefore it has a continuity of light throughout the day and there is no need to make it dark. I like to start the decoration of a room with something that originates from the owner. In this case, it was the carpet, which we found in the attics at Badminton, and which, with its strong colour and busy pattern, immediately suggested ideas for the rest of the room.

———·———

I balance pattern and colour to achieve harmony, and also use colour to restore balance. Consequently, I use a lot of tertiary colours, although red, as a primary colour, is also often in my palette. Nancy Lancaster once said that every room should have a touch of red. It is such a fantastic, saturated colour and one to which everyone responds. In its diluted form, red is pink and my client indicated early on that he had a penchant for pink.

———·———

Colour is also rhythm, used in stripes and pattern. Yet rhythm can so often be spoiled by repetition. In music, rhythm can be broken up: a colonnade, if it is too repetitive, can risk becoming tedious, while on the other hand an enfilade affords you intriguing glimpses into other rooms and, as you get closer, so a little more is revealed each time. There is a tension in the heightened expectation.

———·———

I think I am spatially aware and I have never had to measure anything – somehow I know whether a piece of furniture will fit or not. As with Fritz's approach to photography, I can achieve a sense of space by distancing the objects in a setting, and then I endlessly frame and edit what I have created.

———·———

Before I consider the actual space in an empty room I need to understand what that space will be used for and what will happen in it. If a client wishes a room to perform ten functions, it will invariably do none of them well.

———·———

We no longer live in the same way as our forebears. Contemporary rooms don't have the same architectural vocabulary as their historical counterparts and, as a consequence, I think it is often unnecessary and sometimes pretentious to introduce stray architectural elements that are stylistically unreal.

———·———

Textiles are the starting blocks in all of my designs. If I am to understand what a client wants of me at the outset of a project, then they are obliged to go through my storeroom of old textiles. This is huge, and can take some time, but it provides me with an opportunity to get to know a client, albeit on a superficial level by discovering their likes and dislikes. Watching their pleasure at finding things they love and want to use tells me everything I need to know to ensure a happy and successful collaboration. Obviously this is only from one particular perspective, for I am not a mind reader, but an individual's response to textiles is the clue to all sorts of emotions and memories associated with comfort and style.

———

I have found very few clients unable to identify with textiles. The majority identify, both positively and negatively, with the colour and the texture of a certain textile. I have had a few who hate the feel of silk, while others respond to the coarseness of linen. The emptier and more minimal the house, the more atmosphere I feel required to create. My textiles contribute to this; it's in the suggestion. Old textiles have all had another life, and that other life gives a resonance and a sense of history to wherever they end up.

———

A passion for textiles is often the spur for me to do my best efforts. I am quick to visualize how a room should look and to decide what will give a client pleasure, together with the furniture, objects and things that will bring this about.

———

Style is just a term and doesn't describe a person. A room that is only style doesn't tell you anything about its owner. Style is a fashion and might not last long.

———

I have always been a huge fan of William Morris – I have one of his hand-knotted Persian- and Turkish-influenced rugs in my living room at home. Morris started the Royal Society for the Protection of Ancient Buildings and his restoration techniques are second to none. Nobody did textiles better, nor understood the influence of the East more than he did. He travelled a great deal and employed some of the best artists to interpret his designs for stained-glass windows, textiles, tiles and furniture. He learned how to restore, how to print: there was nothing he could not do!

———

We are all in the habit of reinterpreting, since there is nothing new under the sun.

———

Sir John Soane is a great man who reworked the vocabulary of architecture. Just as in literature T. S. Eliot used exactly the same words as you and me, yet was able to give them a completely different meaning, so in architecture Schinkel and Soane re-organized, re-spaced and re-drew the essence of Classicism to mean something completely new. Robert Adam did the same, as did Sir Christopher Wren, Sir John Vanbrugh and Andrea Palladio, and this success will be built on and changed in its turn.

———

Working at Swangrove was much the same as working at Alnwick, Floors, Goodwood or Clarence House, because they all had very good attics to choose from. The successful re-creation of a room is about the mixing together of the memories associated with the furniture, the textiles, the client and the architecture. 'Minimal' for me is not about emptying a room, but about getting the function so right that even an ornament, because it contributes to the overall look, becomes part of the whole atmosphere I am trying to achieve.'

ABOVE The painted panelling with grey faux-marbling surrounded by bands of painted birds and chinoiserie in soft gold in the Belvedere Bedroom at Swangrove is original, from the early 18th century.

OPPOSITE Designer Robert Kime introduced an 18th-century Persian carpet as a table cover. The daybed in the alcove was designed in his workshops and is covered in indigo and white ticking and French Provençal ikat from his vast stock of textiles.

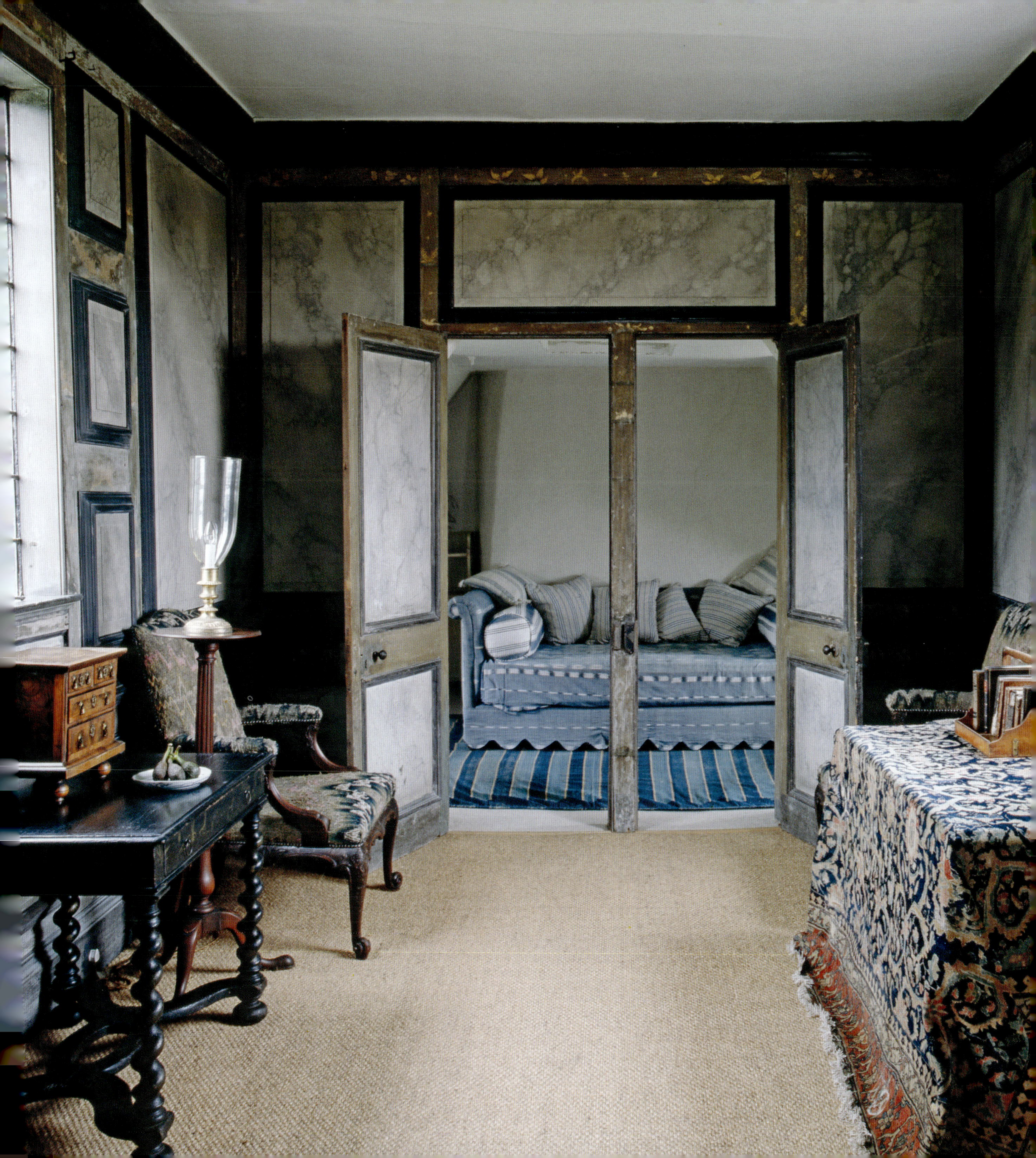

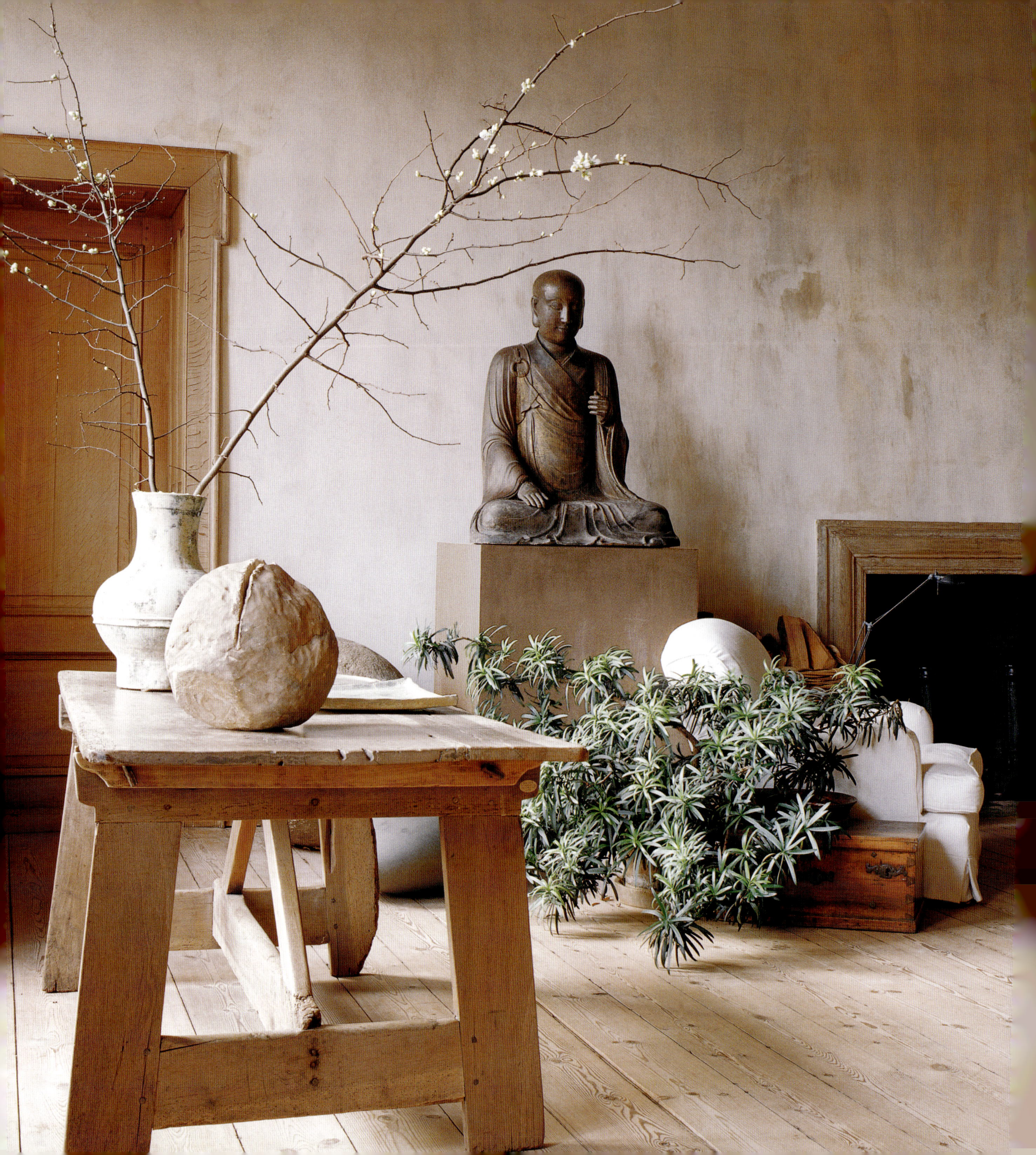

OPPOSITE In Axel Vervoordt's 'withdrawing' room, a statue of Buddha is combined with an arte povera table displaying a branch of blossom from the garden.

ABOVE A collection of Pi, all of jade and symbolizing heaven, is displayed against the chimneybreast in another of Vervoordt's pared-down living rooms.

COMPOSITION

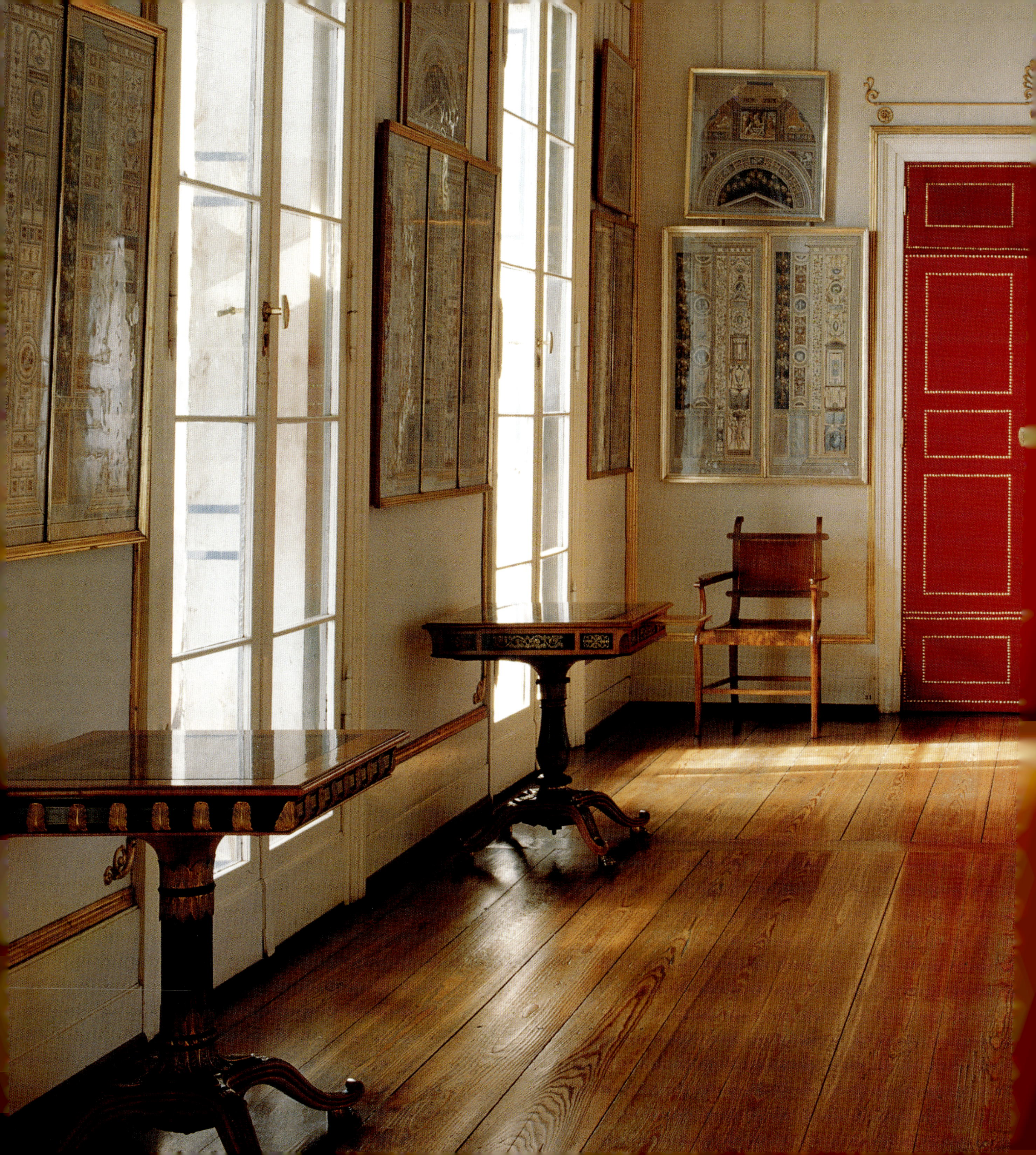

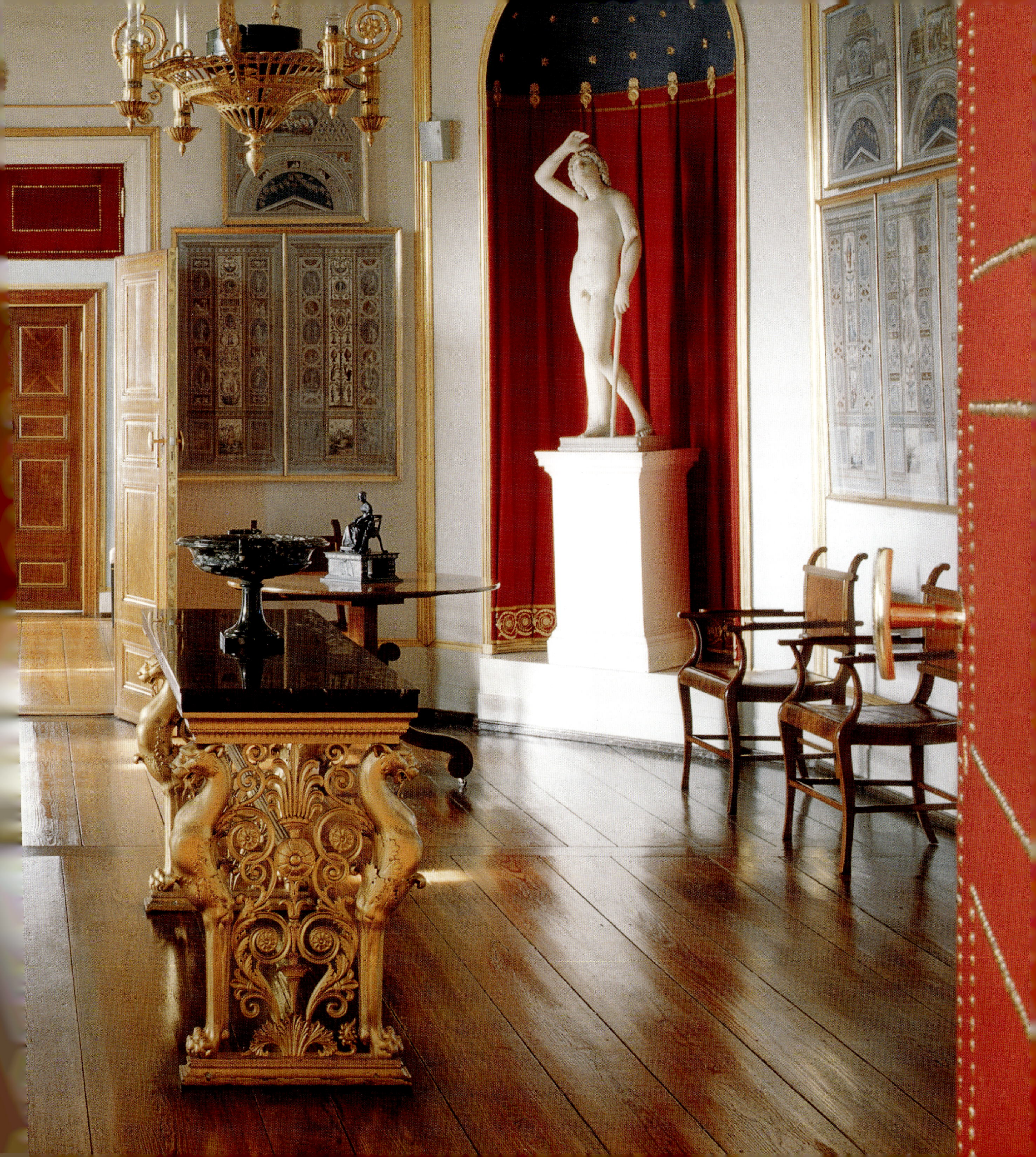

PREVIOUS PAGES Charlottenhof in Potsdam's Sanssouci Park is a summer palace, redesigned in 1825 by architect Karl Friedrich Schinkel for Crown Prince Frederick William of Prussia. The dining room, with its ostentatious table and elaborate furnishings, is the essence of Minimalism in the Grand Style and incorporates the four main concepts of space, light, colour and composition.

ABOVE AND OPPOSITE Axel Vervoordt enjoys the tension between different objects and cultures, and often combines Oriental ceramics and sculpture with European furniture and contemporary artwork.

COMPOSITION

COMPOSITION 297

ABOVE Designer Mimmi O'Connell has transformed a contemporary bookshelf into a composition by wrapping a number of books in white paper.

ABOVE The entrance hall of a house in Cape Town, once owned by antiques dealer Keith Skeel, is a composition of different woods. The floor is made of railway sleepers sliced into boards, while bare weathered tree trunks act as decorative columns.

ABOVE Displaying items alone or in combinations and collections requires confidence and experience. This eye-catching African mask with a blue-painted face (LEFT) is unexpected in the hallway of an Italian villa on the shores of Lake Garda. Antiquarian Axel Vervoordt combines a Han Dynasty terracotta horse set on a black early 18th-century commode with a contemporary abstract painting (RIGHT).

OPPOSITE Axel Vervoordt's knowledge allows him to juxtapose objects in his collection in an original and creative fashion. Here, he combines a circular Oriental antique with a contemporary artwork.

COMPOSITION

COMPOSITION 301

ABOVE The placing of furniture in a room is as important as the displaying of objects. A contemporary piano, situated in the centre of a New York loft, automatically takes on a sculptural quality.

OPPOSITE The free-standing kitchen units in the centre of architect Chloe Cheese's London warehouse become the focus of the room.

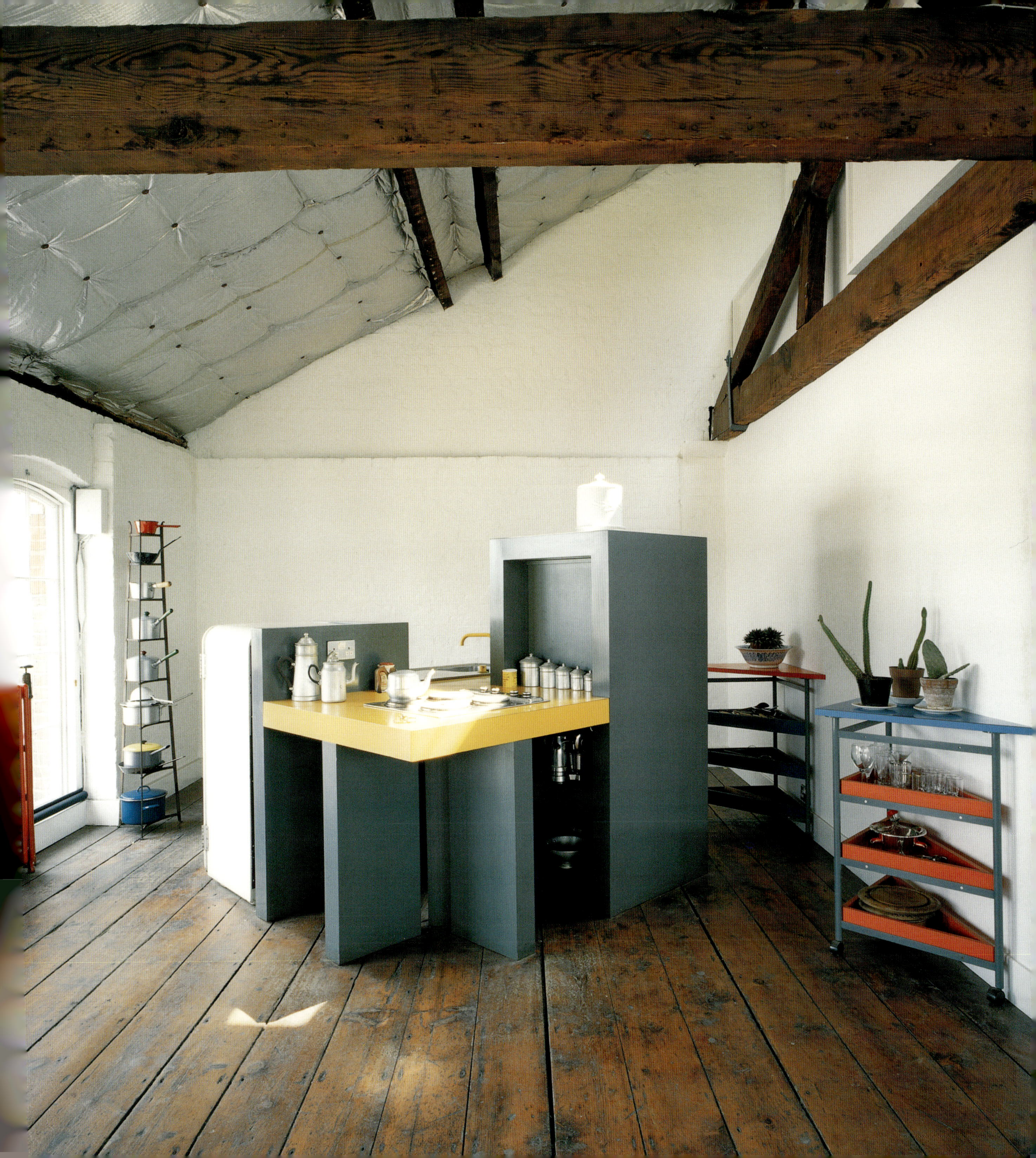

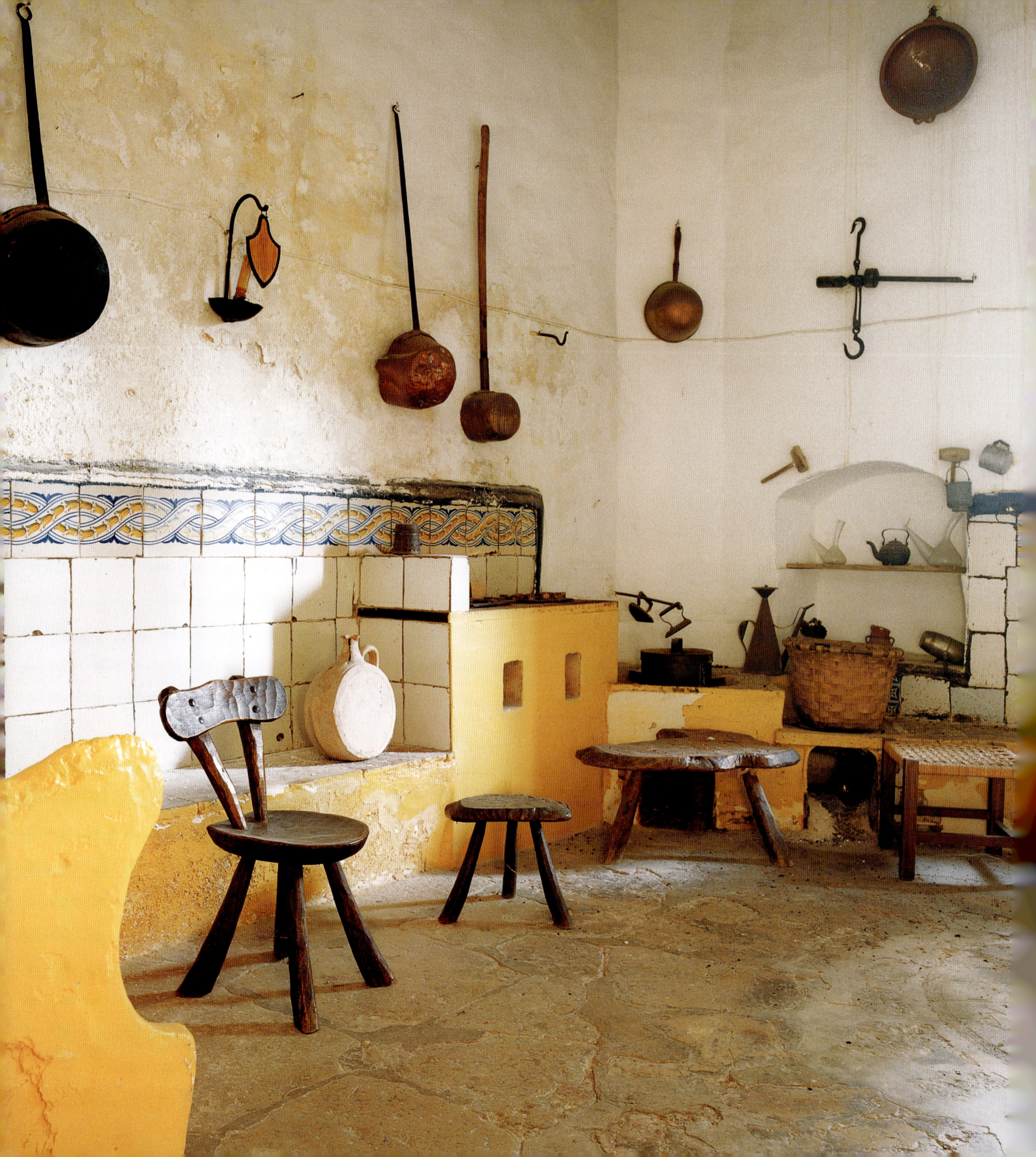

OPPOSITE AND ABOVE Pots, pans and utensils often decorate kitchens in a functional interpretation of composition. As illustrated in the kitchens, both old and new, of Castillo de Bendinat in Majorca, collections of copper pans add texture and also reflect light.

Open kitchen shelves provide an ideal opportunity to combine and display collections of china and glass, silverware, local pottery and other idiosyncratic household items, as illustrated in a Majorcean kitchen (ABOVE LEFT), a butler's pantry (ABOVE RIGHT), and a house overlooking the Thames in London (OPPOSITE).

RICARD
ANISETTE
BERGER
PASTIS 51
ANISETTE BERGER
BERGER
BERGER
BONAL
BERGER
Casanis
BERGER BLANC
BERGER BLANC
RICARD
ANISETTE
RICARD
ANISETTE
BERGER
RICARD
BERGER
PERNOD FILS
GITANES
PASTIS DUVAL
BERGER
PEC
PASTIS 51
BERGER
EPICES
BANANIA
CAFÉ
BANANIA
EPICES
BANANIA

ABOVE AND OPPOSITE Whether a collection of everyday plates and utensils on show in a simple cottage, or polished pewter and brass displayed in an old country house kitchen, the art is in the composition.

Balcony Room
White Room
Cedar Dressing Room
Young Ladies Maids Room
West Door

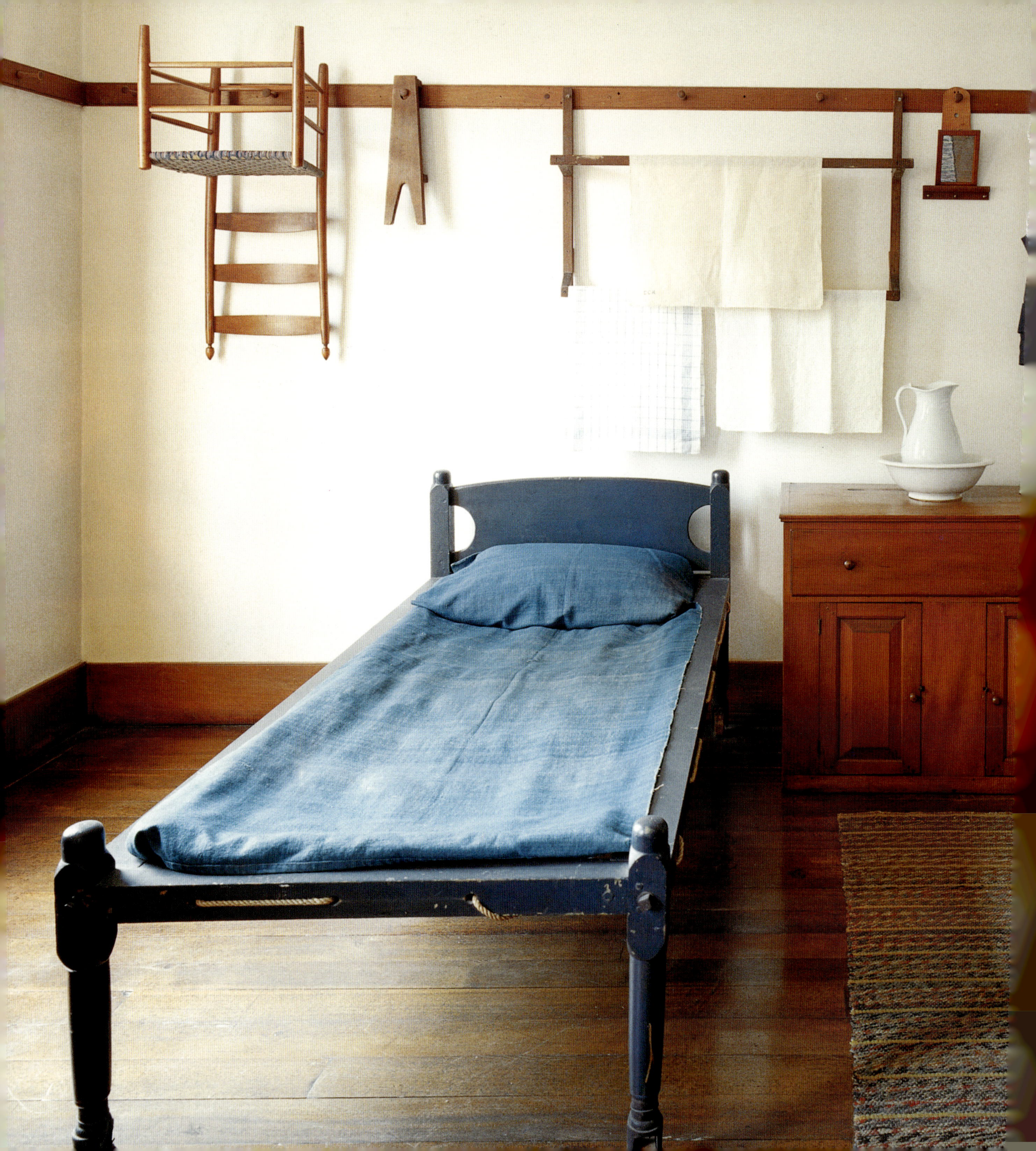

'Architecture is inhabited sculpture.'

CONSTANTIN BRANCUSI, SCULPTOR
(1876–1957)

LEFT Objects and furniture not currently in use are stored on wooden pegs, creating an organic and ever-changing composition in this Shaker bedroom at the Hancock Village in Massachusetts.

COMPOSITION 311

DIRECTORY

ANN BOYD DESIGN LTD
Studio C7, The Depot
The Gas Works
2 Michael Road
London SW6 2AD
+44 (0)20 7384 1660

COLLETT-ZARZYCKI
Fernhead Studios
2B Fernhead Road
London W9 3ET
+44 (0)20 8969 6967
www.collett-zarzycki.com

DAVID COLLINS
David Collins Studio Ltd
The Studio
74 Farm Lane
London SW6 1QA
+44 (0)20 7835 5000
www.davidcollins.com

STEPHEN FALCKE
39 Rosebank Road
Dunkeld
South Africa
+27 11 327 5368
www.stephenfalcke.com

NICHOLAS HASLAM
NH Design
243–247 Pavilion Road
London SW1X 0BP
+44 (0)20 7730 0808
www.nh-design.co.uk

JED JOHNSON
Jed Johnson Associates, Inc.
32 Sixth Avenue, 20th Floor
New York, NY 10013
+1 212 707 8989
www.jedjohnson.com

ROBERT KIME
42–43 Museum Street
London WC1A 1LY
+44 (0)20 7831 6066
www.robertkime.com

CHRISTIAN LIAIGRE
61, rue de Varenne
75007 Paris
+33 (0)1 47 53 78 76
www.christian-liaigre.fr

JOHN MINSHAW
John Minshaw Designs
2/20 Queens Gardens
London W2 3BD
+44 (0)20 7262 9126
www.johnminshawdesigns.com

PAOLA NAVONE

www.paolanavone.it

MIMMI O'CONNELL

8 Eaton Square

London SW1W 9DB

+44 (0)20 7752 0474

www.mimmioconnell.com

JOHN PAWSON

John Pawson Ltd

Unit B, 70–78 York Way

London N1 9AG

+44 (0)20 7837 2929

www.johnpawson.com

ANTHONY REDMILE

The Furniture Cave

533 Kings Road

London SW10 0TZ

+44 (0)20 7352 3775

www.redmile.com

ANNABELLE SELLDORF

Selldorf Architects

860 Broadway, 2nd Floor

New York, NY 10003

+1 212 219 9571

www.selldorf.com

SIR JOHN SOANE'S MUSEUM

13 Lincoln's Inn Fields

London WC2A 3BP

+44 (0)20 7405 2107

www.soane.org

WILLIAM SOFIELD

Studio Sofield

380 Lafayette Street

New York, NY 10003

+1 212 473 1300

www.studiosofield.com

JOHN STEFANIDIS

Unit B, The Imperial Laundry

71 Warriner Gardens

London SW11 4XW

+44 (0)20 7622 4294

www.johnstefanidis.com

SALLY STOREY

John Cullen Lighting

561–563 Kings Road

London SW6 2EB

+44 (0)20 7371 5400

www.johncullenlighting.co.uk

AXEL VERVOORDT

Axel Vervoordt NV

Kanaal

Stokerijstraat 15–19

B-2110 Wijnegem

Belgium

+32 (0)3 355 33 00

www.axel-vervoordt.com

ACKNOWLEDGMENTS

Fritz von der Schulenburg would like to express his thanks
to the eleven architects and designers who agreed to be
featured 'in conversation' in this book.

In addition, particular thanks are due to the team at
Thames & Hudson and to Karen Howes.

INDEX

Page numbers in *italics* refer to illustrations

A

Adam, Robert 62, 124, 125, *176–77, 272–73*, 289
af Sillén, Gustaf *98*
Afra, Corfu *77, 253*
Allcock, Tony 84
Althorp, Northamptonshire *45, 202–03*
Archaeological Museum, Istanbul *56*
Ardgowan House, Scotland *60–61*
Aristotle 152
Art Deco *50*, 124, 125, *148, 182, 313*
Art Moderne 228
Art Nouveau 155
Arts & Crafts *69*, 166, 167, *173*

B

Bargello 261
Baroque 29, *55*, 85
Behr, Gail 254
Beistegui, Charles de *6*
Bernini, Pietro 39
Bicknell, Julian *7*
Biedermeier *43, 80*, 124, *260, 261*
Blake's Hotel, London *195*
Blass, Bill 10, *36, 113, 135, 150–51*, 275
Boll, Otto *271*
Borromini, Francesco 85
Bottega Veneta 229
Bramante, Donato 85
Brancusi, Constantin 311

C

Carlberg, Carl Wilhelm *278*
Carlone, Carlo Antonio *22–23*
Castillo de Bendinat, Majorca *172*, 210, *304, 305*
Charlottenhof, Potsdam 62, *72, 294–95*; *see also* Roman baths, Charlottenhof
Château de Groussay, France *6*
Château de Montmirail, France *247*
Cheese, Chloe *303*
Chirico, Giorgio de 166
Chiswick House, London *205*
Çirağan Palace, Istanbul *170–71*
Classicism 14, *22–23*, 29, *36*, 62, 84, 85, 124, 166, *206–07, 262, 274, 278*, 289
Cobb, Alec *60–61*
Collett, Anthony 110, *166–67*
Collett-Zarzycki 110, *144*, 166, *168, 169, 265*
Collins, David *94, 95*, 124–25, *126*, 148
Connaught, The, London 125
Conran, Jasper *133, 201*
Czainski, Paul 65

D

David, Jacques-Louis 84
Deganello, Paolo *160*
DePadova *82–83*
Destain, Joseph Gabriel *117*
Draper, Dorothy 28, 29, 31, 102
Drumlanrig Castle, Scotland *173, 280–81*

E

Eames, Charles *49*

Elghammar, Sweden *80, 81*
Elkins, Frances Adler *29*
Elveden Hall, Suffolk *18–19*
Erickson, Arthur Charles *186*

F
Falcke, Stephen *78, 79, 149*
Ferguson, Boyd *122*
Ferranti, Sebastian de *7*
Finca Buenvino, Spain *41*
Fontaine, Pierre-François-Léonard *286*
Fontana della Barcaccia, Rome *39*
Fontana, Lucio *268*
Ford, Tom *229*
Frank, Jean-Michel *124, 125, 208, 258*
Frank, Josef *21*
Frulli, Gioacchino *263*

G
Georgian *1, 47, 145, 320*
Germain, Jean-Louis *69*
Gibbs, Christopher *10*
Goldsworthy, Andy *152*
Gray, Eileen *40, 124*
Gripsholm Castle, Sweden *16*
Gucci *229*
Guerin, P. E. *44, 242*
Gunnebo, Sweden *263, 278*

H
Haga, Sweden *216*
Hancock Shaker Village, Massachusetts *33, 91, 310–11*
Harvey, John *246*
Haslam, Nicholas *28–29, 31, 37, 65, 110, 208, 276, 277*

Hawksmoor, Nicholas *47*
Hempel, Anouska *195*
Henbury Hall, Cheshire *7*
Hill House, Glasgow *35, 155*
Hotel Amigo, Brussels *27*
Hôtel de Beauharnais, Paris *287*
Hultgren, Anders *264*
Hylinge, Sweden *279*

I
Ibbotson, Stephen *69*

J
Jim Thompson *230*
Johnson, Jed *50, 120, 225*
Johnson, Philip *85*

K
Kanaal, Antwerp *63, 65, 97, 200, 209, 255*
Kelly, Felix *7*
Killigrew, William *192–93*
Kime, Robert *10, 110, 192–93, 211, 261, 288–89, 291*
Kinross, John *183*
Kremsmünster, Austria *22–23*

L
Lafitte, Louis *286*
Lalique *44*
Lancaster, Nancy *28, 155, 288*
Lao-Tse *152*
Le Corbusier (Charles-Edouard Jeanneret) *110, 125*
Léger, Fernand *166*
Liaigre, Christian *126*
Lorrain, Claude *192–93*

M
Mack, Heinz *270*
Mackintosh, Charles Rennie *35, 155*
Malmaison, France *286*
Manderston, Scotland *182, 183, 219*
Marden, Brice *228*
Marden, Helen *228*
Marot, Daniel *270*
Masreliez, Louis *216*
Matisse, Henri *84*
Melnikov, Konstantin *140, 141, 252*
Michelangelo *230, 259*
Minshaw, John *1, 11, 46–47, 48, 49, 71, 89, 110, 145, 211, 261, 285, 313, 320*
Missoni *126*
Monaghan, William *64*
Morris, William *208, 211, 289*
Mouille, Serge *148*

N
Navone, Paola *164*
Neoclassicism *2–3, 9, 14, 16, 28, 29, 32, 47, 55, 58, 62, 65, 67, 69, 72, 80, 81, 87, 98, 99, 100, 114, 117, 142, 144, 166, 176–77, 178, 189, 197, 205, 222–23, 230, 240, 278, 279*
Neo-Gothicism *26, 196*
Niemeyer, Oscar *84*
Nureyev, Rudolf *241*

O
O'Connell, Mimmi *132, 134, 154, 194, 245, 249, 298*
Oranienbaum, Russia *262*
Östenå, Sweden *112*
Osterley House, London *176–77, 272–73, 273*

P

Painvin, Catherine 217, 238
Palais Sursock, Beirut 24, 123, 157, 163
Palazzo Terzi Martinengo, Italy 206–07
Palladio, Andrea 4, 85, 166, 269, 289
Parthenon, Athens 14, 124
Pavlovsk Palace, St Petersburg 32
Pawson, John 110
Pearce, Gerald 230
Percier, Charles 286
Philip, Paul 72
Picasso, Pablo 62, 84
Piranesi, Giovanni Battista 257
Ponti, Gio 180

R

Ralph Lauren 229
Rateau, Armand-Albert 231
Rauch, Christian Daniel 2–3
Redmile, Anthony 230
Rinaldi, Antonio 262
Rockefeller Center, New York 28
Roman baths, Charlottenhof 2–3, 62, 197; see also Charlottenhof, Potsdam
Roos, Karen 52, 59, 90, 113, 146
Rosersberg, Sweden 98, 108–09
Royal Palace, Stockholm 14, 15
Royère, Jean 148

S

Sadullah Pasha Yali, Istanbul 68, 282–83
Saint-Exupéry, Antoine de 9, 232
St Gumbertus Church, Ansbach 55, 316
St Petersburg Academy, Russia 187
Scharoun, Hans 9
Scherer, Karl-Heinz 51, 73, 106, 147, 261
Schinkel, Karl Friedrich 2–3, 9, 14, 29, 54, 62, 72, 84, 125, 189, 197, 289, 294–95
Schloss Marienburg, Poland 26
Schmarsow, August 155
Selldorf, Annabelle 14, 20, 21, 188–89, 190
Serebriakoff, Alexandre 6
Shaker 33, 91, 310–11
Sharon Temple, Ontario 153
Shiraga, Kazuo 12–13
Sills, Stephen 10
Skeel, Keith 131, 299
Soane, Sir John 30, 47, 125, 229, 289; Sir John Soane's Museum, London 47
Sofield, William 10, 30, 44, 70, 88, 113, 191, 208, 228–29, 231, 242, 256
SoHo Grand Hotel, New York 228
Spoelstra, Renie 259
Stefanidis, John 9, 62, 72, 79, 84–85, 86, 100, 127, 142, 167, 174, 184, 184–85, 220–21, 274, 315
Storey, Sally 113, 116
Stuart, Johnny 87
Sturehof, Sweden 103, 198–99, 246
Swangrove, Gloucestershire 192–93, 246, 288, 289, 290

T

Tanizaki, Jun'ichirō 229
Taverne, Andrea 53
Terry, Emilio 6
Tolstoy, Leo 155
Tullgarn, Sweden 117, 257, 264
Turgenev, Ivan 87
Turpin, André 97
Twombly, Cy 84

V

van der Rohe, Ludwig Mies 34, 84, 124, 125, 189
Vanbrugh, Sir John 4, 47, 289
Verheyen, Jef 258, 268
Verwoordt, Axel 12–13, 47, 63, 65, 96, 97, 129, 155, 158–59, 200, 209, 222–23, 224, 233, 234, 235, 237, 241, 255, 258, 259, 261, 268–69, 270, 271, 292, 293, 296, 297, 300, 301
Verwoordt, Boris 200, 268–69
Vica 188, 190
Vila Viçosa, Portugal 156
Villa Mora, Cortona 76
Vinci, Leonardo da 62

W

Wabi 268
Waite, Joni 25, 212, 227
Walker, Sebastian 121
Wanzenberg, Alan 120
Wootton, John 202–03
Wren, Sir Christopher 289
Wright, Frank Lloyd 125

Y

Yasnaya Polyana, Russia 155

Z

ZERO movement 268, 270

PAGE 313 A Swedish Art Deco statue is displayed on a French radiator cover of the same period in the entrance hall of designer John Minshaw's London home.

PAGE 315 The curved end of this staircase balustrade designed by John Stefanidis is inlaid with mosaic.

PAGE 316 The wooden staircase in the St Gumbertus church in Ansbach is silhouetted against a window.

PAGE 320 The original Georgian iron and brass door furniture on the entrance door to designer John Minshaw's London home.

ABOUT THE AUTHORS

Fritz von der Schulenburg is an internationally renowned photographer, who has contributed to numerous magazines, most notably *The World of Interiors*, published several books and photographed many of the world's most beautiful interiors.

Karen Howes is a well-known interiors writer. Her books include *Living in London*, *Private Ireland* and *Vacation Homes and Perfect Weekend Hideaways*. She also runs The Interior Archive, a London-based picture library and photographic agency.